INSIDE
MAYBERRY

· ·

Dan Harrison and
Bill Habeeb

HarperPerennial
A Division of HarperCollins *Publishers*

To my wife, who establishes order,
and my kids, who provide the chaos
—BILL HABEEB

To all the kids
whose parents told them to turn off the TV—
and who didn't listen
—DAN HARRISON

HarperCollins books may be purchased for educational, business, or sales promotional use. For information please write: Special Markets Department, HarperCollins Publishers, Inc., 10 East 53rd Street, New York, NY 10022.

FIRST EDITION published 1994.

Designed by Jessica Shatan

Library of Congress Cataloging-in-Publication Data

Harrison, Dan.
    Inside Mayberry / Dan Harrison and Bill Habeeb. — 1st HarperPerennial ed.
      p. cm.
    ISBN 0-06-096990-3
    1. Andy Griffith show (Television program)   I. Habeeb, Bill.
  II. Title.
  PN1992.77.A573H37   1994
  791.45'72—dc20   93-43294

---

94 95 96 97 98 PS/RRD 10 9 8 7 6 5 4 3 2 1

CONTENTS

PREFACE

It's an oft-told story. The rookie pitcher stands on the mound facing the hitter he idolized as a boy. An actor lands his first job and finds himself sharing the stage with a giant of the trade. In this case, two writers are sent out to track down a collection of television legends. The fear and the excitement are in taking a peek behind the scenes and seeing if the reality is as appealing as the fantasy.

Our ending is a pleasant one. The experience was very enjoyable, and the legend and joy that is embodied in "The Andy Griffith Show" exist partially because the people who made the show were talented creators and human beings.

During the year spent building this book, we had the great pleasure of speaking to many of the people involved in the creation of "The Andy Griffith Show." These people were not only extremely talented, but also as down-to-earth, accommodating, and entertaining as anyone could hope to find. They were the architects of a tiny fantasy carved into the midst of what has been referred to as a "vast wasteland"—network television.

These individuals deserve credit not only for their work on screen, but also for giving us some of their precious time in order to reminisce about the show. To the following people, we offer our heartiest thanks: Sheldon Leonard, Aaron Ruben, Don Knotts, Jack Dodson, Aneta Corsaut, Hal Smith, Howie Morris, Everett Greenbaum, Harvey Bullock, Bill Idelson, George Lindsey, and Earle Hagen.

Other people who contributed to the book, each in a very individual way, include Ben Starr, Jim Clark, Al and Jessika Corley, Kit McNear, Bev Sweeney, and a host of celebrities who offered their personal tributes to one of television's classic comedies. Of course, our families gave us the kind of emotional support we needed to stay sane while we added the authorship of a book to our two busy schedules. Nancy Peske, Craig Nelson, and Lauren Marino of HarperCollins made the whole process seem easy.

Dan Harrison would like to thank the following people for their support: Larry Gelbart, Stanley Ralph Ross, and Ben Starr for always keeping an eye out for me, and Andy Ross, Rob Lynch, and Sanjay Mani for their innumerable favors and irreplaceable friendship. Thank you all.

Bill Habeeb would like to thank his closest friends and neighbors, who spent a year having every conversation sooner or later turn to "The Andy Griffith Show." Above all, I want to thank my wife, Colette, for her endless support and patience.

As Andy himself once said, "The luckiest thing a man could ever have is friendship." We both have many friends to whom we are indebted—and we'd like to thank the new friends we made in the course of writing *Inside Mayberry*.

We believe that *Inside Mayberry* is as accessible and fun as "The Andy Griffith Show" itself. Mayberry will never become television's version of the lost city of Atlantis. "The Andy Griffith Show" has been a fan favorite for over thirty years—and it always will be.

"THE ANDY GRIFFITH SHOW"

••

8 YEARS
249 EPISODES
OCTOBER 3, 1960, TO APRIL 1, 1968

*"Bob Sweeney once said there was a thread of insanity that
ran through that show, and I think he was right."*

—DON KNOTTS

In the fall of 1960, America discovered Andy Griffith, a new hero who had a
friendly face and a heart as big as his smile. The latest in a long line of TV
sheriffs, he was appointed the benevolent protector of a microcosmic time
capsule of Americana—Mayberry, North Carolina.

On the evening of October 3, 1960, "The Andy Griffith Show" made its
debut, beginning a 249-episode relationship that would last well beyond its
eight-season lifetime. More than thirty years later, a legion of both casual
watchers and devoted fans would still be watching.

Why? "I don't know why," producer Aaron Ruben said. "I think it's a
longing, really. It was built into the show. Even at that time there was a
nostalgia about the show. As Andy used to say, 'This is not a show about
today, this is really a show about the thirties.'" Harvey Bullock concurred.
"We never really designated the period we were writing about, but we were
always thinking earlier . . . back in the amorphous middle age of innocence, if
you will."

In other words, what seems nostalgic now was nostalgic even then. "The
Andy Griffith Show" captured a feeling from a time, as Ruben described it,

"when people left their doors unlocked and used to walk down the street and say hello to everybody."

This is only part of what set the show apart from typical TV fare. It was a show that held to an unusually high standard of quality. The writing, acting, and directing consistently managed to strike a vein of human emotion with the show's remarkable balance of humor and poignant drama. A single episode could be laugh-out-loud funny and yet have moments that leave audiences misty-eyed to this day.

"I can't tell you the letters I used to get," added Aaron Ruben. "They'd write, 'I used to live in a small town that's just like yours, and I remember how warm and friendly the people were, and it brings back such wonderful memories.' Memories. The nostalgia."

In the years since Mayberry first opened itself up to America, "The Andy Griffith Show"—with its familiar characters, warm setting, and time-lessness—has worked its way into American culture like no other show in history. Mayberry has become America's hometown. In the words of executive producer Sheldon Leonard, "It's a phenomenon. It's an American phenome-non." And the phenomenon has shown no signs of abating since Mayberry rolled up its sidewalks for the last time on April 1, 1968.

Add the right creative people to a good project and *voilà*, instant classic.

No one can say exactly why things happen the way they do, or why one show would produce such a fine combination of talent all at the same time. In the opinion of Aaron Ruben, "Every once in a while, things come together. I don't know how it happens, it just happens. We all came together at the right time. Sheldon, Andy, and I, and all the other elements . . . Bob Sweeney, Jackie Elinson and Chuck Stewart, Harvey Bullock, and of course Ev Greenbaum and Jim Fritzell. We came together, and it just worked. It just worked."

It's as simple and improbable as that.

In the beginning, there was Sheldon.

A great deal of the credit for "The Andy Griffith Show" belongs to the show's creator, Sheldon Leonard. Given the assignment to create a vehicle for a rising young comic named Andy Griffith, Leonard dreamed up the idea for the show and formed the core of the cast and crew.

According to Leonard, " 'The Andy Griffith Show' began and was nurtured on 'The Danny Thomas Show,' where I had been hired to write. I had written for radio and had a good deal of success selling half-hour comedy material to the then infant television industry. It was then like $350 for a script. But it was writing. What the hell, I'd sell it to anyone who wanted it. All I had to do was change it a little and sell it again."

Leonard went from writing to directing, becoming the second director to be indoctrinated into the new technique of the multiple-camera show. The method of filming using several cameras in front of a live audience was developed by Desi Arnaz for use on "I Love Lucy." "The Danny Thomas Show" was the second series to use it. After proving he was adept at handling this kind of comedy, Leonard was asked to take over as the show's producer.

Leonard remembered, "We were shooting 'The Danny Thomas Show' on stage five and were doing very well. The third year, the producer, Louis F. Edelman, resigned because he said he'd scraped the bottom of the barrel for story premises. He was not going to beat a dead horse and wanted out. So they asked me to try and revive the dead horse, and I kept it on its feet for another eight years."

And Sheldon said, "Let there be another show."

In the process of reviving "The Danny Thomas Show," Leonard would become known as the man who invented the television spinoff.

"It's true," Leonard admitted. "I invented the spinoff, but it wasn't a big deal. It was economics—money. I had been directing 'Danny Thomas' when Abe Lastfogel, head of the William Morris Agency, came to me and asked if I could do anything for a new client he'd signed in New York. The client was Andy Griffith. Once we came up with the idea, I had a perfect platform to expose it. All I had to do was bring Danny Thomas to Mayberry. Why spend $50,000 or $60,000 on a pilot? That's what it cost then. Instead, not only did it not cost me anything, but I also got paid for the show. So inadvertently I invented the spinoff. Nobody knew what it was. It was an episode of 'The Danny Thomas Show' exposing Andy Griffith."

And Sheldon created the sheriff and gave that sheriff a town.

Before the spinoff could come about, Leonard first had to develop the concept that would highlight his new star.

"Andy had a new record out called 'What It Was, Was Football.' It happened that I'd just heard it, and that's all I knew about him. They said they'd signed him. So they asked me if I had any ideas for him. I said, 'Ideas? What the hell, you want ideas? I'll give you a dozen. How many do you want?'

"At the time, my editor on "The Danny Thomas Show" was a guy named Artie Stander. So I said, 'Artie, let's get together and make up a premise for this

Griffith guy.' We had no guarantee yet. There were several people bidding for him. Bob Banner and Associates, for example, was pleading for Andy because the young television medium was hungry for talent. He was one of the more attractive ones. There was a good deal of competition, so it behooved me to come up with something attractive enough to seduce him into my operation rather than that of someone else."

Since the comedian was well known for his rural style of comedy, Leonard and Stander decided to set the comedy in a rural area.

Leonard described how the genesis of the show was developed: "We asked ourselves, 'What rural things can we use and exploit?' In my opinion, the most important thing about a rural environment was the characters you were going to meet—the people. So we wanted a central figure, someone whom we could surround with colorful, eccentric characters. So we settled on the idea of a sheriff. We decided it might also be funny to give him a multiplicity of jobs. So we decided to make him editor of the paper and the justice of the peace as well."

After using the introductory episode on "The Danny Thomas Show" as a kind of out-of-town trial, Leonard and Stander realized that giving Andy many different duties—including being the paper editor—would not work. "It was excess baggage," Leonard said.

And he said to him, "Son, have I got a deal for you."

The next step was to take the concept to Griffith himself. Leonard recalled their first meeting: "We met with Andy and his business manager, Dick Linke, at an apartment in the Essex House. I pitched the idea, and, much to my surprise, Andy bought it. I found out later that he'd said he bought me, not the idea. Now we had to do the show."

· ·

"Andy is just like you want

him to be."

—CAROL BURNETT,

actress

· ·

Then Sheldon said, "Let there be quiet!"

Griffith, at that time, was on Broadway starring in the musical *Destry Rides Again*. Taking a hiatus from the show, he traveled to Los Angeles to shoot television's first spinoff.

"He sat down at the table with Artie Stander, Danny Thomas, and myself," Leonard recalled. "We read the script and started expressing our opinions and reactions: There's too much dialogue here, and it isn't clear enough there, those sort of things. You have to realize, with Danny Thomas at the center, everything was conducted at a very high decibel level. Danny was not only loud, he was a screamer. So Andy, who's very quiet and laid back, is here in the middle of this group of screaming maniacs. Normally, I'm not a yeller, but in order to exercise any authority I had to yell as loud, or louder."

Late in the afternoon of that day, after several hours of screaming during the creative session, Dick Linke took Leonard aside to tell him that Andy wished to talk to Leonard privately.

"Something was wrong, but I didn't know what. So I went outside and met Andy out by the gate. I said, 'What's the problem?' Andy said, 'Look, Sheldon, I'm gonna do this thing. I said I'm gonna do it, then I'm gonna do it. But I can't make no series. I just can't do all that yellin' and screamin'.' So I said, 'Andy, it's not inherent in the medium. Every show has its own personality. That *is* Danny. When we design this show around you, it will reflect your personality. *We* adapt to *you*, and it will be built in a way so that you can live with it.' "

Fortunately, Griffith accepted Leonard's assurances. Otherwise, according

Andy Griffith and Aaron Ruben confer on the Desilu Cahuenga Studio lot.

to Leonard, "The show would never have happened. At that point the whole thing was over with. He was ready to walk out the door—and he was never coming back."

And he saw what he had created and said, "This'll sell."

The resulting episode of "The Danny Thomas Show" appeared to be a hit. At a time when sponsors, not the networks, were the powers that be in television, General Foods took an instant liking to Mayberry's sheriff. As Leonard said, "The print was still wet. I had Ronnie Howard in it. I had Aunt Bee and Andy. That's all. From that point we went right into production."

Once the show was sponsored, Leonard needed to find a producer to manage the show. Leonard again did something that had never been done in television before—he created the first "hyphenate." Aaron Ruben became TV's first writer-producer.

Leonard discussed the hiring of Ruben: "I went to New York to get Aaron Ruben . . . You don't really need a producer on a television show because traditionally a producer assembled all of the components, hired actors, supervised set design, etcetera. I wanted someone with a comedy background in charge. Too many times, when producers began cutting they'd cut a punch line and leave the straight line. They didn't know where the hell the comedy was. Finally, for "The Andy Griffith Show," I decided, no more."

Pick a pilot, any pilot.

Credited by many as the driving force behind "The Andy Griffith Show," Ruben was the perfect person for the job—even though Leonard only knew him by reputation. The only hitch: Ruben had to accept Leonard's offer. Then a new client of the William Morris Agency, Ruben recalled his first contact with the show: "I went up to the Morris office in New York, and they said, 'Look, we'll show you three pilots that have all sold, and you have your choice of producing any one of the three.' They showed me a pilot that had been done with Tom Ewell, who had done *The Seven Year Itch*. The premise was a guy living with his wife and two daughters and a half-dozen female cats. That was the premise."

The second show was built around the husband-and-wife nightclub team of Peter Lind Hayes and Mary Healey. The third and final series Ruben viewed was "The Andy Griffith Show."

"I didn't have to think twice. I said 'The Andy Griffith Show.' The other shows lasted maybe half a season, and the one I picked, well . . . I don't often make good choices, but boy, I picked right that time."

And they saw the dailies and said it was good.

Those involved with "The Andy Griffith Show" all agree that they never had the slightest idea that it would be as popular as it is now. Don Knotts always felt that they were creating a good show.

"I'll tell you the truth," Knotts said. "I felt from the very beginning that it was going to be a big hit. We'd done a number of shows before it got on the air, and by the time it premiered we all felt good about it."

In fact, not everyone was so certain.

I don't know . . . maybe we need more cats.

Leonard's decision to hire someone who knew comedy for the day-to-day operations proved to be a good one. Since this show was shot like a small film—there was no audience by which the producers could gauge the material—it was imperative to have someone who knew comedy at the helm. Still, there were doubts about the show's quality, so Leonard invited an audience in for a screening to see how they would react.

The screening was well received, but, as Ruben recalled, "Even after that we weren't certain. Early on, even Andy wasn't certain. I remember we were sitting around the table. Andy, who might have been feeling a little negative that day, started saying he wasn't so sure about what we were doing. Now here's who's sitting around the table: Don Knotts; Frances Bavier, who was not the most secure person in the world; and Ron Howard, who was all of six years old. And Andy was expressing some doubt. I spoke to Bob Sweeney about it. We were worried about keeping these people's morale up. Bob said maybe I should talk to him. That was another thing. Another reason it worked. We talked things out. We didn't let it fester."

Ruben went right to Griffith and asked him if he would drop by his office after the day's shoot. Ruben shared what happened: "He came in, and I said, 'You know, you're the star of the show, and they look to you, and if you're going to express misgivings about where we're going, how do you expect Don, or Frances, or the kid, or the kid's father to get up that energy and that morale that we need?' And he understood. He was apologetic, and it never happened again. Of course, once we got rolling and it took off, that stage was one of the happiest of all. I'm sure 'The Dick Van Dyke Show' was, too, but our stage was particularly warm, filled with good humor."

You beat everything, you know that?

With its premiere in 1960, "The Andy Griffith Show" took out an eight-year lease in television's top ten as part of the CBS Monday-night schedule. It started at 9:30 P.M., right behind "The Danny Thomas Show."

Remembering that first season, Don Knotts recalled, "It was very special. It only got better as it went along, but it was such an unexpected thing for me to fall into. Looking back, I would have to say it was definitely my favorite year."

Through the years that followed its debut, rival networks continued shuffling their Monday-night schedules looking for a formula to rival that of CBS's.

Even city slickers have been known to tune in.

Because "The Andy Griffith Show" was set in the fictitious town of Mayberry, North Carolina, it was not unusual for people to mistake it for a thin comedy whose stories were limited to the experiences of the rural South. But even the most casual scrutiny proved that the show had universal appeal.

Aneta Corsaut, who joined the show in 1963, told of her first impressions: "Before I worked on the show, I hadn't watched it much because I was under the impression it was a country show, and I wasn't particularly interested. Once I started watching it, I realized it was a very sophisticated comedy played on several levels, and yet it was truly simple."

Ironically, although several of the cast members (Andy Griffith, Don Knotts, Aneta Corsaut, and George Lindsey) were from small towns, many of the key creative people knew very little about small-town life and nothing about the South.

"We all drew from our experience," as Aaron Ruben put it. "What the hell did we know about living down South. Most of us were from big cities."

Jim Fritzell, who was from San Francisco, wrote with partner Everett Greenbaum, who grew up in Buffalo, New York. Harvey Bullock hailed from Binghamton, New York, and Sheldon Leonard was a Brooklynite. The woman who epitomized the Southern aunt, Frances Bavier, was from New York.

"I was from Chicago," Ruben said. "What the hell did we know about small towns? And yet I remember using a line that my father used to say to me in Yiddish when I was going out to look for a job. He would say, 'Go out on your right foot so everything will work.' " Later, Ruben would use that very line for Aunt Bee as she sent Andy and Barney off on a trip to the big city.

The debate over the secret of the show's success has continued, however, and goes beyond the commonality of life's experiences. "You know what the secret of the show is?" asked writer Bill Idelson. "You know why everybody loves it? It's about man's *humanity* to man rather than man's inhumanity to man. He's a sheriff, the police—the symbol of oppression, brutality, and ignorance throughout the world—and here's a guy who treats his neighbors and the people on the street as if they were human beings. I think people hunger for that so much that it transcends all of culture."

Don Knotts, director Bob Sweeney, and Andy share a laugh on the set between takes.

Idelson is correct: that theme underlies almost every episode. "In [Episode #109] 'Barney and the Cave Rescue,' Andy goes back into the cave so that his friend won't be embarrassed. There was always this thing of being good to your fellow man," Idelson stated.

"And above all," Corsaut added, "it was honest. What they always wanted to say was: Be nurturing, care. . . . The true beauty was in telling it in a way that everyone would understand. Be nice to strangers, don't kill little birds— under every story you'd find those simplest of messages."

Corsaut was acutely aware that it was largely "a guy's show." As she put it, "The ladies had to fight for personalities. I think for the first few years I didn't say much other than 'Did you remember to bring the salt and pepper?' " The show's central relationship was the one between Andy and Barney. Corsaut continued, "There were two dynamics on this show. The friendship between Andy and Barney was one. The love those two had for each other was wonderful."

That friendship was a part of what Harvey Bullock explained as one of the essentials of good comedy and drama: "You have to give the audience an experience they normally don't get or one they long for in their everyday lives. I learned so much from doing this show. It wasn't mechanical. This show got into emotions. I thought, 'Wow, that's where the mother lode is.' Maybe it's a cliché, but if you overlook it, you end up with a product that leaves the audience feeling cheated."

This strong bond between the characters is what Corsaut believed made the show work so beautifully: "Barney was impossible. He was adorable, but impossible. But Andy, as impatient as he would get, truly loved the man. It was a friendship that many people aren't lucky enough to ever have, and on this show it was an honest friendship both on and off the screen."

The other dynamic of which Corsault spoke was Griffith's creation of a "fatherly persona." "When I go to these fan conventions," she said, "men will come up to me and say, 'Andy was my father. My father left when I was a boy, and Andy was my father . . .' Or young people say, 'If it hadn't been for Andy, I wouldn't have had a role model.' No one set out to do that."

Let's not make a big mélange out of this.

Sheldon Leonard's respect for his writers' instincts fostered a healthy creative environment. Harvey Bullock said, "We didn't overly analyze things. We trusted our feelings a lot."

"Sheldon was like the big daddy," Bill Idelson said. "He supervised 'Dick Van Dyke,' 'Gomer Pyle,' 'Griffith,' and 'Danny Thomas' all at the same time. When anyone got in trouble they would call Sheldon. He'd walk down the hall, stand in the doorway, and give them the answer. 'Well there's three ways you can go with that,' he'd say. He'd lay them out, go back to his office, and the story conference would continue."

How about we have them swimming in the water tower? Okay, how about . . .

Practicing what he preached is why Sheldon Leonard was considered a genius by those who worked for him. The opening shot of Andy and Opie carrying their fishing poles, which Leonard conceived and filmed, typified the sort of seat-of-the-pants decision making common to the show. Musical director Earle Hagen recalled, "Sheldon listened to a demo of the show's theme and said, 'That's great. I'll just have Andy and Opie walking along the lake with a couple of fishing poles.' He bought it right away." According to Leonard himself, he had decided on the shot simply because "it was just an easy way to take care of it. We went out, got the shot in a couple of hours, and we were done. We didn't have to worry about it again."

Another version of Hagen's theme was later done with lyrics written by actor Everett Sloane, better known to "Andy Griffith Show" fans as Jubell Foster, the farmer and part-time moonshiner who burned down his own barn in Episode #46, "The Keeper of the Flame," and tried to lay the blame on poor little Opie.

Without much planning, the opening shot immediately established what Aaron Ruben claimed to be the most important element of television comedy: "It's the relationships. The most important ingredient in a sitcom or any dramatic piece are the relationships because from those relationships will come your stories." The jokes, Ruben has always believed, "can be put way down on your list of priorities." In fact, as Don Knotts remembered, Griffith always said, "If it sounds like a joke, throw it out." Ruben agreed, "You can sometimes do an entire story without one joke. Someone once said, 'If you can't be funny, you should at least be interesting.' In other words, you don't have to have a big yuk in every other line."

From your head down to your feet, there's nothing half so sweet.

Griffith has given Ruben credit for the style of the show, and he was also responsible for the creation of television's most memorable unseen characters: Sarah, the phone operator, and Juanita, Barney's favorite waitress. "I always loved the unseen characters," Ruben admits. "We would never have shown them. The idea was to leave it to the audience's imagination. Sarah, you could have pictured a lot of different ways, but Juanita? Well, you can imagine what Juanita looked like."

Interlopers!

Since the 1960s, many things have changed in television, including the networks' approach to selling their time. Jack Dodson, who played Howard Sprague, put it simply: "In those days the sponsor was in control." Today, the network is in control of the programming, and it is the decision of a company whether it wants to advertise during the series.

The debut season of "The Andy Griffith Show" was not an overwhelming success in terms of the ratings. Still, Dodson recalled, "General Foods was very happy with the audience it was reaching. Their only concern was that their show reached coffee drinkers and cereal eaters." So, pleased with those demographics, the sponsor never questioned whether or not it would continue backing the show. Today, however, the scenario might be different. "Since then," Dodson said, "the networks learned they could make more money by taking the shows away from the sponsors and selling blocks of time to several different advertisers."

Of course, an all-powerful sponsor could cause the demise of a show under the old ways of doing business, but "The Andy Griffith Show" was lucky.

Aaron Ruben remembered that the show never had any problems in this regard: "The sponsors were never around. The most you'd get was a memo: 'Please avoid commercial mention of something or other.' If they did show up it was just to bask a little in the success and offer congratulations."

Another reason the show may have been spared any pressure was the imposing presence of Sheldon Leonard, who recalled, "I wouldn't stand for it. They took their hats off when they came by. Don't get me wrong. We had a very good sponsor, although part of it was they may have been intimidated."

We just gave them the big freeze.

With a happy sponsor and a hit show, CBS stayed out of the day-to-day operations of running the program. Asked if they ever interfered with the production, Leonard answered, "They didn't dare."

Ruben's recollections were much the same: "We never saw anyone from the network. Nor did we ever consult them on anything."

Network television is a much bigger business in the electronic age. The freedom enjoyed by "The Andy Griffith Show" would never occur today. "Today," Ruben stated, "you can't hire a wardrobe person without the network's approval. Today they have a say in everything."

Well, that explains where all those gangsters came from.

The exteriors for the town of Mayberry were shot on a studio back lot called Forty Acres, located in Culver City, California. Long since bulldozed and redeveloped, it was the same lot used for the streets of "The Untouchables" and several films, including *Gone With the Wind*.

Oddly, several of the dummies had been tagged with tickets for loitering, jaywalking, vagrancy, and illegal assembly.

Jack Dodson said, "Many of the sets had been refaced, but they were the same basic structures. Part of the *Gone With the Wind* set was just a few feet away from where we shot. The first time I went to Forty Acres, I was wandering around. I had nothing to do for a couple of hours, and I turned a corner and thought, 'God, that building looks familiar.' So I went inside and I saw all these burlap packs with shovels and cooking pots made out of rubber, and I thought, 'Wait a minute. This is the train station from *Gone With the Wind*. It had never been used since then because there were still props left inside. Shovels, rifles with rubber bayonets on the end, and even the dummies they used for the bodies."

. . . .

"The shows were so well written that you felt like Andy and Opie lived just down your street. Growing up where I did in Canada, you could still identify with the characters as everything good about middle America."

—WAYNE GRETZKY,
hockey legend

. . . .

Sheldon would make up for it with "I Spy."

Fans of "The Andy Griffith Show" find it hard to criticize the program, but one area that has been noted is the lack of an integrated cast. Responding to this, both Sheldon Leonard and Aaron Ruben admitted that there was an obvious lack of black actors in leading roles. It is easy to see this as a glaring omission today. But the producers were not prejudiced, they just reflected a racial sensitivity common at the time. Sheldon Leonard was later responsible for bringing Bill Cosby to network television, making him the first black to be cast in a leading series role.

Dodson explained the dilemma that faced the producers. "I've found in my experiences that the show is very popular with black audiences," Dodson began. "The reason is, I think, that it represents the goodness and the decency that is in all of us. They don't see these characters as being of any color. There is a universal quality to them. Back when we were doing the show I know that there were frequent questions of why we didn't use black characters, but if you look at the show and remember what it was like in the 1960s, blacks were first getting an opportunity to be on television. Before then they hadn't been portrayed with the dignity that they understandably desired. Looking at our show, you have to realize that it would have been impossible for us to do it with an integrated cast because the characters we played were all fools. If you picture a black Goober, a black Howard, any of the characters as black, it would have been regarded as a negative stereotype."

Episode #215, "Opie's Piano Lesson," was the one show in which a black actor, Rockne Tarrington, was used in a leading role. Tarrington played the role of Coach Flip Conroy, a former New York Giant who also played classical piano. The episode is a good illustration of the dilemma that Dodson described. Dodson explained, "Watching the show, you see the problem was just the opposite then. The character was almost too good to be true."

And Chief Nugatuk said, "We will call this place Happy Valley."

The happiness that "The Andy Griffith Show" brought to the small screen was due in large part to the happiness that the cast shared. As Aneta Corsaut remembered, "Everyone was very comfortable there. It was a family. It truly was a family. Andy himself, even if he wasn't in the first shot of the day, was still there." Then, after twelve or fourteen hours of work, Corsaut said they would all meet in the prop room and talk, "as if we hadn't seen enough of each other already."

For many members of the cast and crew, this was their first experience in television. It was also their best, Corsaut said. "I don't think anyone at the time realized it was that unusual. We were having a wonderful time, but we were all fairly young and assumed that things would either go on that way or the bad experiences we'd had before were the aberration."

It truly was, Bill Idelson said, "lightning in a bottle."

Idelson, who has worked as a writer, story editor, and producer for dozens of programs since "The Andy Griffith Show," found that his experience was completely unique. "It was a very close-knit operation. Nothing like it exists today. This was like a family. An absolute family."

Andy observes between shots while Ron Howard stays loose.

Aneta Corsaut

Writer Everett Greenbaum shared similar feelings: "We didn't realize we were on such a happy show. We thought they were all like that." Harvey Bullock, who admits he is not objective when it comes to "The Andy Griffith Show," simply said, "I loved it."

A fan to the very end.

One of the unsung heroes of "The Andy Griffith Show" was producer Bob Ross, who guided it after Aaron Ruben left in 1965 to produce "Gomer Pyle, U.S.M.C." Ross inherited a show that had also lost Don Knotts to a budding film career, yet he was able to guide it to the top of the ratings for the first time in the program's history. The actors who worked with Ross have nothing but kind words for him. George Lindsey recalled, "I loved Bob Ross. He knew the Goober character very well. He wrote scenes for me that were so good you didn't even have to learn them." Aneta Corsaut also praised his leadership. "He was greatly organized and worked wonderfully with Andy. I was heartbroken when he died. In any book on this show, the name of Bob Ross should go down with stars all around it."

Jack Dodson recalled, "Bob Ross was an extraordinary man. He was a well-read, well-rounded, educated man with a broad range of interests who really understood humor. He knew Mark Twain. He knew Shakespeare. He was a very bright, talented man. A true gentleman. Ironically, he had sat down to watch the show when he died."

Hal Smith:

"I've worked on many series, with many stars, and I've never worked on a show that was as pleasant as that."

Jack Dodson:

"There really never was, nor will there ever be anything like "The Andy Griffith Show," and that's because of Andy. Andy is a very brilliant man in many ways. He's not remotely like the character of Andy Taylor. He looks like him, he sounds like him, he gestures and moves like him, but inside he is an entirely different human being. He is very smart and very talented with a natural gift for story—for writing."

Who needs prizes anyway?

"The Andy Griffith Show" never won an Emmy. Andy Griffith never received one, either. Don Knotts won five, Frances Bavier one, but the show did not get the attention of the critics. Because the show had a country smell to it, it was never given the credit it deserved at the time it aired. Since the show entered reruns, it has consistently been one of television's most beloved—and most watched—programs.

That's the prize of the game, isn't it?

Was it fun? Ask Sheldon Leonard. "If it wasn't fun, I wouldn't have done it. I was at a stage of my life when enjoying what I did was the only reason for doing it. I wasn't doing it to make a career. I wasn't doing it for financial reasons. I was doing it because I would rather be doing it than be playing golf or fishing or what have you. That was a very important factor in assembling a company. When you assemble a company, it's my opinion that it's not enough just to assess their talents. You also have to make a judgment of how they fit into the big picture."

ANDREW TAYLOR

. . . .

SHERIFF AND JUSTICE OF THE PEACE
OF MAYBERRY COUNTY
CREATED BY ANDY GRIFFITH
249 EPISODES

"He's still a country boy, but he's the smartest damn country boy that ever lived."

—BILL IDELSON

Two Andy Taylors? How did one small town have such good fortune?

Fans of "The Andy Griffith Show" are well aware that there were actually two Andy Taylors. The first Andy Taylor wore a perpetual grin, spoke with a thick Southern accent, and disappeared after the first thirty shows. He was replaced by Andy Taylor number two: a staid but fun-loving stalwart lawman. Don Knotts, referring to Griffith's memorable film character in *No Time for Sergeants*, explained, "Andy was playing Will Stockdale at first, but we did change a lot from the first season. I really notice that when I see it now. I just think we matured into the parts over a period of time."

Aaron Ruben, who credits Griffith with insisting on having a shift in the character, added, "Andy doesn't like to look at those first shows." Ruben also referred to the reprise of the Stockdale character: "In the first year's shows he was playing this rube, this goofy kind of guy, and he was behaving in an absurd fashion toward these women that we were trying to work up some romance with. We had a different county nurse on the show every week to try and get him involved romantically. He thought that was his character. He'll tell you himself. To his credit, he realized he couldn't do that anymore. He realized he had to play poppa, not only to this little kid, but to this whole town."

Knotts commented further on the change. "There was no ego problem," he said. "In the beginning Andy thought he was going to do all the comedy, but after the first show or two it became clear to him that Barney was going to be the funny one, so he switched his attitude a little bit, and as time went on he switched it entirely to be the straight man."

Names out-of-towners called Andy

Hiram	by Bobby Fleet
Rube Sheriff	by Horton, State Police
Curly	by Daphne's boyfriend, Al
Constable	by Malcolm Merriweather
Home Wrecker	by Dud Wash

He was a man of few words—two, to be precise.

After being hired to produce Sheldon Leonard's new show, Ruben followed Leonard's advice and went to Griffith's home in Rye, New York, to introduce himself and to familiarize himself with his new star. Ruben recalled, "Sheldon had said, 'Go out there. You guys ought to sit down and talk.' So I went out to his place. He had this wonderful house, but I don't think I ever saw the inside of it. Conversation was not that easy to come by. When you get to know Andy he can unload, and he can be voluble, but with strangers, as I found out, he was reserved. So I pulled up, and we sat out behind the house on the back stairs that led to the kitchen. It was summer, and there were flies, and I don't think he said 'Hello' or anything. He just said, 'Hunt much?' "

His haircut may have been city-style, but his heart was shaped in a bowl.

Watching the show, it is easy to forget that Griffith was not only the show's star, but the owner of an interest in the series as well. In the television industry, such a combination often spells trouble. Don Knotts, however, said that this was not the case. "Andy was a good boss, and one of the reasons the show had such good rapport was because of that. Andy was simply a good guy. He had a great sense of humor. He was laughing all day long. He invited me in to help with the scripts. So a lot of the credit should go to Andy, really. He set the tone."

Griffith did not just invite Knotts to attend script meetings. The two became so close that Griffith insisted Knotts sit next to him at the table readings of every script. "Whenever a guest would come in and sit there," Knotts said, "Andy would tell him, 'You have to get up. That's Don's chair.' " After Knotts ended his regular stay on the show, Griffith made sure no one sat where his old friend had and he sent Knotts the chair as a gift. "He had it bronzed. It was so heavy you could hardly pick the thing up," Knotts said.

It was a token act from a man who hated to see one of his best friends leave. "When Don left," Aneta Corsaut said, "well, that was unbelievable. Don will tell you he never really wanted to leave, but he was offered the moon . . . Andy was devastated to lose Don, but I don't think he had any idea we would go such a long stretch without Don, or he might have reacted even worse. He hated to see Don go, but I don't think Andy would have ever tried to hold him back."

And you got seconds of Bee's apple pie, for good behavior.

The jailhouse closed on Sundays, so prisoners would usually come back to the Taylor house and have dinner with Andy, Opie, and Aunt Bee.

Will you help us?

Griffith, with one of the best natural senses of what makes a good screen story, was there to help his close friend Knotts even after he left "The Andy

Don Knotts

Don Knotts's chair, used during table readings, was bronzed and sent to him by Andy Griffith as a gift.

Griffith Show." "We were in trouble right from the beginning with the story line of my first picture after I left," Knotts recalled. "We'd talked and talked and talked about the story line, and Jim Fritzell and Ev Greenbaum wrote a treatment that missed. Our producer at Universal said we had to do something about it. So, knowing how good Andy was at this kind of thing, I got Universal to pay him to come over and sit down with us. He actually sat with us for two weeks—every day for two weeks—and we hammered out a new outline, and he had a ball."

The gift that keeps on giving.

There were some scenes that Andy and Don never forgot and never tired of performing, long after the show left the air.

"They would do them at parties," recalled Everett Greenbaum. "One of their favorites was the porch scene Jim and I wrote for [Episode #90] 'Barney's First Car.' They would do the scene where Barney tells Andy he is buying his parents a septic tank. They loved that. They would do it word for word. 'They're really hard to buy for, and besides it was something they could use.' 'You're a good son, Barn.' And then Barney says, 'I try.' Nobody else ever gave Don a chance to relax like this with his acting."

The original idea for that scene came from Greenbaum's wife, Deane. The writer explained, "She grew up in the Ozark Mountains of Arkansas, and her parents still lived in a house with no indoor plumbing. Not long after we were married I decided to give them a present—a septic tank. Jim said, 'Why do you want to do that?' And I told him, 'Well, my father-in-law has cataracts, and when he goes out to the john, he falls down a lot.' Jim thought that was pretty funny. 'A gift for the man who has everything,' he said."

Here's the plan: home, nap, Thelma Lou's for TV.

The porch scenes that became one of the signatures of the team of Andy Griffith and Don Knotts were an invention of the two actors.

"Now if memory serves me," Knotts said, "I think Andy and I were talking one day about how farmers talk. A lot of my family were farmers. Andy and I had very similar backgrounds as kids. We were both from small towns. I wasn't from a real rural area, but I was from a small town in West Virginia. Andy is from North Carolina, of course. And we both had similar experiences with some of these small-town people, particularly rural people. That is, they don't talk a lot. And I was telling him about how my family would take me out to the farm to visit, and we'd sit around Sundays on the front porch or wherever, and no one would say much. You could sit there with them all day, and they'd hardly talk at all. And we started a little bit of that. We gradually worked it into that front-porch thing—particularly that bit I did where I'd say, 'I think I'm going to go down to the gas station, get a bottle of pop, go home, take a nap . . .' Directly from that came those scenes on the porch."

Just a couple of pals.

Andy and Don had so much fun doing "The Andy Griffith Show" together. Knotts's role involved more physical humor than Griffith's, and it tended to wear Knotts out. Andy would good-naturedly rib his friend about running out of energy. Knotts remembered: "Playing Barney, I talked all the time. I had more lines to learn, I think, than Andy, and I was running around all the time. Andy very often was sitting there at the desk. One day I said, 'I'm exhausted.' And Andy would say, 'Well, I don't know why.' He used to tease me a lot because I'd get tired and cranky."

Names Barney called Andy

NICKNAME	EPISODE
Boy	#19, "Mayberry on Record"
Kid	#24, "The New Doctor"
Gardenia Blossom	#27, "Ellie Saves a Female"
Chickie-baby	#72, "The Mayberry Band"
Chief	#78, "The Bank Job"
Screw	#106, "Citizen's Arrest"
Daddy Long Legs	#132, "Opie Loves Helen"

It's just not regulation!

Very few things that happened on "The Andy Griffith Show" occurred by accident. Even Andy's habit of not carrying a gun as he patrolled the streets of Mayberry was deliberately incorporated into Sheriff Taylor's character. Speculating on its origin, Aaron Ruben said, "That came from Andy himself. I don't think he was comfortable carrying a sidearm. And I know he *hated* wearing a hat. He hated wearing hats—he refused to wear them—and I think he felt uncomfortable wearing a gun."

If forced to do so, Griffith would occasionally don a hat. He had his head covered in Episode #8, "A Feud Is a Feud" (nightcap); Episode #89, "Andy's English Valet" (officer's cap); and Episode #195, "The Ball Game" (umpire's cap).

Andy practices for the ill-fated call at the plate in "The Ball Game."

Aneta Corsaut

Some rules were made to be broken.

Sheriff Taylor may not have wanted to carry a gun, but he was not "nave." He knew that there were times when he needed to bring his weapon—or perhaps Fast Gun Fife—along if the situation warranted. The following is a list of episodes in which Andy conspicuously is carrying his gun.

- Episode #2, "The Manhunt." Andy first carries his sidearm while tracking an escaped convict.

- Episode #8, "A Feud Is a Feud." Andy wears a sidearm while umpiring a duel between two mountain families.

- Episode #21, "Andy and the Gentleman Crook." Andy tries to convince a thief that there are no bullets in his gun—and to prove it he fires a bullet into the ceiling. Nice shooting, Sheriff.

- Episode #30, "Barney Gets His Man." Andy wears a sidearm and carries a rifle to pursue an escaped convict on the loose near Mayberry.

When the fugitive is spotted by State Troopers making an attempted escape on Myer's Lake, Andy prevents one of them from firing by lowering the barrel of his rifle. Unintentionally, the barrel ends up pointed at the back of Opie's head.

• Episode #50, "Jailbreak." Andy wears a sidearm while rounding up some escaped prisoners.

• Episode #55, "Aunt Bee, the Warden." Andy carries his gun while rounding up the Gordon boys.

• Episode #80, "High Noon in Mayberry." Andy reveals a handgun that he keeps in the top of the china cabinet in case of emergency. He is worried that ex-convict Luke Comstock is coming to exact some revenge for Andy's shooting him during his capture in 1952, even though Luke shot at Andy first.

• Episode #95, "The Big House." Andy carries a pump-action shotgun while on the lookout for bank robbers.

• Episode #102, "A Black Day for Mayberry." Andy uses a sidearm while he is protecting the big gold shipment.

• Episode #171, "Aunt Bee Takes a Job." Andy borrows Warren's pistol to shoot out the tire of a station wagon carrying fleeing counterfeiters.

• Episode #228, "Tape Recorder." Andy needs a shotgun in order to hunt down a bank robber who has just pulled a heist in Raleigh.

I just hated it when he was obtuse.

Sheldon Leonard, who writer Harvey Bullock claimed was in love with the English language and polysyllabic words, was a man Griffith found amusing in his own country way. Griffith did not want to lose an opportunity to have some fun at the executive producer's expense. As Don Knotts recalled, "When we were in meetings with Sheldon, he'd come to one of those big words of his and Andy would raise his hand and say, ' 'Scuse me. . . . What does that mean?' "

I never met a man I didn't like . . . except for maybe . . .

There were few people in Mayberry or who passed through who Andy did not like, but a few come to mind:

• Episode #111, "Aunt Bee, the Crusader." Mr. Frisbee. Andy never was crazy about Mr. Frisbee.

• Episode #130, "Aunt Bee's Romance." Roger Hanover. Andy couldn't stand Roger Hanover.

• Episode #191, "The Barbershop Quartet." Sheriff Wilson in Mount Pilot. Andy didn't like saying it, but he didn't like him just the same.

Lyrics, lyrics everywhere.

Andy Griffith was not only a talented actor but also an accomplished musician. Don Knotts remembered, "Andy liked to work music into every show he could." The Dillards, who were found by Griffith and worked into the show as the Darling Family, became regular performers. Sometimes the songs were played on the porch of the Taylor home. Singer Jack Prince and Andy himself also added to the musical memories. The music was not just confined to on-camera moments. As Knotts recalled, "We sang harmony together all the time off camera too. We both loved to do that, and Lee Greenway, who was our makeup man, would join in on a five-string banjo. The three of us would do a trio." According to Knotts, "We'd usually sing hymns. Now, I'll tell you, that was a strange thing to hear in Hollywood."

Aneta Corsaut, who sang three times on camera, remembered a special moment from the final show: "The last time, Andy put in one of my favorite songs, and we did it around the piano: 'Darling you and I, know the reason why' . . ."

> **"Andy Griffith is so down-home and lovable that you want to invite him in for a piece of apple pie."**
>
> **—BURT WARD,**
> **actor**

Names Ellie called Andy

NAME	EPISODE
Sheriff Honey	#7, "Irresistible Andy"
Sheriff Sweetie	
Andy-pie	
Special Favorite Sheriff Lamb	
Big, Brave Hero	
Baboon	

Andy with Thelma Lou
(Betty Lynn) and his girl
Helen (Aneta Corsaut).

Names other women called Andy

NAME	EPISODE
Bad, Bad Sheriff	#6, "Ellie Comes to Town" (by Emma Watson)
Doll	#155, "The Arrest of the Fun Girls" (by Daphne)

We got trouble with a capital "T" and that rhymes with "D" and that stands for darts.

"It was a very happy set," Hal Smith, memorable for his portrayal of town drunk Otis Campbell, said. "They had a dartboard there, and whenever I was working I always wanted to play for money. Well, the most they ever wanted to play for was a dime. I wanted to play for dollars, but they never would until one day after I'd been gone for a couple of weeks, Andy comes up to me and says, 'Hey, Hal, let's play some darts.' Well, they'd been practicing, and Andy cleaned me out. He must have hit the bull's-eye every time."

Most likely to . . .

Andrew Jackson Taylor was clearly destined for greatness if the Mayberry High yearbook is any indication. The Cutlass listed the future sheriff as Second Vice President, 4H Club. He was also the secretary of the Philomathian Literary Society.

That's him there, but don't get too close.

It is difficult to gauge the effect of "The Andy Griffith Show," but one story told by Bill Idelson helps put in perspective the impact its star had on America: "I was fishing in Table Rock Lake, which is half in Missouri and half in Arkansas. I was at this lodge, and I was talking to this guy who ran it who asked what I did and where I was from. He could tell from my license plates that I was from California, and, at the time, I guess that was very exotic. Well, I told him what I did and told him I had written some for 'The Andy Griffith Show.' Well, the word spread around that area. I went down to go fishing, and there were guys standing on the hill a couple of hundred yards away, looking at me. They wanted to look at a guy who had shaken hands with Andy Griffith. They didn't come any closer or try to talk to me. They were too afraid, or too polite, to come up and say hello, but they just wanted to look at a guy who was associated with Andy Griffith. That's what kind of appeal that show had."

BERNARD P. FIFE

MAYBERRY DEPUTY

CREATED BY DON KNOTTS

141 EPISODES

411 ELM STREET

JOINED SHERIFF'S OFFICE MAY 16, 1959

BIRTHSTONE: RUBY

HEIGHT: 5'8" (WHEN STRETCHED)

WEIGHT: BETWEEN 138 AND 138½

SOCK SIZE: 10½   SHOE SIZE: 7½B

FAVORITE PIZZA—MAZZERELLA (MOZZARELLA)

FOREIGN LANGUAGES: SPANISH, PIG LATIN,

SOME FRENCH, AND BIRD

"I wish we had a psychiatrist in town. I bet Barney would be a real study."

—ANDY TAYLOR

For my next trick, I will reach into a milk bottle and pull out an egg.

"I had always wanted to be an actor, ever since I can remember," said Knotts. "When I was young I was trying to do magic—magicians were real big. I sent in to one of those little mail-order houses. They advertised a 'Ventrilo' for a dime. It was a little leather thing—you put it in your mouth and you were supposed to be able to throw your voice. Now it's a birdcall. Then I sent in for this little booklet on ventriloquism. I got hold of a dummy, and I started doing it. Pretty soon I started playing at parties, and people paid me a little bit. I was about thirteen. That's how I started entertaining for a living."

Harvey Bullock:

"You can't say enough about Don Knotts. He's a magician. Barney Fife—a totally self-involved, transparent character. Every emotion's on his face. People read a lot of psychological things into it. He represents the downtrodden 'Mr. Little Guy.' We didn't go into that stuff. It was a perfect match of a performer and a role."

Hal Smith:

"Don is absolutely perfect. Don has the best timing of any comic I have ever seen. He knows when he starts a scene just what he's going to do, and he doesn't waver."

Bill Idelson:

"He's the kind of actor—and Barney Fife was the kind of character—that writers dream about."

Everett Greenbaum:

"Don is about 60 percent Barney Fife in real life."

Names Barney called himself

NAME	EPISODE
Reliable Barney Fife	#1, "The New Housekeeper"
Barney Sucker	#19, "Mayberry on Record"
Eagle-Eye Barney	
Barney "Tibbs" Fife	#25, "A Plaque for Mayberry"
Barney the Bulkhead (explaining what he has become when using his body as a weapon)	#30, "Barney Gets His Man"
Sadder but Wiser Barney Fife and Level-headed Barney Fife (said to Thel)	#36, "Barney on the Rebound"
Fast Gun Fife (a name he couldn't seem to shake)	#41, "Crime-free Mayberry"
Puddin' Tame, Fingers, Chopper, and Mad Dog	#50, "Jailbreak"
Barney the Rabbit (because of how fast Barney was when he was a kid)	#51, "A Medal for Opie"

Names Barney called himself (continued)

Ol' Eagle-eye Barney

Big Barn (said to Aunt Bee)

Tweekie

Mr. Independent Wheels

Tight-lips Barney Fife (re: the
gold shipment)

Ol' Sharpshooter Barn (from Barney's letter to Andy)

Bernard P. Fife, Attorney at Law;
Dr. U. T. Pendyke, D.V.M.

Scoop Fife

Rifle Fife

The Scamp (supposedly the
name Mr. McCabe used
to call him), Your
Man in Mayberry

#59, "Three's a Crowd"

#80, "High Noon in Mayberry"

#82, "Class Reunion"

#90, "Barney's First Car"

#102, "A Black Day for May-
berry"

#119, "Andy Saves Gomer"

#122, "A Deal Is a Deal"

#153, "Opie's Newspaper"

#157, "Opie Flunks Arithmetic"

#240, "Barney Hosts a Summit
Meeting"

**Don Knotts and Andy
Griffith in "The Ghost
Story."**

TAGSRWC Collection

There once was a deputy named Fife.

Knotts demonstrated his comic genius with his creation of Barney Fife, an invention of his own.

"I've been asked about my early influences a lot," said Knotts. "I've really tried to think who I patterned the character after. To tell you the truth, I really didn't pattern the character after anyone."

The big time.

"I got to know Andy doing the play *No Time for Sergeants* on Broadway. My first job in New York, though, was in radio. I was in radio for five years doing a western. Then I did television, and I had tried stand-up. And then I just got the part, my first part, in the Broadway show. Andy and I got acquainted there."

A wink is as good as a nod.

Bill Idelson recalled, "When 'The Andy Griffith Show' first went on the air, the network was going to dump it instantly—and then Sheldon Leonard brought Don Knotts into it."

"The Andy Griffith Show" owes its early success to a phone call Knotts made to Leonard. "Barney wasn't in the original idea," Knotts stated. "I called Andy when I found out he was going to do the series. I hadn't seen him in a long time. He was back in New York doing *Destry Rides Again*, and, knowing he was doing a sheriff, I said, 'You're going to need a deputy.' And he said that's a good idea and told me to call Sheldon Leonard. That's where it all started."

You'd better gird your loins, fella, you got a fight on your hands.

Leonard added Knotts to the series, but not as a regular member of the cast. "I never knew he would become such an 'important element on the show," said Leonard. "I thought he would be there for one or two episodes. We introduced him as Andy's cousin. The joke was 'I want to thank you for giving me the job on my merit, and I know there was a lot of competition, and I'm happy that I overcame all the competitors. Thank you, Cousin Andy.' "

After seeing that scene the next day in the rushes Leonard realized the show had discovered something special. "We recog-

> **"Barney Fife was my original role model when I started bodybuilding, even though I knew I could never develop the same type of physique that he possessed."**
>
> **—PETER LUPUS,**
> **actor-bodybuilder**

nized that there was such a chemistry between the characters that we'd better go ahead and tie Don up—make him a part of the show."

Names Andy called Barney

NAME	EPISODE
Cousin Barney	#1, "The New Housekeeper"
Reliable Barney Fife	#2, "The Manhunt"
The Adolphe Menjou of Mayberry (after Andy saw Barney in the ol' salt and pepper)	#7, "Irresistible Andy"
Turncoat	#10, "Stranger in Town"
Bucket Mouth	#14, "The Horse Trader"
Casanova	#22, "Cyrano Andy"
Tiger	#27, "Ellie Saves a Female"
Subtle Barney Fife (he is about as subtle as a pig squealing for his supper)	#37, "The Perfect Female"
Phantom Fife	#59, "Three's a Crowd"
Barney the Beast, Fife the Fierce, and Crazy-gun Barney (to the truck farmers)	#73, "Lawman Barney"
Mr. Marconi	#85, "The Great Filling Station Robbery"
Baron Von Ricktoven	#112, "Barney's Sidecar"
Mr. Fix-it	#123, "The Fun Girls"
Ol' Tiger Fife	#212, "Barney Comes to Mayberry"

The one-bullet theory.

"We had good writers," Knotts acknowledged. "Chuck Stewart and Jack Elinson were the original writers. Chuck is one of the guys I've lost track of. The one bullet—they invented that." Andy only allowed Barney to carry around one bullet for his gun—and the bullet could not be loaded in the gun. This characteristic spawned many funny moments.

History—that's my subject.

"I have to give Don a lot of credit," Aaron Ruben said. "He contributed an awful lot. He came up with some notions that to me are classic bits."

One unforgettable scene involves Barney handing Andy a piece of written material for him to test how well Barney can memorize something. "That was Don's idea," recalled Ruben. "The preamble to the Constitution, the sheriff's rules . . . it all started when he came in. I'll never forget it. He said, 'You know I had an idea . . . they're offering a test in the sheriff's department for a raise or some kind of higher-up job, and you have to know these rules.' That was the very first one (Episode #6, "Ellie Comes to Town"). And Don had suggested it, so we put it together, and from that came the preamble. They're classic bits because he doesn't know one damned word. And then when it's over Andy says, 'You wanna go over that again?' and Barney says, 'What for? I got it.' "

The main thing is eternal vigilance.

To outsiders, the position of Mayberry Deputy Sheriff might have appeared somewhat glamorous. As difficult as it is to believe, the job had its demands. Following is a short list of some of the important duties:

- Emptyin' the trash

- Sweepin'

- Coverin' the school crossin' at 3:00 P.M.

- Dustin', fly killin', and changin' pillowcases

- Watchin' the bicycles at the movie theater

- Checkin' doorknobs

- Takin' in laundry when folks are out of town

- Runnin' the waitin' room and takin' notes

- Fixin' Otis's breakfast, which consists of:
  two soft-boiled eggs (four minutes),
  one piece of toast,
  coffee, black, with sugar

- But mostly just answerin' the phone

Let's stop laughing long enough to shoot this scene.

Two of the scenes Howard Morris will never forget:

"One I directed was when Barney was hanging in the closet with his head in a harness [Episode #131, "Barney's Physical"], and the other would have to be the 'amenanies' scene [Episode #113, "My Fair Ernest T. Bass"], when Barney comes into the imaginary party to show me the proper way of entering a room. Unparalleled, hilarious—he's a genius." In that scene, Barney mimes how Ernest T. should enter a party. After entering with a flourish, Barney pretends to tip his hat, shake hands, and carry on conversations with imaginary partygoers—in an exaggerated way.

Hal Smith concurred: "I used to laugh at Don so much. In [Episode #115] 'Hot Rod Otis,' when we are playing with the cars, he was so funny. You had to work to keep a straight face. But he's the kind of actor you loved to work with. His character was so solid, so true; he never slipped."

"I know the easiest shows we ever wrote," according to Bill Idelson, "were the ones where Barney was the initiator of the problem. Like [Episode #128] 'Barney's Bloodhound,' where Barney gets the idea that he's going to use this dog and the dog falls in love with the crook. Stories always seemed to be easier to write when you worked around Barney."

· ·

"Don Knotts as Barney Fife for me is the funniest comedy performance in the history of television, and when he and Andy work together, it doesn't get any better."

—BOB MACKIE,
costume designer

· ·

Like mother, like son.

• Like his mother, Barney could not stand to wear a hat after it had been on somebody else's head.

• Barney has his mother's frame.

• One of the marks of the Fifes was everything they ate turned to muscle. Barney's mother was the same way. She could eat, and eat, and eat. It never went to fat—just muscle.

• Mrs. Mendelbright reminded Barney of his mother.

• Barney, like his mother, was not superstitious—just cautious.

Mr. Independent Wheels.

"My son Paul's favorite episode," Bill Idelson said, "is where Barney buys that car."

One unforgettable moment from Episode #90, "Barney's First Car," was another bit taken from real life. Everett Greenbaum recalled, "You remember where the grease comes out of the steering column? A friend of mine who later became a doctor was working his way through medical school, and they told him to get under a car. It was a Packard, a great big convertible, a beautiful car. So my friend was under the car trying to get the grease in the grease fitting, and he said to the boss, 'It won't take the grease,' and the guy says, 'Just turn it up full strength, and push as hard as you can.' So he spent twenty minutes on this one grease fitting on the steering column. The guy who owned it gets in after—in this white suit—and a snake of grease comes out with the horn button on top of it."

Other'n that, it's a real peach.

Wally's list of things that Barney's car needed: Plugs, points, bearings, valves, rings, starter switch, ignition wires, water pump, fuel pump, oil pump, clutch, clutch bearings, clutch plate, brake lining, brake shoes, brake drums, radiator hose, and radiator hose cover. And, as Gomer suggested, it could use a good wash, too.

Some people want it and can't get it. I got it and had to get rid of it.

"You'd get some unexpected goodies out of these guys," Harvey Bullock remembered. "You'd see Barney Fife temper a word just right. When you'd see the actors do your stuff, Don, Ron, Andy, whatever shadings they would give to your stuff, it was always right. It was always wonderful to watch."

One thing Bullock could not recall was the origin of one of Barney Fife's signature lines. " 'Nip it, mollycoddle,' I don't know where that came from. This show just gave you free reign to go back into those stuffy old-maid, old school-time words you'd used."

Deane Greenbaum, Everett's wife, gets credit for one of Barney's popular sayings, "Nip it in the bud." Everett explained how "Nip it" was born: "We were on our honeymoon. She's from a very rural background and knows very little about machinery to this day. When we were first married she thought that if you flushed the toilet too many times the electric bill would go up. But anyway, I had a '57 T-Bird, and we were on our honeymoon. We were going to go down a mountain, so I put it in low gear, and it started to whine. And at the bottom of the hill I shifted back into drive, and the noise stopped. And she said, 'Well, you nipped that in the bud.' And I started using that in scripts."

Don Knotts said, "We'd started working on running gags. We had so many things to draw on after a while. The bullet, the front-porch stuff, and also the fact that you never saw Sarah, the telephone operator. Morelli's was a good running gag. And Barney being so cheap. And then, of course, 'Nip it.' We played a lot with that."

" 'Nip it' became very much like the literary equivalent of a Ping-Pong ball," Bullock added. "You use it a couple of times, and then you say, 'Well, let's see if we can put a little spin on it.' You throw out a couple of 'Nip it in the buds,' and then you reverse it, 'Bud nippin'—they're all in favor of bud nippin'.' I mean, you'd giggle when you'd type it. You had such freedom with this guy [Knotts], this magician. Who would have known something you just throw in at the time becomes immortalized? It's incredible."

Great minds.

The legend of "Nip it" makes a great story. But the only problem is "Nip it" was first used in Episode #45, "The Farmer Takes a Wife," written by Jack Elinson and Charles Stewart—not Everett Greenbaum.

At least they never called me "Tattletale."

"One of the other things we always had going were these nicknames," Knotts recalled. "Every week it seemed like Barney had another nickname. I don't know how many we must have used."

. . . .

"I lived for Barney Fife.

Barney Fife was my male role model. He was a true man. He could carry off lines like 'You know, Ange, when you've been trained as long as I have, sometimes the instincts just take over.' Then he'd sniff and hitch up his pants. This was my idea of John Wayne. He was bigger than Wayne. He was more man than Wayne."

—JERRY SEINFELD,
comedian

. . . .

Names other folks called Barney

NAME	EPISODE
Weak-kneed, Chicken-livered, Yellow-streaked Turncoat (Sam)	#12, "Ellie for Council"
Wild Bill Fife (Mayor Pike)	#16, "Andy Saves Barney's Morale"
Ol' Buddy Buddy (Otis)	#45, "The Farmer Takes a Wife"
Little Buddy (Big Jeff "The Skipper" Pruitt)	
A Sap, a Great Big Sap (Henry Bennett)	#49, "The Jinx"
Barney Fife—Hero (the Mayberry *Gazette* caption)	#50, "Jailbreak"
That Caterwallering Tenor (John Masters)	#52, "Barney and the Choir"
Ol' Eagle-eye Barney (Judd)	#76, "Barney and the Governor"
That Stupid Deputy (Mr. Meldrin)	#78, "The Bank Job"
That Lady Sheriff (Ernest T. Bass)	#94, "Mountain Wedding"
Hick Deputy (Doc and Tiny)	#95, "The Big House"
Barney Fise (the phony producer and director)	#150, "TV or Not TV"
Barney Fike (the article in *Law and Order* magazine)	
Dropout (Mr. McCabe)	#240, "Barney Hosts a Summit Meeting"

It hangs just right when you dip.

What else but the ol' salt and pepper? It was Barney's one and only suit, and, according to Everett Greenbaum, one actor was green with envy: "Howard McNear thought that was the best-looking suit he'd ever seen. He'd say to Don, 'Don, oh, I—I love that suit . . .' and then he'd feel the lapel and say, 'That cloth'll—ohh, last forever. I love that suit.' He was serious."

"Howard did like that suit," Knotts recalled. "He'd ask me, 'Is it yours?' My wardrobe only took up about three hangers, I think."

But they got the best use of it. The suit first appeared in Episode #7, "Irresistible Andy." Impressed, Andy called Barney "the Adolphe Menjou of

Mayberry." Unlike Barney's suit, the Menjou reference is one of the very few things that didn't wear well with age. Menjou was a Hollywood actor known for being a natty dresser.

Even a suit needs a stunt double.

During the eight-year run, the suit appears in forty different episodes, including two in which it has its own scene. In Episode #104, "Up in Barney's Room," the suit is hanging in Barney's open closet; in Episode #135, "Barney's Uniform," it hangs in wait on the gun rack in the courthouse. "Barney's Uniform" is the episode in which Barney, threatened by Fred Plummer (Allan Melvin), decides to remain in uniform all the time so Plummer won't beat him up. Later in that episode, a stunt suit doubling for the star's was worn by judo instructor Mr. Izamoto, who took care of Plummer in short order.

Knotts's deputy uniform also makes one solo appearance. In the final episode of the fifth season [Episode #159, "Banjo Playing Deputy"], Knotts's last as a regular member of the cast, the uniform hangs from the hatrack in the back room of the courthouse, a salute to the actor who had become a television legend.

I'd like to thank the Academy.

And the winner is . . . Don Knotts, who won five Emmys for "The Andy Griffith Show."

Knotts remembered: "As far as the Emmys go, I was not only surprised, I was totally shocked! As a matter of fact, I was painting my fence when they called me. My wife called me in and said I was wanted on the phone, and they said they were notifying me because I had been nominated for an Emmy. I said, 'What?' I just couldn't believe it. I thought it was a joke. By the last one I was almost embarrassed. I think it was a record at the time. I don't think it is anymore."

From the *Bernard P. Fife Handbook of Pioneering Moxie.*

• Fires started pioneer style are bound to be hotter than fires started with ordinary matches.

• Wild pheasants may be the toughest bird to ensnare.

Names the girls called Barney

NAME	EPISODE
Naughty Deputy (said by Emma Brand after her arrest for jay-walking)	#1, "The New Housekeeper"
Barney, Parney, Poo (Hilda Mae and later Andy)	#11, "Christmas Story"
Barney Honey, Sugar, Cream Puff (Ellie)	#12, "Ellie for Council"
Frank Sinatra (Elizabeth Growley)	#35, "Andy and the Woman Speeder"
Squirt (Melissa Stevens and later Andy)	#36, "Barney on the Rebound"
Bernie (Skippy)	#68, "Barney Mends a Broken Heart"
(Skippy)	#123, "The Fun Girls"
(and Skippy again)	#155, "The Arrest of the Fun Girls"
Barney Boy (Juanita)	#69, "Andy and the New Mayor"
Al (Sally, Maude, and Floyd)	#74, "Convicts at Large"
Rat (Sally)	
Bartender (Ramona Wiley)	#82, "Class Reunion"
The Sucker of the World (Mrs. Lesch)	#90, "Barney's First Car"
Rabble-rouser (Aunt Bee)	#148, "Barney Runs for Sheriff"
Barney, Baby (Teena Andrews)	#212, "Barney Comes to Mayberry"

Soused!

Barney never intentionally let alcohol pass his lips. Occasionally, however, some managed to sneak through—and the effect was often hilarious.

• Barney first gets drunk in Episode #46, "The Keeper of the Flame." Andy and Jubell Foster haggle over the amount of damage Jubell claimed Opie and his friends did to Jubell's barn. They had reached $450 when Barney sways up with a snootful.

• Episode #76, "Barney and the Governor." While they are waiting for the governor of North Carolina to arrive, Barney gets drunk on spring water, unaware that Otis has spiked it with moonshine.

• Episode #104, "Up in Barney's Room." Barney gets drunk on sweet cider while waiting for news about Mr. Fields, who was going to marry Mrs. Mendelbright. Barney did not like him for the following reasons: "A. A guy moves into town,
2. He has no job, and
C. He wants to marry Mrs. Bendelmright."

• Episode #139, "The Darling Baby." Barney gets drunk on mulberry squeezin's during the contract signing for the marriage of Opie to Andilina Darling Wash.

• Episode #141, "Otis Sues the County." After Otis files suit against the county, Barney gets smashed in the cell with him while trying to loosen his tongue, culminating with the two of them crooning a moving rendition of "Sweet Adeline."

• Episode #149, "If I had a Quarter Million Dollars." Barney passes out cold during a stakeout at the Mayberry Hotel after the crook Hennessey (played by Al Checco) puts knockout drops in Barney's nonfat milk.

From *The Fife Dictionary for the Modern Deputy*.

Exactilioso: A fancy lawman way of saying exactly.
It's therapetic: You should get it off your chest.
C'est la vie, Man: That's the way it goes.
A big mélage: 1. Making a big thing out of something. 2. A plaster cast.
Onvicts-kay ere-hay!: A coded Mayday call used when being held in a cabin by three escaped female convicts.
A-pa-thee (pronounced with the accent on the second syllable): The reason there is so much crime.
Inarculated: What happens when the doctor gives you a shot.
Reveng: Well, you know what he means.
Electronally: Things that operate on electronals, as in "The age of science," "know-how," and "electronal marvels."
La Amour Toujour Zamour: A little lovestruck.
Uno, Duo, Trey . . . Four, Five: How to count in French.
And this little trick for remembering how to spell: "I" before "e" except after "c" and "e" before "n" in chicken.
Nave (naive): Used to describe the kind of guy needed to go with Thel's

cousin, Mary Grace Gossage, to Saturday night's big annual Chamber of Commerce Dance.

E.S.P.: Extra sensitive perception.

Petula obendala: Part of the brain.

El truckos: Highway Patrol talk for truck drivers.

Fusitious: Similar to facetious.

Scram-a-voo: Lawman talk for getaway.

Spliced: Married.

Weddsville: See *Spliced.*

He's so suave and worldly.

The fact that Don Knotts was a bit of a ladies' man might seem inconsistent with the memories of Barney Fife, but according to Everett Greenbaum, there was a bit of "the tiger" in him.

"Ev and Jim Fritzell wrote my first three pictures. That was no coincidence. I had Universal hire them," Don Knotts said. Everett Greenbaum picked up the story. "Jim and I wrote three pictures starring Don. In the years when we were doing those movies, when I'd be on the road with Don, I always felt that I was with a naughty younger brother.

"He kept trying to fix me up with girls when we were on the road, you know. Oh, it would be awful. We were in Cape Canaveral, and he tells me he has two wonderful girls that we're going to take dancing. And we go to this *awful* nightclub with these two *awful* girls—and the next thing I know, Don has disappeared. And suddenly he turns up in the floor show dancing and singing. Then he comes back, and these two girls ask us if we mind if they go to the ladies' room. So they go, and they never came back. They climbed out of a window, and we saw them later with two pimply sailors. I said, 'Look at that! They prefer them to two big shots from Hollywood.' Don said, 'Don't tell anybody about this or I'll kill you.' "

From *The Bernard P. Fife Deputy Manual.*

Regulation Salute:

The right hand is held rigid by your side, the thumb flat against the forefinger. With the elbow out, the arm is brought up at a forty-five-degree angle with the tip of the index finger touching the visor of the cap, whereupon contacting, it is immediately released with a snap to its original position.

High yup puh-hah!

High yup puh-hah!

Episode #63, "Deputy Otis."

Asleep at the switch.

• Episode #42, "The Clubmen." Andy catches Barney sleeping on a cot in the back room of the courthouse, so he hides Barney's shoes, slams the door, and then sends Barney out to fix a stop sign on Elm Street.

• Episode #54, "The Merchant of Mayberry." Andy finds Barney napping on the bench in front of the courthouse. Andy shaves off the tip of Aunt Bee's lipstick, puts it in Barney's open hand, tickles his nose with a broom straw, and then tells him to deal with Joe Waters, who has parked his truck too close to a fireplug. Joe blows Barney a kiss. Barney's reaction to Andy's gag: "Why don't we go up to the old folks' home and wax the steps?"

• Episode #62, "Cousin Virgil." Barney is again caught napping in the back room of the courthouse. Andy stealthily pulls the blanket over his head and tucks the corners under the legs of the cot. He then goes back and slams the door to wake Barney, who is trapped under the blanket like a cat in a bag.

• Episode #94, "Mountain Wedding." Andy finds Barney asleep at 4:00 A.M. on the morning they need to go to the Darlings to deal with Ernest T. Bass. Andy tries to wake him with an alarm clock, by picking him up, slapping his face, shaking him, yelling, and blowing Barney's whistle. He finally rouses him with a snap of the fingers.

• Episode #122, "A Deal Is a Deal." Barney is caught sleeping at his desk when Opie and the boys enter to find out what a blacklist is.

• Episode #146, "The Lucky Letter." Andy walks in and catches Barney napping in the back room. He switches their hats before waking him up.

• Episode #147, "Goober and the Art of Love." Barney is caught asleep in the desk chair by Goober just before his 8:00 P.M. date with Lydia (Josie Lloyd).

We defy the Mafia . . .

Barney's first arrest: Emma Brand. Violation: jaywalking. Result: Andy lets her go. *Episode #1, "The New Housekeeper."*

Barney's biggest haul: The Mayberry 20. Conspirators included most of the known citizens of Mayberry, among them:

- Judd Fletcher, disturbing the peace, Municipal Code 721-8

- Franklin, the bank president

- Otis Campbell, drunk and disorderly

- Mayor Pike, vagrancy and loitering, Municipal Code 439

- Aunt Bee, unlawful assembly and inciting a riot, Municipal Code 421

- Opie. Aunt Bee couldn't leave him home alone, could she? The arrests all occurred in Episode #16, "Andy Saves Barney's Morale," when Andy left Mayberry for the day and put Barney in charge. Cases dismissed.

It's definitely no fun when that iron door clangs shut.
Number of times Barney locked himself in a cell: ten.

- Episode #13, "Mayberry Goes Hollywood"—three (twice alone and once with Andy)

- Episode #24, "The New Doctor"—once alone.

- Episode #26, "The Inspector"—once with Andy.

- Episode #44, "Sheriff Barney"—once (though it was the third time he had done it that week, but we won't count that).

- Episode #79, "One Punch Opie"—twice (once after giving the boys a speech about being "inarculated" and a second time after asking Leon to shut the door while he was cleaning a cell. Leon thought he meant the door of the cell).

- Episode #99, "Ernest T. Bass Joins the Army"—once with Andy (after discovering what Barney thought was Ernest T.'s hidden key).

- Episode #128, "Barney's Bloodhound"—once with Andy (after jailing escaped con Ralph Neal, played by Arthur Butanides, Blue picked up the key and Andy and Barney had to struggle to convince Blue that they, not the convict, should have the key. Barney and Andy won by blowing the dog whistle).

The people who can wear a badge nowadays.
The number of times Barney was arrested or jailed: 3.

• Episode #33, "Barney's Replacement." Barney is jailed for violation of the Green River Ordinance (peddling merchandise within the city limits without a license).

• Episode #36, "Barney on the Rebound." Barney is charged with breach of promise to Melissa Stevens.

• Episode #106, "Citizen's Arrest." Barney is jailed after committing a 9-11 (illegal U-turn) and refusing to pay the fine.

It was a local rock.
Barney's Daddy's Rock had a lot of good memories attached to it. The rock used to sit right on his daddy's desk. When Barney was a boy, his father used to let him strike kitchen matches on it and hold it to his pipe. That was a big thrill for Barney. The fact that Barney kept the rock from his father's desk said a good deal about how sentimental Barney was. His memory of striking the matches as a little boy added a very real, warm dimension to a comic character. The irony, as Everett Greenbaum tells it, is that the rock had no significance to the writers. "We did a lot of things with rocks on this show, but this was totally made up. Rocks just always struck me and Jim as funny. But to find actors who would understand these things was a real joy."

No wonder Thel went for him.
In Episode #22, "Cyrano Andy," Knotts hits his stride as Barney Fife solidly for the first time. He shows levels of shyness, anger, suave womanizer, and scared rabbit. That episode was also the first with Betty Lynn as Thelma Lou.

No more peanut-butter-and-jelly sandwiches.
"It wasn't easy leaving the show," Knotts said, "but the reason I left was that Andy all along had said that he was only going to do five years. I had a

five-year contract, so in the middle of the year I began looking around, as you have to in this business. I had several offers, but I got a good one from Universal. I had always wanted to be in the movies because there was no TV when I was a kid. Then Andy, like at the very last minute, he comes up to me, and he says, 'You know, I'm going to stay on.' And I said, 'Oh, well, great.' And he said, 'You wanna stay?' And I said, 'Well, I've already kind of told Universal . . .'

"It wasn't easy to do, but I thought I better go while I had a good offer to do pictures. It wasn't easy, but I was also excited at that point about the deal, and that was it. I remember I came back to do the first guest shot, and all the crew cheered, and I said (as Barney), 'So you're still working on this small screen, are you?' "

"The Andy Griffith Show" stands out for Knotts as the personal highlight of his career: "The overall memory was that it was the best experience of my career. To go into a relaxed show with a great cast—and Andy was so great that it stayed that way for five years. That's my memory."

BEATRICE TAYLOR

. . . .

**AKA BLOODY MARY,
FIFI, THE UPSTAIRS MAID,
THE FOSTER LADY, MISS GAD-ABOUT,
AND, OF COURSE, AUNT BEE
CREATED BY FRANCES BAVIER
173 EPISODES**

"Beatrice, in Latin, means 'she who makes happy.' "
—PROFESSOR HUBERT ST. JOHN,
Episode #230, "Aunt Bee and the Lecturer"

I'm giving her twenty-four hours.

Aunt Bee arrived on a Tuesday, having told Andy that after he called, she got down on her knees and thanked God she had somewhere to go and something to do. On Wednesday, Opie decided to run away.

A New Yorker played the perfect southern aunt? Gol-ly.

Of all the regulars on "The Andy Griffith Show," Frances Bavier was the most experienced actor in the cast. A native of New York City, Bavier attended Columbia University and was a graduate of the American Academy of the Arts. After completing her training, Bavier spent more than twenty years on the New York stage. She starred in both vaudeville and Broadway productions, including *Kiss and Tell, Point of No Return,* and *The Lady Says No.*

Imagine if she had a niece or nephew.

"She was an ingénue," Hal Smith recalled. "She was a beautiful young lady, and I think she always saw herself that way. One day she came to me and said, 'This isn't for me. This is not my show.'

"I said, 'What are you talking about?'

"And she said, 'I just don't feel comfortable with it.' I asked her why, and she said, 'Oh . . . I'm not an aunt.'

" 'You're the perfect aunt,' I told her. But of course, even though she won an Emmy for her role as Aunt Bee, she never saw herself that way."

It might look good on the wall.

Since Bavier's early years were spent on the Broadway stage, it is difficult to find images of the young Aunt Bee. The careful observer can still get a glimpse of the young Bavier by paying attention to any one of five early "Andy Griffith" episodes.

A framed publicity photo of the ingénue Bavier can be seen hanging in the Taylor living room in each of these shows. For no apparent reason, the photo is never in the same spot.

Frances Bavier in her days as a Broadway ingenue.

"One of the things Aaron Ruben used to do," recalled Don Knotts, "was move pictures around. No one knew why, but he was always shifting and changing pictures. I guess he must have had one of those picture-hanging compulsions."

The photo first appears in Episode #1, "The New Housekeeper." Just after Aunt Bee arrives, she and Andy pass the photo as they cross in toward the kitchen. In the final scene of Episode #8, "A Feud Is a Feud," the photo can be seen hanging in the same spot, on the wall around the corner from the entryway to the kitchen.

Later that season, in Episode #18, "Andy, the Marriage Counselor," when Cliff (Forrest Lewis) comes over to report that Fred Boone just punched him in the nose, the portrait shows up on the back wall over the side table.

In Episode #23, "Andy and Opie, Housekeepers," Bee stands just to the left of the photo as she is preparing to leave for the bus.

Finally, in the show's second season, the photo emerges again. In Episode #38, "Aunt Bee's Brief Encounter," the photo can be seen very clearly, hanging over Henry Wheeler's (Edgar Buchanan) right shoulder on the wall next to the front door.

• •

"I always considered that cast of characters the epitome of comedic craziness. And don't you know that Aunt Bee's pie was killer!"

—LISA HARTMAN BLACK,
actress

• •

And the winner is . . .

Though in Episode #219, "Goober's Contest," Aunt Bee claims never to have won anything in her life, she must have had a very short memory—she was the hands-down champion when it came to winning sweepstakes.

In Episode #165, "Aunt Bee on TV," Aunt Bee was on "Win or Lose," starring Jack Smith, and she won the sweepstakes.

Aunt Bee's Prizes
Washing machine
Dishwasher
Ice crusher
Television set
Garbage disposal
Dryer
A genuine Ranch Mink from Darcey Furs, Hollywood, "Furrier to the Stars"

The value of Aunt Bee's prizes
$4,850.00

The tax based on Andy's income
$1,138.72

In Episode #219, "Goober's Contest," Bee won $5 in the big "Grab Bag for Cash" promotion at Wally's filling station.

In Episode #227, "A Trip to Mexico," Aunt Bee won the Tampico Tamale Contest. First prize was an all-expense-paid ten-day trip to Mexico for two.

In Episode #234, "Aunt Bee's Cousin," it was mentioned that Aunt Bee's ice cream won first prize at the County Fair.

Aunt Bee, the diplomat.

"Every once in a while, Jim Fritzell and I would go on the set," said Everett Greenbaum. "We loved Sweeney, Don, and Andy, just about everyone there, but we never really got along with Aunt Bee . . . I'll tell you what she'd do to me. Whenever there was a party—a wrap party or something, she'd say to me, 'You know there's only one thing really wrong with this show.' I'd say, 'What is it, Frances?' 'The writing.' she'd say. 'The writing is vile.'"

He was such a nice young man until he met the Greenbaum boy.

In 1986 Harvey Bullock and Everett Greenbaum were called upon to write the script for the long-awaited film *Return to Mayberry*. The telefilm reunited all of "The Andy Griffith Show"'s major characters with the exception of two—Howard McNear, who died in 1969, and Frances Bavier, who was then eighty-four.

"Originally," Bullock explained, "there was a lot of talk about using Frances, do we . . . do we not? And it was finally decided that she was a little too old and a little too sickly. She was living in North Carolina, and it was the decision that Aunt Bee die. Now this has been dissected—when death came to Mayberry, you know—this was an unusual thing, but it was primarily a decision made just out of practicality." The first death to strike Mayberry did not occur until Episode #238, "The Church Benefactors," when Jared Hooper went on to his reward.

"So, we thought we would have Bee's voice come from the grave. This is where Everett was marvelous. He would say those little things like, 'Well, it's the sleep before eleven o'clock that counts, and always wear your clean underwear because you might get in an accident.' All those little things they just spout out. So we wrote this thing—some advice for them that she could record as a voice-over—and it ended with her saying, '. . . and always wear clean underwear. I know it doesn't show, but it's what we think of ourselves that counts.' "

It seemed like a simple-enough solution, but things did not work out as the writers imagined. Bullock continued, "We sent her the script, and she was outraged. She said, 'I will not say underwear. I have never said underwear. And I will not say underwear now!' Ev and I had no idea, so ultimately we had to find another actress to do her voice."

She told Andy to keep it brief.

As Aunt Bee went off to see Aunt Louise (Episode #65, "Andy and Opie, Bachelors"), she said the word "underwear" not once but *twice*. She first told Andy where his clean ones were—a strange thing for a grown man not to know, even in Mayberry, and then she admonished him to change his underwear when he got home.

And speaking of that voice . . .

"Bee was a very strong character, too," Aneta Corsaut remembered, "and like myself Frances was rather strong-willed. Though they still did all the fluffy things with Bee, which was hysterical considering Frances was playing her. The voice of course, was a character choice. She had that flutey tone . . . that wasn't her normal speaking voice."

It wasn't just the poetry, but her reading.

In Episode #96, "Briscoe Declares for Aunt Bee," Briscoe Darling falls for Bee after she recites "My Fading Flower of Forgotten Love" by Agnes Ellicot Strom.

If at first you do succeed . . .

Considered by most fans of "The Andy Griffith Show" to be one of the classics, Episode #43, "The Pickle Story," will forever be linked with Aunt Bee.

As the writer of "The Pickle Story," Harvey Bullock, recalled, "If I had done 'The Pickle Story' first I don't think I ever would have worked again."

As is common in television, a cast's first exposure to new scripts comes at a table reading, a closed-door meeting in which each member of the cast reads his or her part aloud around a table. Although the producer and director were allowed to be present, in the case of "The Andy Griffith Show" there was an unwritten rule that writers were not invited.

"That was lucky for me," Bullock said. "It was the second script I'd written for them. ["Opie's Hobo Friend" was the first.] I had no idea until years later when Aaron Ruben told me that when they read it around the table it was received with dead silence. Aaron was thinking, 'Hey, I thought we found a new writer in this Bullock guy, but this—this is terrible.' At the time, though, they were still shooting thirty episodes a season, a third more than now, and knowing the appetite of the camera was so tremendous, they went ahead and shot it. And to their surprise, it worked."

> Aunt Bee's first pickle victim—Clara
> 2nd—Barney and Andy
> 3rd—A fly that made the mistake of landing on one

> Single batch = 8 jars
> Double batch = 16 jars
> Total that Aunt Bee made = 24 jars

She probably refused to fly in coach, too.

Members of the cast and crew were aware of a need to be careful of how they acted around Bavier. "She was a rather spooky lady, personally," one writer recalled. Even when out of character she expected everyone to behave as proper ladies and gentlemen.

"You had to tiptoe around her on the set," Harvey Bullock said.

And whatever you do, don't ride a motorcycle.

In Episode #112, "Barney's Sidecar," Barney's obsession with his new motorcycle conjures up some fond memories of a war movie for Aunt Bee. In the film, the Nazis were riding along on motorcycles, prompting the Allies to set up piano wire across a road. That finished off the enemy.

But then Aneta never asked her to say underwear.

One cast member Bavier became very close to was Aneta Corsaut. "She was wonderful to me on the set. We got along very well. In fact, I think she's a wonderful actress for any ingénue to watch."

That was before you got that motorcycle.

Don Knotts, whose rapport with Bavier translated well on the screen, concurred: "Frances and I never had any problems. They'd tell me she could get a little difficult, but she never showed it on the set."

Now that you mention it, we did have to run her in a couple of times.

Aunt Bee was arrested in Episode #16, "Andy Saves Barney's Morale," for violating Code 421, Unlawful Assemblage, and for inciting a riot. According to the police report, she was talking to some women in front of the courthouse when Barney asked them to move along. Unable to control themselves, the ladies kept talking and when Barney insisted, one woman raised her umbrella to him.

In Episode #87, "Aunt Bee's Medicine Man," Andy had to lock up his own Aunt Bee and five members of the Ladies' Aid Church Committee for drunkenness.

From *The Mayberry Cookbook.*

Lillian's Meatballs
1 percent meat
99 percent bread crumbs
Cook in the oven until vulcanized

Rabble-rouser.

Mayberry's first sign that the 1960s would be the age of protest came when Aunt Bee led a demonstration in front of the courthouse. She was not protesting military advisers being sent to a foreign country but the construction of a new highway.

Sometimes art really does imitate life.

Aunt Bee had a few problems with directors. John Masters never measured up to Bee's high standards. That fella who worked on the Foster Lady commercial did have a very commanding voice, although Aunt Bee did not mean to criticize him.

Frances Bavier also had her own quirks when it came to dealing with directors. When Howard Morris started directing episodes of "The Andy Griffith Show," there was a little tension between the two of them.

"You had to direct her in a certain way," Morris said. "I love actors, and I think that a show is only successful if the juice of an actor is allowed to flow. Your job as director is to do that. Now she was an old pro. She was a star on Broadway and all that. I'd say, 'Now take it easy, and listen good.' I'd never say 'Action.' I'd say, 'All right, ready . . . go.' She wanted somebody to say, 'Ac-tion!' I was embarrassed to say that. It was like a Hollywood movie. I couldn't do it!"

Give the guy a break. He passed it, he didn't heave it.

"She was a strange lady," Howard Morris, legendary for his portrayal of Ernest T. Bass, recalled. "Very good. A brilliant talent, perfect for the part, and as real a character portrayed as you'll ever see anywhere . . . but she was strange."

Morris was the only member of "The Andy Griffith Show" who both acted with and directed Bavier. "I don't think she liked me. I was too crude. As Ernest T., she resented me terribly. The scene where we're sitting at the table, and I grab the potatoes [Episode #113, "My Fair Ernest T. Bass"], she thought that was terrible. She tried to get that cut from the show."

It must have been the liver. She looked right at it and started crying.

Little things that make women cry:

• Sounds

• Smells

• Songs on the radio

• And, according to Opie, liver

I think Aunt Bee knows all the words to "You Make Me Feel So Young."

One show that Morris specifically recalled was Episode #130, "Aunt Bee's Romance."

"She wasn't easy during the shooting of that, but suddenly you know, there was Wallace Ford as Roger Hanover, and he was flirting and kissing her on the back of the neck, and suddenly she started bouncing around like an eighteen-year-old. She was being wooed. Look at it. You can see it happen."

Back then Log Cabin syrup actually came in a log cabin.

"Frances was a little eccentric," Jack Dodson admitted, "and she would get in a snit occasionally, but no more than that. I had a very cordial relationship with her, and I think what most people don't realize is that her parents were in their forties when she was born. When you think about how old Frances was

[Bavier died December 6, 1989, at the age of eighty-six], that would mean her upbringing reflected the proprieties of the middle of the 1800s. Frances was a woman who was brought up with a completely different type of values than we had then and especially different from a Hollywood television environment."

OPIE TAYLOR

....

AKA BIRDMAN
CREATED BY RON HOWARD
177 EPISODES

"He should make a fine dentist."

He was so mature, he was like a short adult.

Aaron Ruben, who shares a birthday with Ron Howard, commented on his feelings toward the then child actor. "He was one of the most professional actors I've ever worked with. You know who deserved all the credit for that? Ronnie's parents. They were so unlike any stage parents. He also had the benefit of having his father on the set as well as Andy—who became somewhat of a surrogate father. They became very close. Andy would talk to him. If there was something Ronnie was doing that Andy thought Ronnie could do better, or differently, Andy would lean over and tell him quietly. They developed a wonderful relationship. There truly was a genuine affection and warmth between the two of them."

Other members of "The Andy Griffith Show" cast, crew, and creative team have made it clear that parental influence kept Ron Howard grounded and made him such a pleasure on the set. The credit, Don Knotts said, went largely to his father, Rance: "Ron Howard was so easy to work with, and his dad was such a good person. He wasn't at all like many of the other kids I've worked with, and that was probably because he had such great parents."

Remember it was the middle of the 1960s.

Hidden under Opie's pillow:

- A slingshot

- An apple

- A peanut butter sandwich

- A matchbox containing "The Sacred Candle" and kitchen matches

Jerry Mathers was booked, and the Bonaduce kid wasn't born yet.

Without Ron Howard in the role of Mayberry's favorite son, Opie Taylor, "The Andy Griffith Show" would have been like a cake without icing. Sheldon Leonard, who cast Howard in the role, told of the way in which he discovered Ron Howard, which was easier than convincing his father to let him star in a television series. "I had seen Ronnie Howard doing a pilot with Bert Lahr. The pilot failed, but the kid was so obviously charismatic that I filed it away in my mind, and when time came to cast the pilot, I had my casting director look him up. He was five years old. He came in with his father, Rance, and while I was convinced that I wanted him, Rance wasn't convinced that he wanted us.

"He wasn't sure that he wanted his five-year-old boy to get committed to show business. This was different than a one-shot thing. This was a commitment of several years. I said, 'Look, if you're worried about him losing his childhood, don't. I have kids on my other shows. I have kids on 'The Danny

Ron Howard gave producer Aaron Ruben a sketch on March 1, 1962—the date of the birthday they share.

Thomas Show,' I've always worked with kids. We'll create an environment where he can be a kid. His friends can come visit him, he can bring his skates to the set with him, ride his bike, whatever he wants.'

"Reluctantly, Rance said he could do it. What if he had said no?"

And he didn't even want creative control.

Even at his tender age, Ron Howard was present at all the script meetings. Did he ever complain that a six-year-old wouldn't say this? Aaron Ruben emphatically answered, "No."

All in the family.

"The Andy Griffith Show" was often a Howard family affair. Ron's family spent a great deal of time on the set, which enabled his father, Rance, and brother, Clint, to get a few moments in the limelight, as well.

Clint Howard appeared as Leon in the following episodes:

Episode #49, "The Jinx"
Episode #78, "The Bank Job"
Episode #79, "One Punch Opie"
Episode #102, "A Black Day for Mayberry"
Episode #117, "The Shoplifters"

Rance Howard played several bit roles in the following episodes:

Episode #62, "Cousin Virgil," as the bus driver
Episode #76, "Barney and the Governor," as the chauffeur
Episode #102, "A Black Day for Mayberry," as the T-man. His line: "We'll wait."
Episode #125, "The Rumor," as a guest at the surprise party thrown for Helen and Andy

No wonder he felt so comfortable in Hollywood.

• Autographs Opie brought back from the Taylors' Hollywood vacation:

Audie Murphy
Tony Curtis

Doris Day
Rock Hudson
Kirk Douglas
Dean Martin
Dave Schneider (a necktie salesman—his sunglasses fooled Opie)

• Andy and Opie also had their first picture in Hollywood taken while holding Cesar Romero's newspaper.

• Darlene Mason—the leading lady in *Sheriff Without a Gun*—signed an autograph for Opie. "She sure has good penmanship."

Names Andy called Opie

NICKNAME	EPISODE
The Shortest Gun in the West	#4, "Runaway Kid"
Cannonball, Diamond Jim, Charley Money Bags, and the Big Philanthropist	#5, "Opie's Charity"
Tonto	#64, "Opie's Rival"
Tex	#66, "Mr. McBeevee"
Brother	#71, "Floyd, the Gay Deceiver"
Lefty	#85, "The Great Filling Station Robbery"
A Regular Mr. District Attorney	#130, "Aunt Bee's Romance"
Mr. Rockefeller	#136, "Opie's Fortune"
The Dancin' Boy	#181, "Look, Pa, I'm Dancing"

Early on he knew about the value of good entertainment.

In Episode #131, "Barney's Physical," Opie charged his friends a nickel to take a look at Barney hanging himself.

Aunt Bee didn't have to worry about sharing her kitchen.

Opie's recipe for boiled eggs:

Take an egg and put it in a pan of boiling water. When the water evaporates, add more. If your pa isn't awake by the time that water evaporates, add more again. Repeat for forty-five minutes.

Sandwiches Opie prepared for runaway kid George "Tex" Foley (Pat Rossen) to take on his trip to Texas:

Peanut butter and sardine
Peanut butter and bologna
Peanut butter and liverwurst
Peanut butter and peanut butter

He was a wizard with a jar of peanut butter. Episode #4, "Runaway Kid."

Names other kids called Opie

NICKNAME	EPISODE
Dopey, and Dopey Opie (Steve Quincy)	#79, "One Punch Opie"
TX4 (Tommy)	#170, "A Man's Best Friend"

. . . .

"I've always had a crush on Opie. Now I have a crush on Ron Howard."

—BEVERLY JOHNSON,
actress-model

. . . .

He should've been nominated for an Emmy.

In Episode #93, "Dogs, Dogs, Dogs," Barney tries to explain to Opie why the stray dogs he released into an open field will be all right. Reviewing a tape of that segment, Everett Greenbaum—the co-author of the episode—was amazed at the polished performance of the then eight-year-old actor. "To tell a kid to look at Barney so you don't quite believe him and have him do that so perfectly . . . well, no other kid in the world could do that. Ron Howard was just quite marvelous."

It's like a regular zoo in his room.

Opie was never without some form of animal friend, real or imagined. It was very natural for a country boy to enjoy playing with animals, as Opie did. Opie had several pets, including:

- Dickie the parakeet

- Gulliver the dog (not seen)

- Blackie the imaginary horse

- and a pet frog

Aneta Corsaut

Ron Howard suits up and is ready for "The Ball Game" in 1966.

Opie learns a valuable lesson.

Fans often cite Episode #101, "Opie, the Birdman," as one of their favorites. "That one I recall with great warmth," its writer, Harvey Bullock, said. "That was a wonderful story because it had within it all the right ingredients and that very touching final moment. You have Opie, who doesn't want to let the birds go, but his father tells him, 'You've got to, son. You gotta let go.' "

"Opie, the Birdman" has since been scrutinized as a story that uses the birds to symbolize Opie himself. "I've found people read a lot into these stories," Bullock said, "but I wasn't thinking about a boy without his mom. It was never meant to be allegorical."

You can do it!

In the final scene of "Opie, the Birdman" Andy utters one of the most memorable lines from the whole series.

"I remember it occurring to me," Bullock recalled. "You know, sometimes you're never quite sure how a script is working, and other times, the plot starts turning, and the characters start talking, and it all gets a little spooky. I remember coming to the end of that scene. I was right at the end, a couple of lines from finishing, and it just came out. Opie says, 'The cage is awful empty, Pa.' Andy says, 'But aren't the trees nice and full?' I thought, 'Hey! That's what I'm trying to say!' "

All creatures great and small.

What Bullock was trying to say through Opie and Andy may also have captured the feelings of others associated with "The Andy Griffith Show."

"I think that story is a perfect example of what we were trying to do," said Aneta Corsaut. "Harvey was able to say it so simply and so beautifully. We have to take care of each and every living thing, and at the same time we have to give them the freedom to live their own lives. He said it all." And Bullock said it using the youngest character on the show, a tribute to both the writer and Ron Howard.

It was not just sentiment that made "Opie, the Birdman" memorable. Bullock, who was a master of the misty moment, was just as good at making the audience laugh. In the script for "Opie, the Birdman," Bullock broke the tension with a scene in which Barney lectures Opie on the language of birds: "The whistling scene, you know, 'Here comes a cat!' That's an example of something we used to call a treacle cutter. It relieves the drama, so it doesn't seem like all violin music. It worked so well with Barney because he was the world's authority on *everything*."

Names Aunt Bee called Opie

NICKNAME	EPISODE
Naked Savage	#120, "Bargain Day"

A modern man's guide to modern women.

After watching Big Jeff Pruitt search for his bride in Episode #45, "The Farmer Takes a Wife," Opie came into the courthouse and told his pa that he had learned the technique for picking up girls. As Opie understood it, whenever a woman walks in, all you need to do is pick her up, then set her down, and say, "Excuse me, ma'am, just checkin' your weight."

A name Opie called himself

NICKNAME	EPISODE
The Taylor Dummy	#100, "The Sermon for Today"

One minute he's a young boy, next minute he's a big-shot director.

After "The Andy Griffith Show" ended, Ron Howard appeared as the teenage star of another hit series, "Happy Days," and has performed in many films. Eventually preferring a role behind the camera, Howard has become one of the most commercially successful directors in Hollywood.

Directing feature films has afforded Howard the opportunity to renew some old friendships from "The Andy Griffith Show." Actor-director Howard Morris recalled one such experience: "Ron and I would meet occasionally. He was a big fan of Ernest T.—he loved the character and still does. I was called to Disney to meet with them about a small part in a movie called *Splash*. We met, we embraced, as we do . . . We read the scene a few times, and he said, 'Hey, thanks very much, Howie. Thanks for coming in.' And I said okay, and I left. And I was just getting into my car in the parking lot, and I hear someone running like mad across the lot yelling, 'Howie!' It was Ron. He said, 'Hey, I didn't want you to leave without knowing I want you for the part.'

"He took the trouble to leave the office, go outside, run all the way across the parking lot to talk to me personally. Pretty nice kid. And he got that from his father and mother, who were good, God-fearing people who treated you decently."

MAYBERRY MILESTONES

· ·

Over the course of 249 episodes, there have been many milestones. The following is a catalog of some of the more important "firsts" that happened in Mayberry, a town where change occurred reluctantly.

Episode #1, "The New Housekeeper"

• First line: "Anybody here know why these two should not be wed, speak now or forever hold your peace."

• Opie was first sent to his room.

• First misty moment: Opie saying that Aunt Bee needs him.

• First song lyrics: *"You get a line and I'll get a pole / Crawdad hole."*

Episode #2, "The Manhunt"

• First person sent to jail: Otis Campbell. He let himself out.

• First phone call to Sarah, the operator.

• Barney couldn't find his bullet the first time Andy allowed him to load his gun.

• Barney first accidentally discharged his pistol—into the courthouse floor. He had to give back the bullets.

• Barney first tied up: runaway convict Dirkson (Mike Steen) got him with Barney's own gun belt and gagged him with his kerchief.

• Andy first carried sidearm.

• Andy got in his first "10-4."

Episode #4, "Runaway Kid"

• First shootout: Opie, Tommy, and Steve at the corner in front of the courthouse. Shot down the sheriff, but he was too busy to fall down and die.

• First sacred trust: between Opie and George "Tex" Foley.

Episode #5, "Opie's Charity"

• First reported death: Tom Silby, allegedly killed when run over by a taxi while on a business trip to Charlottesville.

Episode #6, "Ellie Comes to Town"

• First outsider: Ellie May Walker, Ph.G. (Pharmacy Gal).

• First reported murder: Emma Brand, reported by Emma Brand.

Episode #7, "Irresistible Andy"

• Barney wears the ol' salt and pepper for the first time. Andy is impressed enough to call him the Adolphe Menjou of Mayberry.

Episode #9, "Andy, the Matchmaker"

• Barney resigns for the first time, turning in:

1 badge
1 notebook
1 pencil
1 gun belt
1 holster
1 revolver
1 bullet

1 whistle
1 tie clip
1 tie
1 cap
1 flashlight
(and 1 pair of handcuffs, which he forgot to mention)

Barney resigned as a matter of principle: He claimed Opie teased him. Barney claimed he wrote a derogatory poem on the wall of the bank. The only problem was Opie had not yet learned how to write.

• Barney's first date: Miss Rosemary. Sealed with a handshake.

Episode #12, "Ellie for Council"

• Barney's first date with Hilda Mae, his second girl.

• Otis jailed for the first time for something other than drunkenness. He took a swipe at his wife with a leg of lamb. Although he missed his wife, he struck his mother-in-law in the mouth. Ironically, the theme of this episode was feminism.

• First woman to run for town council: Ellie May Walker. Mayberry took a big leap forward.

Episode #16, "Andy Saves Barney's Morale"

• First time Barney was made Actin' Sheriff. Barney had one duty: Cover the school crossin' at 3:00 P.M. This was also the first time Barney was guilty of trying too hard.

• First flashback: Barney's date with Hilda Mae the night before. She laughed at his hair after running her fingers through it.

• Barney's second resignation. He turned in one cap, one badge, one revolver, one bullet, and was up to one gun belt when he rescinded his resignation—the "Mayberry 20" had decided to turn themselves in for reincarceration.

Episode #17, "Alcohol and Old Lace"

• First shots taken at a lawman: Ben Sewell (Jack Prince) took two shots at Andy and Barney.

• First mention of Mayberry as a dry county. Andy mentions it despite the fact that Ben Weaver had said in Episode #11, "Christmas Story," that he had sold "spirits" in his store. Maybe he was just too cheap to advertise.

Episode #18, "Andy, the Marriage Counselor"

• Barney's first try at judo. Professor Matsu Matto's book, *The Art of Judo,* led Barney to two failed attempts at demonstrating the ancient art on Andy.

• First thing Fred Boone says to his wife, Jennie, each morning at the breakfast table: "Yegghh!"

Episode #22, "Cyrano Andy"

• First appearance of Betty Lynn as Thelma Lou.

• First time Thelma Lou concocts a scheme to make Barney jealous. That didn't take very long.

Episode #24, "The New Doctor"

• Barney duck-walks for the first time. He is behind the drugstore counter, hiding from Ellie and the new doctor.

Episode #25, "A Plaque for Mayberry"

• First "You beat everything, you know that?" Barney said it to Andy after he confessed that he did not get a substitute for Otis at the acceptance ceremony for the plaque honoring Otis's descendant, Nathan Tibbs.

Episode #27, "Ellie Saves a Female"

• First make-over: Francine Flint by Ellie May Walker.

Episode #28, "Andy Forecloses"

• Barney's first mention of his phobia with hats. He did not like anyone touching his hat, just like his mother.

• First mention of Juanita Beasley, the new waitress at the truck stop, the Junction Café.

Episode #29, "Quiet Sam"

• First baby born: Andy Becker, born to Sam and Lilly Becker. Named after Andy Taylor, who performed his first baby delivery.

• First of many rocks in the episodes written by Jim Fritzell and Everett Greenbaum. It was held by Floyd, who was waiting outside the house, armed but not necessarily dangerous.

Episode #30, "Barney Gets His Man"

• First surprise party for Barney. In future episodes these parties served as a harbinger of bad luck. This one ended before it began when the announcement was made that bad guy Eddie Brooks had escaped and was heading for Mayberry.

Episode #31, "The Guitar Player Returns"

• Barney gives his first police escort: to Jim Lindsey. He drove him from the courthouse three doors down to the Mayberry Hotel.

Episode #35, "Andy and the Woman Speeder"

• First official female prisoner: Elizabeth Crowley. There were other women locked up prior to this, including Aunt Bee, but those were just regular folks, not real lawbreakers.

Episode #41, "Crime-free Mayberry"

• The new map in the courthouse, first seen in this episode.

Episode #43, "The Pickle Story"

• First victim of one of Aunt Bee's pickles: her friend Clara Johnson.

Episode #44, "Sheriff Barney"

• Andy's first assignment as acting deputy under Acting Sheriff Fife: Go out and chalk some tires.

• Barney's first case as sheriff: Sid Osgood v. Huey Welch. The chicken-wire case. Osgood put up a fence on Welch's property line, blocking sunlight from reaching Welch's layin' hens. Precedent: Willoughby v. Perkins.

Episode #45, "The Farmer Takes a Wife"

• First recorded "Nip it in the bud!"

Episode #47, "Bailey's Bad Boy"

• First bad rock-and-roll: heard on Ron "Bad Boy" Bailey's transistor radio.

Episode #68, "Barney Mends a Broken Heart"

• Andy's first "You beat everything, you know that?" to Barney.

Episode #69, "Andy and the New Mayor"

• First time Andy's jaw muscles were visibly working: when Mayor Roy Stoner threatened him for letting Jess Morgan go home for three days to harvest his crops.

Episode #70, "The Cow Thief"

• The phrase "Let's get busy," made popular by late-night talk-show host Arsenio Hall, was first used by Mayor Roy Stoner: "Let's get busy, Sheriff."

Episode #73, "Lawman Barney"

• First appearance of Wally, the owner of the filling station.

• First time Andy gave Barney a direct order: Go out and get the truck farmers to move.

Episode #74, "Convicts at Large"

• First and only use of pig Latin in Mayberry: Barney tried to warn Andy by yelling "Onvicts-kay ere-hay!"

Episode #77, "Man in a Hurry"

• Jim Nabor's first episode filmed, although his TV debut was actually on Christmas Eve of 1962 in Episode #78, "The Bank Job."

• First porch scene: Barney decides he's going to go home, take a nap, go over to Thelma Lou's, and watch TV.

Episode #80, "High Noon in Mayberry"

• Gomer first deputized. He got his first taste of serving his country—or at least his county. He loved guns, he loved being a deputy, he loved riding in the patrol car.

• Barney "took a lock" for the first time.

Episode #82, "Class Reunion"

• Andy's first real love scene—shot with a filtered lens, the only such shot in the series.

Episode #85, "The Great Filling Station Robbery"

• Gomer's first "Shazaam!"

Episode #86, "Andy Discovers America"

• First appearance of Aneta Corsaut as Helen Crump.

• First sign of the Crump temper.

Episode #92, "A Wife for Andy"

• Andy's first date with Helen: to Mount Pilot for Chinese.

Episode #123, "The Fun Girls"

• First episode with actor George Lindsey. This was the first and only episode featuring both George Lindsey as Goober and Jim Nabors as Gomer Pyle.

Episode #136, "Opie's Fortune"

• First divorce: Lorraine and Howard Fletcher. Why? Because she could not stay off the sauce.

Episode #137, "Goodbye, Sheriff Taylor"

• First episode in which Otis appears and is not either drunk or jailed.

Episode #141, "Otis Sues the County"

• First time the phantom footsteps are heard covering Floyd's entrance after Howard McNear's recovery from a stroke.

Episode #160, "Aunt Bee, the Swinger"

• First episode broadcast in color.

Episode #170, "A Man's Best Friend"

• Goober's dog Spot's first line: "Nope."

Episode #192, "The Lodge"

• Howard's first words as a member of the Regal Order of the Golden Door to Good Fellowship: "I sure could use one of those root beers."

Episode #195, "The Ball Game"

• Andy's first called strike was a pitch way over the kid's head—you had to know there was going to be trouble.

Episode #215, "Opie's Piano Lesson"

• First African-American in a speaking role. Flip Conroy (Rockne Tarrington) returned to work in his father's business after college and a professional career with the New York Giants.

Episode #218, "Opie's Most Unforgettable Character"

• First voice from someone's brain: Goober responding to Andy's comment that he guessed Goober had done some living in his time. Goober thinks out loud, "You can say that again."

Episode #221, "Goober, the Executive"

• First look at Emmett's Fix-It Shop.

Episode #222, "Howard's Main Event"

• First love montage: Millie and Howard at lunch, walking down Main Street, on a hilltop, next to each other pointing, walking down the lane.

. . . .

"Doing what I did in a complex, crime-ridden city like Gotham City for all those years, I sought the simple easygoing escape to Mayberry whenever I could get away. Andy and Don and the others were warm and amusing hosts even to a millionaire philanthropist."

—ADAM WEST,
actor

. . . .

Episode #229, "Opie's Group"

• The Sound Committee's first gig: Brenda Roach's birthday party. They were paid $5 a person.

Episode #235, "Howard's New Life"

• First dream sequence: Howard dreams Bee and Andy come to the island and find him tearing newspapers at the general store.

Episode #238, "The Church Benefactors"

• First actual death: Jared Hooper passes on and leaves $500 to the church.

WHERE IN THE WORLD IS . . .

. . . .

During the run of "The Andy Griffith Show," several characters disappeared without explanation. Since milk was delivered in bottles in Mayberry, there was no great way to locate missing persons. As a service to the good citizens of Mayberry, the following is a brief dossier on the missing.

Episode #10, "Stranger in Town"
Missing: Floyd I.

Description: The first town barber.

Reportedly had an argument with Deputy Fife regarding his sideburns.

Last seen: At barbershop.

Whereabouts: Unknown.

Episode #10, "Stranger in Town"
Missing: Ed Sawyer.

Description: Average height, black hair, overbearing, claimed to be from New York.

Believed by some to be from the supernatural world or maybe even a spy.

Last seen: Outside the courthouse speaking to gas station owner George Safferly. Safferly asked Sawyer to drop by the station to discuss his interest in purchasing the filling station.

Whereabouts: Unknown.

Episode #24, "The New Doctor"
Missing: Dr. Robert Benson.

Description: Young, Caucasian, six feet tall, dark hair, could be considered handsome.

Expressed definite intentions of moving with his fiancée to live in Mayberry.

Last seen: Speaking with Sheriff Taylor and druggist Ellie May Walker.

Whereabouts: Unknown.

Episode #29, "Quiet Sam"
Missing: Sam Becker.

Description: Farmer. Had a striking resemblance to the father on "The Patty Duke Show." Displayed peculiar behavior attributed to worry over the impending birth of his first child.

Last seen: Standing on the porch of his farmhouse with Sheriff Taylor, Deputy Fife, and the "new" Floyd.

Whereabouts: Unknown.

Episode #31, "The Guitar Player Returns"
Missing: Ellie May Walker.

Description: Young, attractive, female. Worked as Mayberry town pharmacist.

Last seen: Speaking with traveling bandleader Bobby Fleet.

Whereabouts: Unknown.

Episode #39, "Mayberry Goes Bankrupt"
Missing: Frank Myers.

Description: In his seventies, Caucasian, whiskered. Formerly in the business of making wooden berries for ladies' hats.

At one time was believed to be owed in excess of $350,000 by the city of Mayberry.

Last seen: Standing in front of his newly remodeled home with several Mayberry citizens.

Whereabouts: Unknown.

Episode #48, "The Manicurist"
Missing: Mayor Pike.

Description: Short, round, balding. Spoke with a squeaky voice.

Last seen: Getting a manicure at Floyd's Barbershop.

Whereabouts: Unknown.

Episode #54, "The Merchant of Mayberry"
Missing: Ben Weaver I.

Description: The first Ben Weaver and the owner of Weaver's Department Store.

Last seen: Going fishing with Andy Taylor.

Whereabouts: Unknown.

Episode #152, "The Case of the Punch in the Nose"
Missing: Charley Foley.

Description: In his fifties, Caucasian, male. Owned and operated Foley's Market.

Reportedly had differences with barber Floyd Lawson.

Last seen: At courthouse patching up differences with Floyd Lawson.

Whereabouts: Unknown.

Episode #201, "A New Doctor in Town"
Missing: Dr. Thomas Peterson.

Description: Young, Caucasian, professional male.

Reported to have once worked for the IRS.

Last seen: Taking Opie Taylor into the operating room.

Whereabouts: Unknown.

Any information about the whereabouts of these citizens should be reported immediately to the Office of Missing Persons in Mayberry, North Carolina.

GOMER PYLE

· ·

AKA GOME, BOOB, NUTSY, NO. 3, HOUDINI, AND
MR. OPIE TAYLOR SENIOR
CREATED BY JIM NABORS
SPECIAL SKILLS: PUMPING GAS AND SINGING
FIELDS OF INTEREST: MEDICINE, AUTO REPAIR
23 EPISODES

"Andy, I know he's green, and he's raw, but I can bring him along. He's learned a lot from me already."

—BARNEY FIFE

Someone that has not been around too much, really nave.

The name "Gomer," first uttered in January 1963 in Episode #77, "Man in a Hurry," soon became part of the American vernacular as a name synonymous with simpleton.

"It's absolutely astonishing," Everett Greenbaum said. "I'll go to a movie and hear someone call another character Gomer. It's absolutely become a part of the language. It was a name invented in this house."

Tall, and quiet . . . and tall . . . and dark, and nice . . .

Greenbaum told how Gomer came into being. "We created Gomer, but in actuality it happened because we were asked to create Wally for 'Man in a Hurry.' We labored over that trying to make it funny, but Jim Fritzell and I were never really satisfied."

According to Greenbaum, the idea of using Jim Nabors belonged to Andy Griffith. Nabors had no previous acting experience when he was cast. "We didn't know Jim Nabors, but Andy had told us about this young guy who was singing at a local club called The Horn. He wanted to bring him into the show."

Having an actor is easy; finding a way to use him is another matter. Greenbaum explained, "The idea came when I was on my way to a story meeting. My car wasn't working right, so I pulled into a gas station, and the guy pumping gas said, 'Well, sometimes she'll say F when she's E.' There it was. So when we started writing, we thought, 'Well, Andy's got this young guy . . . Why not?' "

"He came on, really, to do a single shot," said Aaron Ruben. "We were just going to use him in that one show as the gas station attendant, but after seeing him we thought, 'This guy's not bad, let's use him again.' And then the singing voice came up, and that character was formed.

"He was a lucky discovery. The name was taken from Gomer Cool, a writer, and Denver Pyle, who played Briscoe Darling. The dialogue we wrote like Percy Kilbride's Pa Kettle . . . 'I don't make the rules, you know. Cows gotta have salt.' And that's the way we wrote it. Jim came in, and his voice and way of speaking became another thing altogether."

Somebody has to make Barney look good.

In Episode #80, "High Noon in Mayberry," Gomer gave a birdcall signal. Barney signaled with the venetian blinds.

In Episode #118, "Andy's Vacation," while he and Barney were pursuing an escaped convict, Gomer suggested he do his hoot owl imitation and Barney go "chick-a chee, chick-a chee," like a squirrel.

In Episode #125, "The Rumor," Gomer plans on doing his hoot owl as soon as he sees Barney and Thel drive up with Andy and Helen. He cannot do it until after they all enter because he has his mouth full of food.

He's a wonderful man.

When it came to motors, Gomer said Wally had a green thumb.

Once you know where the gas and oil go, the rest is easy.

By the time the character was sighted on the small screen, he was a local boy working only part-time at Wally's while saving money for medical school.

The script for "Man in a Hurry" did not reach the air as written. In the original script, Gomer reveals the extent of his knowledge. He knows where to put the gas, how to check the oil, he can make change and has no problem opening and closing the money drawer.

Would that make it the grandchild of "The Danny Thomas Show"?

After "Man in a Hurry," Nabors appeared in another five episodes that season, and he would reprise his role as Gomer Pyle the following season seventeen times before leaving for his own spinoff, "Gomer Pyle, U.S.M.C.," in 1964.

> " 'The Andy Griffith Show'
> represented an ideal to
> millions of people. It
> confirmed that there could
> be an extended sense of
> family in a community—and
> that unconditional love really
> existed."
>
> **—VICTORIA PRINCIPAL,**
> **actress**

Gomer's buying spree . . .

For Gomer's first date, Episode #105, "A Date for Gomer," he went wild and bought a whole new set of accessories:

• A necktie

• Yellow socks

• Brown belt with a horseshoe buckle and imitation mother-of-pearl

• An $8 pair of shoes with brass buckles on the side

• A purple tie with "acerns" on it.

I said it, and I ain't takin' it back.

The cry of "citizen's arrest" will forever be associated with none other than the inimitable Gomer Pyle.

"We didn't make that up," Everett Greenbaum said. "That was based on fact, but we never imagined it would turn into such a popular phrase."

How do you do that?

In 1964, the writing team of Bill Idelson and Sam Bobrick sold their very first work together, "The Shoplifters," which became Episode #117, to "The Andy Griffith Show." They were then faced with a reasonable challenge— what would they do for a follow-up?

"I had the idea for 'The Shoplifters,' " Idelson said, "and Sam was kind of stung by that. So he said, 'Hey, I got the idea for the second show. How about the boys having to sell a salve?' That was Sam's idea. It was one of the things we used to do when we were kids. The prize was always a pony or a motorcycle or something. Something that was completely unattainable."

Things the Miracle Salve was good for.

• Athlete's foot

• Prickly rash

• Complexion

• Spring itch

• Crow's-feet

• And, according to Dr. U. T. Pendyke, D.V.M. (practice limited to small animals . . . dogs, cats, birds of all kinds and small sheep), it was also good for the mange.

Prior to this script he'd been using Molly Harkin's Mange Cure.

The mange idea was one Idelson added to Bobrick's original notion. "I used to raise dogs, and the mange was incurable. So we thought that would work on these crooks who were pushing it on the kids."

That's a great name, by the way, "Miracle Salve."

From those two notions came one of the many unforgettable scenes between Don Knotts and Jim Nabors.

"The Dr. Pendyke scene," recalled Idelson, "where Barney disguises his voice and then Gomer decides this thing Barney's doing is so great that now he's going to give it a try—most of that came from Aaron Ruben. That's the way his mind worked. He would get these little touches that were so funny— and still in character. He had such a line on all these characters. He would know just the right reaction for them. He taught me quite a lot about writing."

The Lives Of Gomer and Sport, a story of a mechanic and his dog.

Gomer's dog was known by two names, one of which was Sport. As Gomer himself said, he was a dumb dog. When the house caught fire, he got up and went next door until the fire burned out—without telling or warning anyone.

You can't trust him with just anyone.

Of the twenty-three episodes in which Gomer was featured, ten were written by the team of Everett Greenbaum and Jim Fritzell. The only other writers who scripted the character of Gomer Pyle were Harvey Bullock (6), John Whedon (3), Bill Idelson and Sam Bobrick (2), and Aaron Ruben (2).

You get to carry a gun and ride around in a squad car . . . It's fun.

Gomer was first deputized in Episode #80, "High Noon in Mayberry."

And get that gun out of your mouth.

Gomer was deputized a second time in Episode #95, "The Big House." When his gun wasn't in his mouth, Gomer was dropping it (a total of three times) from the roof.

Wasn't anybody else available?

In Episode #102, "A Black Day for Mayberry," Gomer was called into service again to help protect the big gold shipment.

Now, which is cell #1 again?

By now a seasoned deputy, Gomer got his fourth call to duty in Episode #109, "Barney and the Cave Rescue." This time Gomer's regular duties were expanded to include patrol coverage, watching out for stolen autos, cooperating with state and federal officials to provide for the common defense, assuring domestic tranquillity, and maintaining law and order in the entire area. Mostly this translated into answering the phone.

You think Barney is any better?

In his final stint as a Mayberry deputy, Episode #118, "Andy's Vacation," Gomer managed to lock himself and Barney in the cell, cuff the two of them together, and allow a prisoner (Allan Melvin) to escape twice.

Also considered—a show called "Mr. Schwump, U.S.M.C."

In Episode #123, "The Fun Girls," Aaron Ruben brought back the original girls who just wanted to have fun, Skippy (Joyce Jameson) and Daphne (Jean Carson). He also introduced the man who would replace his cousin Gomer at the filling station, Goober Beasley Pyle. Though this episode aired first, it was the second of two scripts Ruben wrote featuring the character of Gomer Pyle, and it was the only episode to feature both Gomer and Goober in the same show. Ruben's first episode (#107), both written and filmed, was "Gomer Pyle, U.S.M.C."

Ruben recalled how the notion of Gomer going off to join the marines began: "Andy would mention to me from time to time after Gomer had become a fixed character on the show that he thought Jim could do well starring in his own show. He'd come to me and say, 'We gotta do something with this boy. We gotta do something with him.' "

What the heck does that mean?

Ruben continued: "I wasn't looking for another show. As my old English instructor used to say, 'Sufficient unto the day of evils thereof.' So I thought, 'Who wants to get involved with still another show?' Until at the end of a day's shooting, Andy came into my office. I'll never forget it. He sat down, put his feet up on the desk, and said, 'I ain't leavin' here till we come up with something for Jim.' Those were his exact words."

My daddy always said, "You're going to be challenged someday."

"So being pushed against the wall like that," Ruben went on, "it was something of a challenge. And I said, 'Well, Jim—Gomer—is such an easygoing, peace-loving, sweet guy, I'd like to see him thrust into a situation where he comes up against everything diametrically opposite to his character. Something almost violent. Something that's just like—the marines.' Really, can you imagine this guy, this peace-loving schmuck, in the marines? And I was taking a chance because up until this point the United States Marine Corps had never given permission for a sitcom to use their facilities. I mean, are you kidding, it was like making fun of mother and God—it was really taking a chance. The only one they had ever given permission to do anything with the Marine Corps was John Wayne, but Andy liked the idea, so we went ahead."

Heck, my ma and pa just shook on their deal.

"At the time I had been introduced to a guy named Doug Palmer," stated Ruben. "He'd been a career man in the marines and at the time ran a gun club out in Long Beach where you shot skeet and trap, which I was eager to learn. Bob Sweeney, who was a shooter, put me on to it and introduced me to Doug, and I used to go there with my kids. It was fun. We all learned to shoot there, and I got to know Doug, and I told him about this idea."

From there Ruben found that doors began flying open. "He thought it was a great idea and took me down to the Marine Corps recruiting depot in San Diego. I don't remember why or how they granted us permission, but somehow after telling them what the idea was, suddenly, for some reason it just happened. They said 'Okay, fine.' We were allowed to shoot anything we liked. The opening shot, in fact, on the parade grounds, those aren't actors. Those are real marines."

Not to mention real Teamsters.

The gate used for the Camp Wilson, Wilmington, North Carolina, gate was actually the gate at Desilu Studios. It was also used as the studio gate in Episode #167, "Taylors in Hollywood."

From the halls of Monta-zoomer . . .

Gomer learned "The Marines' Hymn" from the back of a calendar from Nelson's Funeral Parlor. His favorite part of the song: "First to fight for right and freedom . . ."

They never said nothin' about cuttin' hair.

Aaron Ruben recalled the early days of Gomer's stint in the marines: "On the very first 'Gomer' show Jim had long black hair. Of course, when new recruits come in, the first thing they get is a haircut. Well, that's a misnomer. It's not a haircut. They sit down in that chair and that barber takes a clipper and they come out bald.

"They gave us the barbershop, and we were going to bring in a barber from L.A., but they said, 'Why don't you use our barber?' So we said okay, but take it easy on him. This guy didn't know any better.

"Jim was turned with his back to the mirror, and I'm saying to him, 'Now make it like kind of a close crew cut, you know, something the marines would accept.' I'm giving him directions. Well, we started the cameras and he started to go with that clipper, and I couldn't stop him. We were shooting, and he was too far into it. This guy was shearing him, and I was thinking, 'Oh, my God.' And Jim was just sitting there—he didn't know what was happening, and this guy was clipping away, clipping away. When he was all done—and to this day I give Jim credit that he didn't scream—he spun the chair around so Jim could see himself in the mirror. Without missing a beat, Jim looked at himself and said, 'Well, it's not the way Floyd woulda done it, but then you're new.'

"And then I said, 'Cut.' And that's when Jim said, 'Oh, my God!' He was bald."

GOOBER
BEASLEY PYLE

....

CREATED BY
GEORGE LINDSEY
82 EPISODES

"George Lindsey made that character a human being."

—JACK DODSON

For a country boy, he sure does get around.

Originally from Jasper, Alabama, he graduated from the American Theater Wing and then went on to do graduate study at Hunter College in New York City. By 1964, he was already an accomplished actor who had performed in two Broadway musicals, a major motion picture, and about forty television shows. Is this Goober? Well, no. The man of whom we speak is George Lindsey.

When speaking to Lindsey, it is clear that this is a man whose education and experiences go well beyond the character he created for "The Andy Griffith Show." At the same time, he displays a sharp sense of humor and down-to-earth charm.

He was raw, but with a little work, he could be made into a hardened gasman.

Lindsey, who originally read for the role of Gomer Pyle, talked about how the decision to cast Jim Nabors came about. "I had been put on hold for the part, and in the interim Andy saw Jim performing at The Horn in Santa Monica. I guess the consensus of opinion was between going with someone they knew was a trained actor or Jim, who was talented and funny, but untrained."

Goober (George Lindsey) begs his dog, Spot, to say a few words in "A Man's Best Friend."

Before the end of the 1963–64 season, the decision was made to create a spinoff starring Jim Nabors. The producers called Lindsey to ask if he was interested in joining "The Andy Griffith Show." Lindsey was fully aware that his character "was merely a copy of Gomer," but he soon found and expanded the role.

Do you think he'd try sushi?

For dinner, Goober once ordered a peanut butter and tuna sandwich with ketchup—and a milkshake.

It's okay, but it could use just a dash of something.

"The handle on my character," Lindsey recalled, "I got from something Andy said to me. I'd asked him to tell me about Goober, and he said, 'Goober's the kind of guy that would go into a restaurant and say, 'This is great salt.' "

Just don't be comparing us to the Crab Monster.

The actor and writer function much as if they are trying to create Dr. Frankenstein's monster. Their jobs are to take amorphous matter, whether it is an idea or the written word, and shape it into a living, feeling, human being.

Lindsey's creation is unique. Jack Dodson commented, "Goober was a good example of a broad character built on very subtle touches. George had a wonderful way of bringing things of his own to the character."

Therein may lie the secret to the overall success of "The Andy Griffith Show." "Believability," Lindsey said, "was the key to the whole show." The characters were so real that in Lindsey's opinion it may have been to the actors' professional detriment. "Believability is what made it a hit, and at the same time, it was probably the reason the show never won an Emmy. We did it too well. The audience actually thought we were those people."

Just pretend there's no lights, no cameras, no extras, the buildings are real, you're not wearing makeup, and you're not getting paid.

When speaking of the show, fans often express a feeling that it is not a show at all. "The Andy Griffith Show" somehow conveys a sense that it wasn't rehearsed but just happened naturally for the first time in front of the cameras. Strangely enough, as Lindsey pointed out, "That's the definition of good acting."

In the case of "The Andy Griffith Show," the end should not be confused with the means. "It was a very hard show to do as far as the physical rigors involved," recalled Lindsey. "You had to be up all the time because Griffith had you performing at 110 percent. You acted at his level."

With respect to rehearsing, Lindsey said, "We had to learn the script." Many situation comedies do not require the actors to stick to the script exactly, allowing the actors to make the words, to some extent, their own. "The Andy Griffith Show" cast was very faithful to the scripts. Griffith, who, Lindsey said, "is about the best script constructionist there ever was," was very meticulous about story structure. He insisted that all problems be worked out before shooting began. "There was no ad-libbing."

Griffith, Lindsey recalled, "demanded two things: You were always on time, and you always knew your words." Lindsey went on to say that Griffith was a man who drove his actors hard, but "he was always very fair. He gave each actor his due and gave each his day in the sun. He made sure we each had our own segments."

Episode #249, "A Girl for Goober."

Goober ends the episode reading Aristotle.

He may not be too good-lookin', but he ain't stupid.

Lindsey acknowledged that the show brought out the best in him as an actor. In the years since he stopped playing Goober, it has been hard to remember why he did certain things on the small screen. "It's certainly not direction," he explained, "but some of the little innuendo and touches, they weren't contrived. Sometimes I don't know how I came up with some of the things Goober did."

Upon further reflection, he came to the realization that much of what is on screen happened because the actors were so focused they became completely immersed in their roles.

"Somehow or other when the cameras came on and I got into the wardrobe, I became Goober. I think everyone was like that. We had to do that. When I talked to Frances during filming, I was talking to Aunt Bee. I wasn't talking to Frances. It was the same with Andy and Ron. It was a real father-son relationship. What you saw on the screen was real to all the actors. We didn't play those people. We were those people. I don't know how to explain it better than that."

Be careful what you wish for.

One of the curses of success for an actor is that if he or she becomes popularly identified with one character, it can be difficult to escape the identity with that character. In this case, Goober effectively killed George Lindsey's acting career. Lindsey admitted, "That's tough to get used to." Lindsey played mostly heavies before landing his role on "The Andy Griffith Show," but overnight he became known as the gas station attendant who did impressions.

"I still get asked to do Cary Grant wherever I go," Lindsey said. "Two or three times a day I get asked to do Cary Grant. It says a lot about the impact of that show. It was one little moment in the show, but suddenly everyone across the United States was doing, 'Judy, Judy, Judy . . .'"

Lindsey is very proud of his association with the show. He left behind "a legacy of laughter," as he described it. He felt the cast on the show was one of the best acting ensembles ever. "That is directly attributed to Griffith and his staff," acknowledged Lindsey, "because they put it all together."

As far as his feelings about being brought into the show, Lindsey is forever grateful. "You have to be," he said. "Andy brought me into a number-one show and gave me a chance." Lindsey playfully added, "I'm just awfully glad I didn't play a character called 'Snot.' 'Cause for the rest of my life everywhere I'd go I'd hear people calling me that."

That's still thirty-six minutes behind some folks in Manhattan.

Goober's personal record for taking a car apart: thirty-eight minutes and twelve seconds.

You want to talk parts? We got parts.

"The show is bigger than its parts," Lindsey said, discussing its continued popularity. "I guess we made the town of Mayberry live."

Lindsey shed more light on why this happened. "We never did anything that we thought was funny. As far as the characters were concerned, *we* weren't different. The public thought we were different. Goober, for example, didn't think Floyd was funny. They certainly didn't think Goober was funny. If we'd have played it as if we were all these characters in this town that thought we were all so funny, it never would have worked. Think about the way it was done. It was an authentic town. When you go into a small town, you don't see everyone sitting around laughing at each other."

Lindsey cited an excellent example of the point he made, making a reference to Episode #144, "Goober Takes a Car Apart." "If you remember when Floyd was sitting in that car in the courthouse, he says, 'I think I may buy this car.' Now, Floyd didn't think that was funny. It was hilarious, but Floyd was being absolutely serious. He wasn't thinking, 'I look funny sitting here.' He was thinking about buying that car."

That explains the hilarity of cable access.

The other side of comedy is what Harvey Bullock referred to as "its dramatic spine." Lindsey concurred: "That is why one of my favorite shows is 'Goober and the Talking Dog' (Episode #170, "A Man's Best Friend"). On the surface it's funny, but beneath the comedy is the stuff that makes good drama . . . the cruelty of a child to an adult. That's what the show was about. Then in the tag, Goober forgives the kids and becomes a child again when he says, 'Let's play FBI dog.' You could run every gamut of emotion in that show. That's why I liked it."

This approach is what placed these actors on a level of their own. "We all came out of the theater," Lindsey said. "That's where we got our training, and I think that helped us. We weren't television actors per se."

Sometimes you just need a change of scenery.

Episode #195, "The Ball Game," was also one of Lindsey's favorites. Lindsey was pleased that he had one opportunity to put his athletic background to use on the show. "For once, I got out of my Goober gear and got to wear something other than a beanie."

Well, maybe I would have worn my pants a little lower.

Lindsey has no regrets. Looking back, he said, "I think Goober certainly has spread more happiness for me than making me sad. He's a lot bigger than me, and that's good, so there are no minuses, and if I had it to do over again, I would."

HELEN CRUMP

AKA: THE DAME, SOME THIRD PARTY,
MRS. TAYLOR, AND HELENE ALEXIAN DUBOIS
CREATED BY ANETA CORSAUT
65 EPISODES

"She was the original feminist."
—EVERETT GREENBAUM

Wanted: female acrobat who can make the pivot at second base.

Although Corsaut sees herself as a minor player in the battle for women's rights, she has admitted to some unusual early ambitions. "The dream of my life," she said, "was either to be the lady in the circus who rode standing with one foot on each of two horses or to be the first woman in the major leagues."

Born in Hutchinson, Kansas, Corsaut grew up as the classic tomboy. "They used to put me in dresses, and I would scream," Corsaut recalled. "I broke my nose so many times playing sports, the last time they took me to a doctor after getting hit by a baseball bat, the doctor said, 'I'm not going to clean her up until she decides she's a girl.'"

Corsaut, who first appeared during the third season of "The Andy Griffith Show," was the last of several actresses tried as a romantic lead opposite the character of Andy Taylor. In fact, Corsaut stated, "By the time I came along they had decided they weren't going to have a female interest for Andy." Corsaut spoke highly of all the actresses who preceded her, offering her opinion of why she might have succeeded where the others failed. "They were all very talented women," she said. "It certainly had nothing to do with their talent. Elinor Donahue, for example, is a darling, darling woman, and wonderfully talented. I think it was more a matter of chemistry."

Winning the role of Helen Crump through an audition, Corsaut was only

Jack Dodson, Aneta
Corsaut, and Howard
McNear pose before
shooting "The Ball Game."

scheduled to appear as Mayberry's new schoolteacher in one episode, #86, "Andy Discovers America." But the chemistry between Griffith and Corsaut seemed to work on screen, so Corsaut came back. "Andy and I got along very well, and we became very good friends," Corsaut said. "That probably had as much to do with me staying as anything." At first, though, it appeared Corsaut might end up as just another failed match for Andy. Corsaut recalled, "We had a less than auspicious beginning. The first time we met we had a rather heated argument. We were out on location, standing nose to nose in the middle of a road, yelling at each other. I don't recall exactly what started it, or just what it was about, but it had something to do with feminism."

As strange as it may seem, it may have been the best way for this actress to begin work with her new leading man. "Andy was great," Corsaut went on to say. "He ran everything, and he was brilliant at it, but he always respected other people's opinions. There were obsequious people who came on the show who would try to butter him up, and he didn't like that. I think he respected the fact that I stood up for what I believed."

You don't have to call me Andy.

During the run of the series Helen Crump called Andy many things, including:

NAME	EPISODE
The Great Sheriff Taylor	#142, "Three Wishes for Opie"
Mayberry's Answer to Cary Grant	
Hollywood Playboy	#168, "The Hollywood Party"

· ·

"I always enjoyed 'The Andy Griffith Show.' It's a show that brought wonderful entertainment to millions of people."

—TOMMY LASORDA,
baseball manager

· ·

This dame ain't for Andy.

Corsaut was asked back for Episode #92, "A Wife for Andy," and things began to fall into place. This episode, written by Aaron Ruben, involved Barney trying to find the perfect woman for Andy to marry. By accident, the one woman Andy shows interest in is Helen Crump. Barney, of course, does not approve of her at all. Despite his objections, though, Andy finds his mate, and what began with a misunderstanding about history class eventually culminated with the marriage of the two characters in the premiere episode of "Mayberry R.F.D."

Even though Corsaut made six appearances the following season, she did not sign a contract to be a regular cast member until the fifth season. Reflecting on her success, Corsaut said, "The fact that Helen was a bit abrasive might have helped. Andy was such a good man. It created more of a tension that hadn't been there with the other characters because most of the other women were rather sweet."

Corsaut admitted there was a minor backlash from some fans who didn't immediately take a liking to Helen's abrasive side: "There was a lot of positive mail, but in the beginning I also received letters from people who were upset I wasn't Elinor ... she was so sweet. Then, of course, here comes Helen ..."

From the beginning, Helen was anything but sweet. Concerning her own feelings, Corsaut said, "I adore men, I want to be perfectly clear about that. For some reason, though, they liked to have Helen always yelling at Andy."

The writers admitted they had trouble writing for women. Corsaut recalled, "Jim Fritzell used to say we can write for little girls and old ladies, but he'd say, 'I don't know anything about women.' And it was very strange because Jim and I must have talked for thousands of hours about my feelings and feminism, and he was very supportive of it, but somehow he couldn't incorporate it into his scripts."

There was a lot for Corsaut to like about Helen. "I kind of liked Helen. She was real cranky." Corsaut, however, is anything but cranky. But, like Helen, Corsaut was not one to be pushed around. "It was the early stages of women's lib, and we were all fighting really hard to get recognition as equals, and quite a lot of the mail was from women who said, 'Give it to him.'"

You asked for it.

Helen loses her temper with Andy:

• For sticking his nose into her business and causing anarchy with the boys in her history class. *Episode #86, "Andy Discovers America."*

• Because Gomer appeared to have run out on his date with Mary Grace Gossage. *Episode #105, "A Date for Gomer."*

• After catching him and Barney with Skippy and Daphne, "The Fun Girls." *Episode #123, "The Fun Girls."*

• After she hears he referred to her as a "third party." *Episode #134, "Man in the Middle."*

• When she notices he's paying a little too much attention to Gloria. *Episode #151, "Guest in the House."*

• After catching him with "The Fun Girls." *Episode #155, "The Arrest of the Fun Girls."*

• Because of the poor way he dealt with Opie's problems in math. *Episode #157, "Opie Flunks Arithmetic."*

• Because of his jealous behavior toward her visiting friend, Frank Smith. *Episode #163, "Andy's Rival."*

• After seeing a photo of Andy with Darlene Mason in her dressing room and after learning Andy went out to dinner with Darlene. *Episode #168, "The Hollywood Party."*

• Because Warren tried to put the moves on her. *Episode #173, "Girl-Shy."*

• For asking her not to give Opie the prize for best composition. *Episode #188, "The Battle of Mayberry."*

• Because Andy didn't want Aunt Bee to wear her wig. *Episode #194, "Aunt Bee's Crowning Glory."*

• For being more than an hour late for dinner. *Episode #206, "Dinner at Eight."*

• After Andy suggested he might get himself another date. *Episode #213, "Helen, the Authoress."*

• After realizing Andy lied to her about Leigh Drake. *Episode #226, "Andy's Trip to Raleigh."*

Aneta Corsaut and Jack Dodson.

We'll all look back on this some day and laugh.

Although their characters were archenemies on screen, Corsaut was very fond of the two wild women who occasionally paid a visit from Mount Pilot. Corsaut recalled, "We were always delighted when we heard Joyce Jameson and Jean Carson were coming. They were *fun* to work with . . . I loved them both very much, especially Joyce. She was an absolutely wonderful lady. She was so smart and sweet; she was one of those people who just glows. Watch her entrances. Every time you saw her walk in a door, both on screen and off, you just felt good about her. She has such a joy about life."

But did he have to tell me while I was putting?

While playing golf in Palm Springs, Aaron Ruben met former President Dwight Eisenhower, who told him "Andy Discovers America" was his favorite episode.

A big star and he was nice, too.

Quite a few well-known actors passed through the fictional borders of Mayberry. Film and television star Charlie Ruggles, who played John Canfield in Episode #160, "Aunt Bee, the Swinger," was one of Aneta Corsaut's favorites. "Working with Charlie was exciting for me," Corsaut said. "That was like your history coming to life in front of you. I just adored him. I always noticed when people of that stature came on the show, they would totally blend in. Everyone who came on would always say they had the best day on the set. It was true. The people in the cast and the crew truly got along. The group that was there became a real family." Corsaut and the rest of "The Andy Griffith Show" made sure that the family always welcomed its newest, if only temporary, members.

The sound of rain can be so romantic.

One of the common memories for many cast members involved the primitive conditions they worked under at the now demolished Forty Acres in Culver City. Corsaut shared her recollections: "That lot . . . when it rained, there were literally streams of water that would come down. Andy and I did a love scene in one show with a bucket set between us to catch the water. And when there wasn't water, the termites would swarm around and you'd have to shoo them away."

FLOYD COLBY LAWSON

....

CREATED BY HOWARD McNEAR
AKA: WRETCH, POP, FOUR EYES, CHARLEY CHASE
78 EPISODES

"There are a few people in this world who can't not be funny. And he was one of them."

—AARON RUBEN

"Howard McNear was exactly the kind of actor we were looking for. Like Howie Morris, he was totally unique."

—SHELDON LEONARD

The passing of actor Howard McNear was a huge loss to members of the cast and crew of "The Andy Griffith Show." He was remembered so fondly by all of those with whom he worked. All of the comments about McNear echo the same sentiments. In the words of Don Knotts, "Howard McNear was so wonderful. He'd never change the words, but he would change his delivery. You never knew what he was going to do. Andy and I found it hard to work with him without breaking up. A lot of times we would just break out laughing when a scene was all over."

If you want a good suit you gotta go to Mount Pilot.

Often, television actors can seem a disappointment off screen when compared to their popular on-screen roles. Everett Greenbaum claimed that this was not the case with McNear or any other member of the show's cast. "There are people who will fool you," he said, "but that cast was just as wonderful as you'd thought they'd be from watching the show. Howard McNear was a wonderful guy, and he was a lot like the character."

Aaron Ruben had fond recollections, too. "Andy would slide on the floor when Howard opened his mouth, sitting around the table. Not reading the script . . . just talking about something that happened that morning!"

The cast agreed that McNear was nothing less than a true comic genius. "The cast as a whole would agree that Howard was one of the funniest guys around," said George Lindsey. "We all loved to do scenes with him." Hal Smith said. "Howard was the funniest man that ever lived, and he wasn't acting. That's the way he was."

Nothing beats a great pair of legs.

According to Aneta Corsaut, "Howard McNear was everyone's favorite. He was so warm and genuinely a good friend. He was the funniest man in the world, and he had started as a dramatic actor. He was personally as funny on camera as he was off. Andy once told me a story: we were doing a scene in church. I was finished and had come over to say good-bye, and as I walked away, Howard started saying, 'Oh, yes, oh . . . the best legs in the world . . . absolutely, the best . . . oh, yes . . .' He just kept going on like that, and Andy said he had everyone in hysterics."

Don't get cold feet—we'll make you a star.

Episode #71, "Floyd, the Gay Deceiver," was the only script written to feature Floyd Lawson as the central character. Aaron Ruben, who wrote the episode, told why: "Howard was a dear, dear man, and very modest. I didn't realize it at that time, but he was absolutely terrified about doing that show. Shortly before we were to shoot, he called me up, and he said, 'Oh, oh, oh, I don't think you should . . . uhm, uh, make me the ah, ah, star of that story. I— I . . .' He was scared silly. I said, 'Now, Howard, it's gonna work. It's gonna be great, you'll see.' "

Still in the same location after twenty-eight years.

Following the December 1962 filming of Episode #74, "Convicts at Large," McNear suffered a stroke. He lost the use of one arm and had great difficulty walking.

"It was such a shame when he had that stroke," said Bill Idelson. "Howard was a marvelous guy. I loved him and really admired him. It says a lot about the

Andy, Floyd (Howard McNear), and Goober (George Lindsey) in "Goober Takes a Car Apart."

people who ran the show, though. They looked out for their people. After he had the stroke, they could have easily written him out. You get a new barber. Believe me, it can be the most cold-blooded business in the world. They don't think twice about getting rid of someone. Instead, the people on "The Andy Griffith Show" stuck by his side and found a way to work Howard back in."

Returning more than a year later during the spring of 1963, McNear would film another sixty-two episodes. Many of the people closest to McNear believed Griffith's decision to bring him back was the best medicine of all.

Howard Morris said, "I had the pleasure of directing Howard McNear when he actually had to cut hair. It was the first time he'd come back from his stroke. He really couldn't stand up very well. So in back of the barber chair we rigged up what we used to call a boatswain's seat—that's a thing that sailors use when they go up and down the mast, a piece of wood on ropes. And we tied it to the back of the chair, and it looked like he was standing. I'll never forget that. I was so thrilled that he could actually do the scene. And you know what? He was, too."

One other trick was employed to work around McNear's limited mobility:

sound effect footsteps. These were first used in Episode #141, "Otis Sues the County," to cover McNear's entrance.

"Howard had a marvelous sense of humor," Jack Dodson, who worked with McNear following his stroke, said. "His mind was not impeded by the stroke at all." Dodson admitted that his memories are difficult ones. Like the rest of the cast, he was very fond of McNear. In Episode #210, "Floyd's Barbershop," Dodson's Howard Sprague bought the building that housed Floyd's business. Sharing his recollections of that episode, Dodson said sadly, "It was a very difficult experience. Howard McNear had such a hard time during that show. I think he did only one or two shows after that. It was very hard for him. I had to watch this wonderful man struggle so much that it's hard for me to talk about him. It was very sad."

His memory will always be alive in Mayberry.

On January 3, 1969, Howard McNear passed away due to complications from pneumonia. This was a mere eight years after his debut on "The Andy Griffith Show." Actor and old friend Parley Baer delivered his eulogy.

HOWARD
SPRAGUE

· ·

CREATED BY JACK DODSON
"INTELLIGENT, CONSCIENTIOUS, UPSTANDING
AND HE LOVES DOGS!"
39 EPISODES

*"Jack likes to play the crankiest man in the world, and he tells
outrageous lies. He was one of my favorites."*
— ANETA CORSAUT

Yeah, right, and Aunt Bee was an exotic dancer.

In Episode #239, "Opie's Drugstore Job," Howard and Andy talk about
their first jobs. Andy's was as a movie usher. Howard drove a truck for the
Mayberry Transfer Company. He quit after a couple of days, explaining to
Andy, "It just wasn't me."

A fella has to follow his dreams.

Jack Dodson has viewed life this way: "Extraordinary things happen."
After several years of stage work in off-Broadway productions, Dodson was
ready to give up acting. "I couldn't get above Fourteenth street. I couldn't get
to Broadway." Unable to support himself and his wife on acting jobs, Dodson
had to work part-time for a pipe and tobacco company that had offered him a
job at $10,000 a year if he would take on a full-time position. "That was pretty
good money back then," Dodson recalled. "I'd pretty much decided to do it. It
was Thanksgiving weekend of 1964. My wife and I were starting down the
steps of our apartment and the phone rang. I picked it up and it was José

Quintero asking me if I wanted to be in the play *Huey.* I told him no, I didn't want to do any more off-Broadway, and he said, 'It's not off-Broadway. This is Broadway. Just you and Jason Robards.' They were starting rehearsals on Monday. If I hadn't picked up the phone at that moment, he would have called someone else and I would have been selling pipe tobacco."

It was Eugene O'Neill's *Huey* that eventually brought Dodson to Hollywood and to the attention of Andy Griffith.

"I was here in town when they made the decision to drop the Jack Burns character. Andy had it in the back of his mind to create a totally new character, a nondeputy. I happened to be here doing *Huey* with Robards. Andy and his wife saw it, and he came backstage and just raved about it. He really was extraordinarily enthusiastic. I was then strictly a stage actor, but when the play closed I decided to spend some time here to see if I could get work."

Remembering Griffith's reaction to his work on stage, Dodson naturally decided to start his search for work on the small screen by calling "The Andy Griffith Show."

"I mentioned to my agent that Andy had seen *Huey* and liked it, so he sent me in to see his casting director and it was like walking into a brick wall. I was in her office for about thirty seconds and then out the door."

An elephant may never forget, but Andy has been known to every once in a while.

A little confused by the icy reaction, Dodson told his agent what happened. A phone call to the casting director's assistant, Mike Fenton, set off a chain of events that appeared to be a comedy of errors.

"My agent told him the story about Andy seeing the play so Fenton called Andy, and Andy says, 'I don't know who the hell you're talking about.' So my agent gets a return call from Mike Fenton, who's upset because he thinks we're trying to pull something on him. He tells my agent, 'Listen, don't be handing me this kind of bullshit!' So, of course, the next call is my agent to me. 'Dodson, don't be handing me any of this bullshit!' But I insisted that the man had come backstage, introduced himself, and was very enthusiastic. So we tried the whole thing again."

Oh, that Jack Dodson.

"Well the second time Mike Fenton went to Andy, Andy said, 'I told you the first time, don't bother me. I've never heard of the son of a bitch.' "

Andy gives Howard (Jack Dodson) a hand bringing in the legendary silver carp, Old Sam.

Maybe you should call him around 5:00 A.M. and do a speech from the play.

Fortunately for Dodson, Andy received a little memory refresher shortly after the chain of phone calls occurred. Dodson relayed the story: "Well, that night Andy and his wife went to see the picture *Darling* with Julie Christie, and he hated it. On the way home with his wife he said, 'You know, that picture stank. The best acting we've seen in a long time was that play with those two guys in it' . . . and that's when it hit him. 'Oh, geez, that's who that was!'"

Meanwhile, back at the agency . . .

After Griffith realized what had happened, he phoned Dodson's agent to ask Jack to come to the "Andy Griffith Show" stage so they could meet and Andy could apologize. "I was embarrassed to death," Dodson recalled. "I went down. I was very self-conscious. He was very apologetic. We chatted, he introduced me to Don, and we talked, but I was very uncomfortable. Suddenly there was thunder and lightning outside, which you never see in Los Angeles. So we all went outside, and there were these great boiling black clouds overhead. That was my cue to get out of there. I said, 'Oh my gosh, I left all the windows of my car open. It was nice meeting you. Good-bye.' "

By the time Dodson arrived back home there was a call waiting for him asking if he would return the next day to read for the role of the insurance man. As Dodson said, "It happened to be material I could do very well, and after that I was taken in to meet Aaron Ruben."

Ruben, who had already decided to give Dodson a chance, asked him if he would be interested in a recurring role on the show. Dodson recalled, "Aaron described the character as someone who always had a cold, can't play sports, and tries to be one of the guys but can't quite make it. I'd never played anything like that, but it was a time in my life when I thought I could play anything, so I naturally said yes. They called me a few weeks later and we did the first episode with Howard Sprague."

This is a man with too much time on his hands.

After Aunt Bee invested in the Canton Palace Chinese Restaurant (Episode #209, "Aunt Bee's Restaurant"), she was upset when she realized on her opening night that the printer had left the last "Chi" off of Ling Chi Chi, which is Chinese for chicken. Her partner assured her that no one in Mayberry would notice, and no one did . . . except Howard.

Hamlet Shmamlet, I'll take the guy with the bow tie.

Dodson had an opportunity that does not often present itself to actors: He was creating a character for the first time. In many cases, stage actors are continually re-creating characters who have been played many times on stage. Dodson recalled his thoughts after reading the script for Episode #185, "The County Clerk," which introduced Howard Sprague to the show's loyal audience.

"Howard was a guy living under his mother's thumb, and I pictured myself as a kid who lived a couple of doors away from us in Pittsburgh and another person I knew in college who took forever to tell you a story. If it took another person a minute to tell you a story, it would take this guy an hour. So it struck me that this was the kind of guy Howard was. He knew all of the filler stories in the newspaper. He was just filled with all the details—how many salmon go to spawn upstream annually. I thought of him as a guy who would wear a belt and suspenders—little things like that. That basically was Howard, double cautious about everything."

Jack Dodson as Howard
Sprague.

You never know what might happen south of the border.

For Aunt Bee's vacation in Episode #227, "A Trip to Mexico," Howard
loans her his suitcase—which has a secret compartment for keeping money.

Not the intoxicatin' kind, of course.

In Episode #192, "The Lodge," Howard buys a joke book to impress the
guys at the lodge. His first words after becoming a member: "I sure could use
one of those root beers."

You mean to tell me that Mr. Ed didn't really talk?

The job of acting can be a double-edged sword. Actors must convince the
audience that the characters they are playing are real. But if they succeed, as
often happens on hit television series, the actors are typecast into the same or
similar roles. Dodson, like most of the actors on "The Andy Griffith Show,"
had played many roles but had never been seen by as large an audience as
watched him as Howard Sprague.

As a regular cast member on a hit show, Dodson was quickly initiated into
the world of show-biz journalism. "The impression that I was like the character

of Howard Sprague probably started with an interview I did. The magazine took everything I said and turned it completely upside down. They had an angle they wanted to hang the story on, so they wrote just the opposite of what I had said. The headline was something to the effect that Jack Dodson was a mother's boy long before he played Howard Sprague. We had talked the exact opposite."

Explaining that there were some similarities, Dodson told how he rounded out the character: "Some of Howard was what I remembered of myself when I was about fourteen. I wasn't very good at sports. I was tall for my age, but I was slow. I didn't have very good reflexes. My family didn't have a car, and if you didn't have a car, you didn't date. So I was awkward and self-conscious around girls."

The similarities, however, ended there. "I was as far from being a mother's boy as you could get," Dodson said. "In fact, I remember having a fistfight with another boy in the backyard one time, and we'd bloodied each other's noses, and were whaling the hell out of each other. Right in the middle of it my mother stuck her head out the back door and said, 'Lunch is ready. When you're finished with your fight, you come on in.' We must have both been hungry because we immediately stopped the fight and went to eat."

Has anyone seen Norman Bates?

Actors are charged with bringing the words of the writer to life on stage or screen. In television, the actor goes through the unique experience of allowing the character to grow with every new episode. In the case of Howard Sprague, Dodson felt this might be a problem. "Early on, it occurred to me that though Howard's mother provided a wonderful obstacle, if he stayed under her thumb for very long he'd become pathetic." The character of Howard Sprague was not inherently funny. "He was more amusing than funny, but I was afraid he'd cease to be amusing if he didn't get out from under the dominance of his mother." So, following one of the script readings, Dodson went to Andy with a proposition: "I suggested we lose her."

And people think Hollywood folks aren't friendly.

Of course, "losing her" referred to writing a character out of the show. Dodson admitted that this "sounds like a rotten thing for a guy to do, and I had reservations about it." The character of Mrs. Sprague was played by a frequently cast actress named Mabel Albertson, actor Jack Albertson's sister. "She worked a lot," Dodson said. "She wasn't under contract, and she worked constantly, so it wasn't like getting someone fired. It wasn't an easy thing to suggest, but I really felt it was important for the character."

Who we gonna get to write this one? Bullock killed that bird. Call him.

Dodson explained the reaction to his proposal. "This was as good as any example of how 'The Andy Griffith Show' allowed an actor to contribute to the show. They would not allow you to write, but they were always open to changes, or suggestions, and they would then write it."

How come that wasn't in the school's brochure?

In Episode #231, "Andy's Investment," Howard graduated from Bradbury Business College in Mount Pilot, located on the third floor of the Essex Bank Building. He took the full eighteen-month course. Some of Howard's fellow alumni included Cyrus Whitley—who was doing five years for embezzlement.

And we don't validate.

Today, series regulars are almost by definition given a number of per-quisites, including their own personal trailer. In the 1960s, when television was still young, things were a little different. Dodson reminisced, "Forget about getting a trailer—my first year on the show, I didn't have a parking space. It was the number-one show on the air, and I had to go out every two hours and put money in the meter. I was on the show a year before I got my own chair."

Well, what do you want? We pay for all the film and processing.

Another surprise came when Dodson discovered he had to provide his own wardrobe. "When I first came in, the wardrobe guy looked at my shirt and said, 'You haven't had these shirts dipped.' I didn't know what he was talking about. You see, they couldn't photograph white shirts. They had to dip them in coffee or something. And I said, 'Well, that's all I have.' He said, 'Well, if you want to stay in show business, you better get some dipped shirts.' "

I think that's him, but last time I saw him he was wearing a red ascot.

Years after "The Andy Griffith Show" finished its run, the character of Howard Sprague was resurrected for one episode of "It's Garry Shandling's Show." Dodson, reprising his Mayberry role, sat quietly and anonymously in a condo organization meeting until Shandling, faced with a dilemma, realized that Howard Sprague lived in the condo complex. Shandling then approached Howard with the problem, asking him what Andy would have done. Howard,

Jack Dodson cuts a big Hollywood deal using one of the phones from Andy's desk.

Jack Dodson

of course, came up with the perfect answer, remembering a similar problem from the time he lived in Mayberry.

"That was actually the second time I auditioned for "It's Garry Shandling's Show." The first came about a year before we shot that episode. My agency had sent me down to see about a part. I got down there, and there were a bunch of people waiting to go in and audition. The casting director looks at me and says, 'Did you bring a picture and résumé?' I said, 'No. That's my agent's job to give you a picture and résumé.'

" 'Well,' she said, 'we have to have a picture and résumé.' I said, 'Well, I didn't bring a picture and résumé.' Again, I said, 'That's your job, isn't it? Aren't you supposed to coordinate with my agent to get my picture and résumé?' 'Well, you have to write down your credits for these people,' she said. 'Here's a piece of paper. You can write down your credits.'

"I said, 'You can take that piece of paper and shove it up your ass.' I got up and walked out. I was really angry."

Wait a minute, haven't I heard this story before?

Nearly a year later, Dodson got another call. "This time, Garry Shandling himself wanted to know if I'd come in and meet him. So I went in and they said, 'We don't know if you'd be interested in this or not, but we'd like to write a show with Howard Sprague.' I told them I'd be interested. Of course, Andy had to give permission to use the character, which I arranged." Dodson recognized that sometimes lightning does strike twice. "The comparison of the two experiences with the show is really surprising."

Yeah, but how do you explain the Jell-O salad?

Working on a TV series can be compared quite nicely to Thanksgiving dinner. Looking back on a series or on the dinner, most people don't remember the actual food, but they do recall all of the events surrounding it. In this vein, Dodson acknowledged: "My memories are not so much of the show, but of the making of the show."

One show that Dodson clearly remembered making was Episode #235, "Howard's New Life." It is still vivid in his mind because, he said, "It was an absolute horror to shoot. We went down to the beach and I had to fall in the water. The wardrobe man had no change of clothes, no towels. I was furious the entire time. All I can remember about that show, basically, was being very angry. Yet it's one of my favorite shows."

Among other things, this episode marked the first time quartz lights were used on the show. Dodson spoke of that experience. "They had nine lights on a unit, and they used them to balance the light against the sun. They were so incredibly hot. They'd set them up right in front of you, just blasting you with this light, and I could hardly stand it. But you have to realize, I was the only one in front of them. Everyone else was standing on the other side. I kept complaining of the light and the heat. I said, 'I can't do this. I can't keep my eyes open.' And they were saying, 'Oh come on, don't be such a sissy. Quit your moaning, we've got to get this shot!' It was awful."

The following week, "The Andy Griffith Show" was back at Forty Acres. The director was setting up a shot of someone sitting in the front seat of a bus. Dodson told what happened. "They were lighting the person in the front seat, and the lights melted the bus window. Then they realized how hot they were. They realized these things are a little warm."

If that fish could talk, he'd say, "I sure wish I could see Floyd, Goober, and the whole gang again."

Another show he enjoyed was also a fan favorite, Episode #198, "Big Fish in a Small Town." "That was a wonderful show," Dodson said. "I liked everything about that show. It was a pleasure shooting it. I got out in the lake and had those waders on. They filled up with water, and they couldn't get me out. I weighed about five hundred pounds. They had a guy who was the fish wrangler, and they couldn't get a fish big enough. They got the biggest fish they could find, but when you look at that fish you've got to think that the rest of the fish in that lake must be awfully damn small if everyone made such a big deal about that one."

THE WRITERS

....

"Why would anyone be interested in a bunch of ink-stained wretches like us?"

−HARVEY BULLOCK
31 episodes

"I don't know much, but what I know, I've used."
−EVERETT GREENBAUM (partner:
JIM FRITZELL)
29 episodes

"I know where Aaron Ruben parks his car."
−BILL IDELSON (partner:
SAM BOBRICK)
17 episodes

They were the best," Aaron Ruben said of the more than fifty writers who contributed to "The Andy Griffith Show." "We did thirty shows every season—thirty. When you ask, how can you do so many?, the answer is: the writers."

Jack Elinson and Charles Stewart were the writing team responsible for the first three episodes, fourteen of the first thirty-two, and twenty-nine of the first sixty-four. "They were the guys who came up with a lot of the running gags," Don Knotts recalled. "The one-bullet thing, getting locked in the cells, those were their ideas."

The balance of those first sixty-four were written by a combination of individuals that included Harvey Bullock and the writing team of Jim Fritzell and Everett Greenbaum.

When the show moved into its third and fourth seasons these writers, along with the writing team of Bill Idelson and Sam Bobrick, would be responsible for forty-eight (75 percent) of the sixty-four episodes aired. Of the remaining sixteen, six were written by producer Aaron Ruben, eight by John Whedon, and one each by Sid Morse and the writing team of Bill Freedman and Henry Sharp.

. . . .

"Most Americans—at least most of my age—have a memory of just such a small town as Mayberry. Sure, our small-town recollections may have been idealized by the passage of time, but my notion is that the goings-on in Mayberry were so popular because they were essentially so true. A small-town editor in Nebraska told me once, 'Nobody uses a turn signal here because the guy driving behind you knows where you're going anyway.' And: 'A small town is where you dial a wrong number and end up talking for fifteen minutes.' Mayberry is like that, of course."

—CHARLES KURALT,
journalist
. . . .

The phone company ain't easy to work for, you know.

Already a veteran of six episodes, including "The Pickle Story," "Andy and Barney in the Big City," and "The Bookie Barber," Harvey Bullock began his second season as a writer for "The Andy Griffith Show," in the program's third season, with Episode #66, the Mayberry classic "Mr. McBeevee."

"I liked writing that one," said Bullock. "I like writing for old guys, and that one was a dandy."

Named after the central character, "Mr. McBeevee" told the story of Opie's fascination with a fanciful telephone linesman. Played by Carl Swenson, the heart of the story revolved around Andy's assumption that McBeevee was a character fabricated from his son's imagination. When Opie comes home with money he claims Mr. McBeevee gave him, Andy is faced with the problem of forcing Opie to admit his friend is fictitious.

"That story came from one of the seminars," Bullock recalled. "Originally, the idea was a story in which a father has trouble accepting what his child is saying, and Aaron said, 'We're going to have to have Andy straighten out the kid.' I remember it suddenly rose up in me, and I said 'No, no, that's not the way to go. The way to go is the father is going to have to grasp that there are times when he has to accept the unacceptable. Sometimes he has to give some breathing space.' And Sheldon said, 'Bingo.' That was the turnaround they were looking for. That's how I got that story."

The odds are ten-to-one that Opie flunks arithmetic.

The seminars to which Bullock referred were another innovation of Sheldon Leonard.

"When I was directing and producing," Leonard explained, "which is what happened in the third year of 'The Danny Thomas Show,' I knew that my responsibility was to accumulate stories. In those days we did thirty-nine episodes a year as opposed to the twenty-two that they do now. I had to get the stories. I couldn't do it when we were in production because I would be on the stage most of the time directing. So I would invite my core of writers to be my guests in Las Vegas when Danny Thomas was working The Sands Hotel . . . and The Sands would pick up the bill."

Between the slots and our per diem we just about broke even.

"So we'd go there for a week," Leonard continued, "and we'd sit on the patios of the various cottages in Las Vegas, and we'd pitch ideas. 'How would it be if Danny did this, and his wife did that . . .' and so on. Now we'd do this for a week. In that week we'd generate ideas, and the secretary would make a note of them. We'd have four or five writing combinations there—some singles, some teams. None of them knew who was going to get what, but by that point they had all made a rich contribution to all of them. When we had accumulated enough, I'd start handing them out."

We concentrated better without the showgirls.

After Leonard branched out with "The Andy Griffith Show," the trips to Vegas ended, but the idea of the seminar remained a viable one. Aaron Ruben recounted how they were organized:

"Toward the end of the season, when it was a foregone conclusion that we were picked up, Sheldon would call together a meeting in his office of some nine or so writers. We would all pitch in on story ideas. 'How about Aunt Bee makes an awful pickle that she decides to enter in a contest? . . . How about Barney decides . . .' whatever. I would sit there scribbling really fast as everyone chimed in. Then, as best I could, I would write a brief outline and we'd distribute them to the writers. The next day we'd have another group of writers come in and we'd start all over."

The result of all the work was a head start on scripts for the upcoming season. "It wasn't easy," Ruben remembered. "If we got a couple of stories from each group, we felt fortunate. But by the time we finished these seminars, we'd have eight or ten assignments to give out. Guys could go off by themselves and work. Now the season is over and they're already bringing in their first drafts."

Look for the union label.

As practical as it may seem, the seminar is now part of television history.

"It's quite illegal now," stated Everett Greenbaum. "It's against Writer's Guild rules. It would be considered working for nothing, but I kind of enjoyed the seminars."

Will you listen to me? Will you listen to me? Will you do me a favor and just listen to me?

Greenbaum was not the only one who loved the seminars. Bullock, another seminar regular, told his version of one of the lighter moments from those sessions.

"One story I remember involved Freddie Fox, who sometimes worked with a guy named Izzie Elinson. Freddie stammers. He was a classic stammerer and made more jokes about it than anyone. Well, after we'd come up with a good notion, and they'd made a list, on the last day they'd hand them out. Everybody liked the pickle story. Now, it's the end of the week and everybody's supposed to ask for the stories they want. Freddie was one of the most affable, outgoing guys imaginable—and charitable to a fault—but he wanted that story. So Sheldon brings it up. 'Who wants the pickle story?' he says. Freddie can't find his voice. He looks to Izzie because he's helpless—he's hung up, he's trying to find some help. He wants to bid on it, but Izzie is busy writing notes. So Sheldon says, 'Harv, you take that one.' Freddie says, 'F-F-F-For Christ sake, I-I-Izzie, y-y-y-you just b-b-b-b-blew the pickle story.' "

The stories that were assigned in seminars were not fully fleshed out. After writers got their assignments there was still much work to be done.

"We'd each leave with two or three stories," Bullock recalled. "We'd write up a step outline. We'd bring that in to Aaron. And he'd either give you the okay or suggest some changes. That's when you catch the problem stuff. Then you'd leave and do the regular routine. You'd do the first draft, get it to them, and then they'd call you back in again for changes. Then would come the most wonderful words of all: 'We're going to mimeo with it.' That meant your script was approved. They were going to print it and hand it to the cast. That was an epiphany."

I don't want to discuss it any further! Take a lock.

From the point the script went to mimeo, it was no longer in the writers' hands. The producer, director, and actors started work with the script. "The practice we had back then," according to Ruben, "was to read two scripts on a Thursday morning—one was an advance script so that if anything was wrong with it, it could be fixed. That would be the script that would go into production the following week. The second script we read was the script for the current week that had been fixed and was ready for rehearsal."

During these sessions, known as "table readings," the actors were given an opportunity to suggest changes. If something did not appeal to someone, or there was an idea they thought might work better, the comments were considered and often accommodated.

"The table readings were so much fun because everyone had input," said Aneta Corsaut. Corsaut's favorite table reading story involved Rosemary Dorsey, the show's script lady. "I adore comedy writers," Corsaut began, "but sometimes they can overthink things. We were reading [Episode #168] 'The Hollywood Party,' and Andy is sitting on the sofa in the starlet's dressing room and is getting uncomfortable, so he makes a comment on the drapes, saying, 'Gee, those are pretty drapes. What color would you call that?' They were all looking for a funny color, it was the old thing that some numbers and some words are intrinsically funny, and they were going back and forth coming up with nothing. There was this long silence, and Rosemary says, 'Brown.' "

"We were glad to get the actors' input," Ruben said. "Although once, I remember one of the actors got a little out of hand, and Sheldon said, 'I believe I have to warn you. This is not a democracy. What we have here is a benevolent dictatorship.' "

How about this one from _True Blue Detective_.

Though the seminars were helpful in getting a head start on a new season, they still left more than half the scripts to be written. The writers themselves were left to invent the stories for these. "I always worshipped story," said Bullock, "and was in awe of people who knew them. They're hard to come by. They involved a lot of ceiling staring."

You didn't like Aunt Bee's piano wire idea?

"The one story that really had us stuck for an ending," said Everett Greenbaum, "was [Episode #112] 'Barney's Sidecar.' We didn't know how to get out of that one, but I had just bought a little tool for burning words into wood. So I said to Jim Fritzell, 'Why don't we just put a sign in there, and then up earlier we'll have Opie playing with this thing.' It was such a phony thing, but it was all we could think of, and I guess it works."

Writers cannot live by bread alone.

Episode #143, "Barney Fife, Realtor," written by Bill Idelson and Sam Bobrick, was another example of a writer drawing from his own life.

"The great thing about being a writer," Idelson said, "is nothing bad can happen to you—if you can turn it into a story. If you can do that, then every experience you have you can turn into cash.

"At the time I wrote the skit for the Writers Guild Awards Show, I had just left the real estate business. I sat down and decided I'm going to be a writer. I was in my late thirties, and I sold my first script to 'Twilight Zone.' " (It won a Writers Guild Award.)

"I used to call people on the phone. I had a reverse directory, and I'd ask, 'Would you like to sell your house?' I'd usually get the woman during the day, and the answer was always, 'Well, we've thought about it.' I was amazed. Everybody I talked to was interested in selling their house. They'd say, 'Well, if we could get more room, or bigger closets, or a smaller this. . . .' So I got this idea that Barney gets everyone interested in selling their houses but everything is contingent on getting the other guy's house, and of course no one ever moves."

I didn't want everyone to think I was a snob.

Oddly enough, the writing team of Jim Fritzell and Everett Greenbaum began their careers with no background in their craft. They managed, however, to produce some of television's finest moments.

"I never had any courses in writing," Greenbaum said. "I went to MIT but flunked out because I wasn't any good at math. Jim was completely uneducated. Jim's talent was on the penthouse level, but his taste was definitely ground-floor. He would turn on the quiz shows and watch them all day, and he was addicted to sports. He knew everyone's batting average, and so forth. But when we were working he could produce all this wonderful stuff."

"They used to have a ball writing together," said Aneta Corsaut. "I had the wonderful pleasure of writing with Jim on a show called 'Anna and the King.' We wrote two or three of them together, and he taught me their approach to construction. He was so brilliant at building a story."

Writers Everett
Greenbaum (on phone)
and Jim Fritzell (typing)
are working on another
script for "The Andy
Griffith Show." Behind
them is their 1963
Writers Guild Award for
best comedy for "Barney's
First Car."

Corsaut, Andy's girlfriend on the show, was Jim Fritzell's girlfriend off the set.

"Jim was so outgoing," Corsaut remembered, "and absolutely beloved. Everyone who met Jim adored him. He was funny, he was loving, he was attractive. . . . I don't know if he was good-looking or not, but he was beautiful."

"Jim and Ev both were from big cities," Corsaut recalled, "but still they wrote such wonderful rural stories. It was strange, but when you look at the other side of that—Damon Runyon, who had a rural background, became known as *the* 'New York' writer. I think a good part of that has to do with being an outsider looking in. When you're so close to something it's difficult to see things in a fresh way. It becomes so normal it's hard to see the qualities that make a people or a place special."

All of the masters: Shakespeare, Kipling, Ruben.

The "Andy Griffith Show" writers received inspiration for their most memorable work from a variety of sources. Their backgrounds gave a wealth of knowledge from which to draw. Everett Greenbaum provided some examples.

Episode #112, "Barney's Sidecar," gave Barney his memorable speech that followed Andy's refusal to let him use the squad car to patrol Highway 6. Greenbaum, who wrote that episode with Fritzell, recalled the origin of the payoff line to that speech: "Barney gets upset and goes on about how 'it's the same the world over—police departments are the lowest-paid underdog officials of them all,' and then he sums it all up by saying, 'But it's thank you, Johnny Shafto, when the guns begin to shoot!' That's Kipling. It's from *Gunga Din*."

The motorcycle itself was another bit of history from Greenbaum's past: "I had a World War One Harley when I was a kid. I paid eight dollars for it. When I was a young boy my father had a tire supply store, and we had a motorcycle with a sidecar that two of the men who worked for him, Howard and Eddie Ziffle, used to go out in when they did their bill collecting."

Another Greenbaum and Fritzell script borrowed from one of the masters to give Barney one of his most quotable lines. In Episode #93, "Dogs, Dogs, Dogs," after Barney goes out to rescue stray dogs from the dangers of a breaking thunderstorm, bringing them back at the risk of losing much-wanted extra funds, Andy congratulates the deputy on his good deed. Barney's eloquent response? "The quality of mercy is not strained, it droppeth as the gentle rain from heaven."

This catches Andy by surprise. "That's Shakespeare," Greenbaum admitted. "It's from *The Merchant of Venice*."

Greenbaum did not just draw from the classics. He credits Aaron Ruben with creating the "Giraffe" speech that occurs earlier in "Dogs, Dogs, Dogs." Barney and Opie are releasing some stray dogs in a field when it starts to rain. Opie is concerned about the animals being loose in the storm. Barney explains how dogs will handle the storm in a way that other animals could not. Greenbaum continued, "Barney gets on those giraffes and turns on them because they're selfish, 'They run around, lookin' after number one, gettin' hit by lightning.' That was Aaron Ruben's idea. I remember that clearly because I liked it so much."

Ruben, however, avoided taking credit for this contribution to the show. "I don't know why they always want to give me credit for that," Ruben countered. "They really liked that line." Why?

In Greenbaum's words, "It was a small thing, but it really made the whole scene work."

Don't be sorry, that rock had a lot of good memories attached to it.

As is the case with any craft, the life of the artist provides the most fertile ground for creative inspiration.

"These characters were a perfect conduit for us," Greenbaum said. "For example, in high school ROTC, I was a member of 'The Awkward Squad.' And we grew up in a different time than now. We remembered the Depression when we were writing these stories. You never see anyone lock their doors or sleeping on the ironing board when relatives came to visit. We wrote from life, not from other television shows."

One of the many qualities common to the Fritzell and Greenbaum scripts was the great attention they paid to detail. "The lucky penny [Episode #77, "Man in a Hurry"]—we used to do that when we were kids—put them on the streetcar tracks and smash 'em. When Gomer confesses that they took the liberty of taking a picture of Goober with the hood up, that was typical of Jim Fritzell."

One of the great romances of all time.

In Episode #82, "Class Reunion," shortly after Barney becomes sentimental about his father's rock, the audience is treated to the story of his legendary romance with Romana Wiley. Greenbaum tells of the roots of that story: "There was a girl in my fourth grade who I'd had a big crush on. Her name was Jane Clark, and some of the boys knew that. So to play a trick on me, they got a little ivory elephant and put it in a box that they left on my desk with a note that said, 'The tears on my pillow bespeak the pain that is in my heart,' and signed it 'Jane.' I never forgot that. 'The tears on my pillow bespeak the pain that is in my heart.' I believed it was from her, so I gave her a ring. And she liked it."

You know, the raspberry-snow-cone girl.

There was one other girl that haunted Barney's past. Vicky Harmes was in Episode #91, Bullock's "The Rivals." She was the girl Barney had a childhood crush on whom he remembered for sucking the syrup from his raspberry snow-cone. Bullock noted, "Vicky Harmes is my sister's child from Binghamton."

Lamour Toozure Zamure.

"Class Reunion" also included one of the few love scenes involving Andy Taylor. The outdoor scene with Andy and Sharon DeSpain was the only one in the series that used a filtered lens for Griffith's close-up. "That," in Harvey Bullock's opinion, "was probably the most romantic scene in the whole run of the series. Jim and Ev wrote that one, but I think I probably wrote the sexiest." Bullock was referring to Episode #114, "Prisoner of Love," and specifically the bedsheet-over-the-cell scene.

He was no prize, either.

One of the other details lifted from Greenbaum's life was the name of Jack Egbert, the guy who blackballed Barney from the Philomathian Literary Society. "He was my neighbor in Buffalo when I was a kid," Greenbaum said, "but a lot of the stuff—the names Gossage, Blush, and so forth—came from [Greenbaum's wife] Deane's life. They're all relatives and neighbors of hers. She just gave me a long list of all of her friends and relatives, and when we needed a name, I'd use it."

So it wasn't a skin condition after all.

"Leonard Blush was an idea I got from a friend of mine who, once a week, performed as the masked singer on WOR radio," Greenbaum said.

They used to call him Harvey "Scoop" Bullock.

According to Bullock, the idea for Episode #153, "Opie's Newspaper," came from a paper he had when he was a kid called *The Keyhole Journal*.

"We had a shack alongside the garage, and we'd make four or five copies on a gelatin thing. Anyway, it was about 'tee-hee,' what girl did what, juvenile titillation of what we thought was great gossip, and we sold it for a penny apiece and thought we were big-time."

We were just looking for work.

One strange similarity occurred in two episodes written by the team of Fritzell and Greenbaum and involved the births of two babies.

In their first episode of "The Andy Griffith Show," Episode #29, "Quiet Sam," a farmer (William Schallert) exhibited behavior that caught the immediate attention of Deputy Fife. After being called to the farmer's house, Andy saw that Sam was worrying about the coming birth of his first child. The baby—a boy—was delivered by Sheriff Taylor and was named Andy in his honor.

The story in Fritzell and Greenbaum's final script for the show, Episode #139, "The Darling Baby," centered around the Darling family's search for a husband for Charlene's newborn baby girl. The baby, also named for Sheriff Taylor, was called Andilila.

Not to be outdone, Harvey Bullock named his own firstborn Andy. Bullock joked, "I was looking for work."

Say, isn't that Barney Fife?

Episode #117, "The Shoplifters," Bill Idelson and Sam Bobrick's Writers Guild award-winning first script together, came from an idea Idelson had as a young navigator stationed in the South Pacific. "I originally wrote it as a sketch," Idelson said. "I was in Guam, and I used to get bored, so I used to write these little sketches. I was lying on my back in a Quonset hut daydreaming, and this funny notion occurred to me: What if a nerdy clerk in a department store volunteered to catch some clever shoplifters by dressing as a store dummy? The idea went around and around in my head, and finally I wrote it as a sketch. After that, it just went in my footlocker."

Seventeen years later, Idelson, now teamed with comedy writer Sam Bobrick, would find himself in Hollywood, struggling to find work as a television writer.

So that's it, is it? Shoplifters.

Idelson told how he got that first assignment. "I thought that old sketch of mine would be good for Barney Fife. So I told Sam, 'I know where Aaron Ruben parks his car.' "

Ruben, who was producing "The Andy Griffith Show" at that time, happened to park his car in a small lot across the street from the back entrance to his office. He entered the office through the back door. By chance, Idelson saw Ruben one morning.

"Of course, Sam, you know, he's from New York, he says, 'You're full of shit. I don't believe you.' So I said, 'Come with me.' "

I got my eye on our bird right now.

Sure enough, Ruben pulled into the lot that morning just as Idelson had predicted.

"We were standing there on the other side of the street, and we're scared because Aaron is a *big* man on the lot. So he walks up and I say, 'Aaron, can we see you for a couple a minutes, 'cause I got an idea for your show. Could you spare us five minutes sometime?' He gave us a look as he took out his keys and said, 'Come in at eleven tomorrow.' And he went into his office. I pitched the shoplifting idea, and his eyes lit up. He bought it on the spot. He started laying out scenes right away, and we were furiously taking notes. A couple hours later we left his office with a job, and that was it."

I don't think I could have been wrong.

After handing in a first draft, several days passed before the writing team found out whether or not they would ever work again.

"We'd gotten no word from Aaron," Idelson recalled, "but then I went to a party one night and there was Sheldon Leonard, the big man himself. 'That was a funny script you boys did,' he said as he walked by. We were in!"

You made a couple of mistakes back there.

To Idelson's surprise, the work had just begun. "We got a call from Aaron the next day to come in for a rewrite. We were in his office, and he, too, says to us, 'It's a funny script.' Then he proceeded to give us a whole shitpot full of changes. 'God, if this is what he's like when he likes a script,' I thought, 'I'd hate to see what he gives you when he doesn't.' "

You knew all along, didn't you?

The second draft was a success. Idelson told what happened next: "One thing that everyone who has ever worked around the studios knows is that the grapevine is all-powerful. It is strong, and it is fast. How everyone gets the word at almost the same time is one of those mysteries peculiar to the Hollywood film industry, but overnight Sam and I became one of the boys. We were guys who could do it. That's so important. The whole business is divided into those 'who can do it' and those 'who can't.' "

Now part of an elite group, Idelson and Bobrick went on to pen many more memorable stories.

"One of the shows I really enjoyed working on was [Episode #128] 'Barney's Bloodhound,' " Idelson said. "A guy gets a bloodhound, and the bloodhound falls in love with the crook. That's got to be funny. And the crook then gets the bloodhound to guard Barney. It's irony. I love irony. That was what was great about writing for Barney. He was such a wonderful foil for all this stuff. If he gets a bloodhound to catch a crook, wouldn't you know that the bloodhound likes the crook more than it likes him. But the one I think we got the most notice for was the reunion [Episode #176, 'The Return of Barney Fife.'] That was the one where we brought Thelma Lou back and Barney finds out she's married. Don then went on to win another Emmy for his work in that one."

He's a regular Bill Shakespeare.

Episode #135, "Barney's Uniform," also written by Idelson and Bobrick, is a favorite of Harvey Bullock's.

"That's a great script," Bullock said. "Bill was always known in the business as a great construction man. He really was terrific at building a story, and that one is a textbook example on story construction."

And in parting.

In Episode #112, "Barney's Sidecar," when Opie leaves the courthouse with his new wood-burning set, Andy bids him adieu by saying "Abyssinia," to which Opie answers, "See ya Samoa."

"That was all the rage in high school," explained Greenbaum. "Abyssinia— I'll be seeing you. See ya Samoa—I'll see you some more."

After leaving "The Andy Griffith Show," Fritzell and Greenbaum went on to write many episodes of "M*A*S*H." They were responsible for many of the milestone episodes of that classic black comedy set during the Korean War. One of the scripts they wrote was the well-known episode in which Lieutenant Colonel Henry Blake (played by McLean Stevenson) is killed when his plane is shot down. The title of that episode? "Abyssinia, Henry."

Commenting on his career, Greenbaum remarked, "My whole career was very lucky. I guess that's because I wasn't very ambitious. Right now I'm sorry I didn't make more money, but what do you need? You need a roof over your head, a few cars, two planes . . . but you can get old planes and used cars."

According to Bullock, part of the pleasure of working for "The Andy Griffith Show" was the reception the writers received from the show's powers that be. "Sheldon and Aaron treated writers as a favorite nephew. When you came on the lot, they were glad to see you. You'd go in to see Aaron, you'd have a cigar—they wouldn't interrupt you. They wouldn't say, 'What now?' "

Like so many other aspects of the entertainment business, this has changed. Many of the writers would discover that the norm on "The Andy Griffith Show" was the exception on other series. "Writing was different then than it is now," Bullock said. "Everything now is very up front. It's like going to a nude beach. If you ask me, I'd rather go to a beach where there's a lot of good bathing suits. It's much more interesting—leave it to your imagination."

SHOES-AND-RICE TIME

· ·

THE MANY MARRIAGES
OF MAYBERRY

Mayberry was the kind of place where people fell in love, got married and lived happily ever after. Or the network television equivalent of that phenomenon. The following is a brief description of the many weddings that occurred in Mayberry.

• Episode #1, "The New Housekeeper." Rose wed Wilbur Pine. The ceremony was performed by the honorable Sheriff Taylor.

• Episode #8, "A Feud Is a Feud." Josh Wakefield and Hannah Carter tried to elope. The ceremony was interrupted when both fathers arrived with shotguns.

• Episode #24, "The New Doctor." Andy proposed (under duress) to Ellie May Walker. She turned him down.

• Episode #36, "Barney on the Rebound." Barney was sued for breach of promise by Greg and Melissa Stevens. Andy bluffed them out by starting the wedding ceremony.

• Episode #45, "The Farmer Takes a Wife." Big Jeff Pruitt proposed marriage to Thelma Lou. The proposal was called off when Andy convinced Thel to bluff an acceptance.

• Episode #48, "The Manicurist." Manicurist Ellen Brown mistakenly thought Andy proposed marriage. She turned him down.

• Episode #59, "Three's a Crowd." Barney jumped to the conclusion that Andy had proposed to nurse Mary Simpson.

• Episode #96, "Briscoe Declares for Aunt Bee." Briscoe Darling declared for Aunt Bee. Again, the only way out was the old marriage bluff. The wedding was called off.

• Episode #121, "Divorce Mountain Style." Andy was the happy groom (victim?) when forced to marry Charlene Darling. The wedding was called off when the Darlings were tricked into believing Andy was marked with "the curse of the white horse."

• Episode #125, "The Rumor." Barney started a rumor that Andy and Helen had gotten engaged after he saw them kiss in the jewelry store.

• Episode #140, "Andy and Helen Have Their Day." Barney jumped to another conclusion and ran the whole family up to a justice of the peace. He thought Andy and Helen were waiting for him to bring money for a marriage license. Andy was actually fined for fishing without a license.

• Episode #142, "Three Wishes for Opie." It's hard to believe but Barney jumped to another conclusion. Barney thought Opie's wish—the one he was convinced would come true—was that Andy would marry Helen. Opie had much lower expectations: he wished that Helen would be his teacher again next year.

MISTY
MEMORIES
· ·

"A man wrote to me—he was a complete stranger—to tell me he breaks down and cries at the point in Episode #77, "Man in a Hurry," where Opie gives the man a penny."

—EVERETT GREENBAUM

It always makes me cry.

One of the remarkable qualities associated with "The Andy Griffith Show" was its ability to make the audience both laugh and cry.

"We often used the same corny approach that Frank Capra was so good at," said Sheldon Leonard. "I'm not derogating it. It's the result of the indoctrination I got on 'The Danny Thomas Show' of going beyond the joke to evoke a little emotion. It was what we called schmaltz. When it was done right, it was very effective to cap off a comedy routine with a serious stroke."

The following is a short list of some of the show's most memorable misty moments.

• Episode #1, "The New Housekeeper." Opie rushes out to stop Andy from taking Aunt Bee back to the bus station. He told his pa that Aunt Bee can't go because she needs him.

• Episode #2, "The Manhunt." Opie stands up to the state policeman on behalf of his pa and says, "My pa's the best sheriff in the whole world."

• Episode #11, "Christmas Story." Andy plays "Away in a Manger" on his guitar. While Ellie sings, Andy joins in on harmony, and Ben Weaver joins in quietly from behind the jail-cell window.

Later, Weaver comes in with a suitcase full of gifts and gives them to everyone in the courthouse.

• Episode #12, "Ellie for Council." Ellie gives Andy an admiring smile after he admits he was wrong about women.

• Episode #25, "A Plaque for Mayberry." Otis gains stature when he delivers a sober and sentimental speech accepting the award from the Women's Historical Society.

• Episode #34, "Opie and the Bully." Opie returns from his moment of truth, and Andy, the proud father, lifts him up and gives him a hug.

• Episode #58, "Wedding Bells for Aunt Bee." Opie asks Aunt Bee if she has that special kind of feeling for Mr. Goss, whom Opie believes she wants to marry. Aunt Bee cannot bring herself to say that she does, explaining only that everything will be all right.

• Episode #70, "The Cow Thief." Barney returns to the farmhouse to stand by his friend Andy. Barney recalls the time when Andy stuck by him even though everybody thought making Barney his deputy was a harebrained idea.

• Episode #109, "Barney and the Cave Rescue." Barney breaks through the rock and dirt to accomplish what he thinks is a daring rescue of Andy and Helen.

• Episode #120, "Bargain Day." Aunt Bee tells Mr. Foley about a friend who needs to store a freezer full of beef that the "friend" bought from a rival market. Foley, knowing Aunt Bee is the "friend," tells Bee simply, any friend of hers is "a friend of mine."

• Episode #136, "Opie's Fortune." Opie hands over the $50 to Andy after returning a fishing rod for a refund, and Andy tells Opie that he is "really something."

• Episode #161, "Opie's Job." Opie wins the box-boy job at the grocery over Billy but gets himself fired after hearing that Billy's family needs the money. While being scolded by Andy, Opie confesses what really happened and Andy, proud of his son, tells him that he has become a man.

• Episode #223, "Aunt Bee, the Juror." Aunt Bee serves on a jury that is deliberating the fate of Jenkins (Jack Nicholson), who's charged with robbery. Aunt Bee is the only juror who does not believe Jenkins is guilty, and she refuses to cast a guilty vote. Some of the other jurors start to get angry, but Goober, back in the courtroom, comes to her defense. When Jenkins learns that Aunt Bee stood up for him, he walks up to her and says thank you.

MAYBERRY
STATS

....

- The number of times Barney wore a tuxedo: 1

- The number of times Barney wore a dress: 3

- As of 1960, the number of years the Wakefield-Carter feud had been going on: 87

- The number of Carters shot by Wakefields since the feud started: 0

- The number of Wakefields shot by Carters since the feud started: 0

- The number of names Ellie needed to be placed on the ballot for town council: 100

- The number of names Ellie got on the petition: 100

- The number of men known to have signed it: 1 (Barney)

- The number of times Dr. Benson wrapped a sphygmomanometer, the blood pressure device, around Barney's arm: 3.5

- Except for the war bond, the estimated worth, in dollars, of Frank Myers's valuables: not a tiddly-boo

- The estimated value, at 8.5 percent interest compounded annually, in dollars, of Frank Myers's 1861 war bond: $349,119.27

- The value of the Mayberry treasury: just a little over $10,000

• Following the outcome of the Civil War, the actual value of Frank Myers's bond: not a tiddly-boo

• The winning number chosen for the door prize, a portable TV, at the church social: 44

• The number Henry Bennett chose at the church social—in spite of the fact that all the numbers in the hat were 44: 6⅞, the hat size.

• The number of peppermints Gomer bought without getting one prize-winning center: 24

• In Episode #116, "The Song Festers," the number of seconds the choir held that note: 26

• The number of days it took Barney and his cousin Virgil to go through $10 while on vacation in Raleigh: 3

• In Episode #137, "Goodbye, Sheriff Taylor," the number of times Floyd mentions the traffic jam to Andy after promising Barney he wouldn't: 2

• The number of documented cases of malfeasance during Andy's tenure as sheriff that Barney claimed to have in his briefcase: 76

• The amount Barney tipped for the use of Floyd's whisk broom: $1

• The number of times Floyd saw the Exotic Exciting Sultan's Choice, Arabian Dancer: 7

• The number of tries it took Warren using ESP to guess which number Andy had chosen between one and ten: 8

• The number of potatoes in Sharon Dobbins's Potato Queen crown: 10.

• The number of station wagons shot by Mayberry law officers: 2

• The number of times someone said "Shazaam!": 18

• The number of times someone said "groovy": 8

• The number of times Aristotle was mentioned: 1

• The time it took for Barney to get everyone seated for the first ride in his new car: 1 minute, 55 seconds

• The time it took to make the "split-second" change of guard for the gold shipment at Wally's: 17 seconds

• The number of times Barney had his gun taken away by a criminal: 5

• The number of times Barney loaded his bullet: 8

• The number of times Barney accidentally fired his pistol: 8

• The number of times Barney shot a bullet into the courthouse floor: 3

• The number of times Barney shot the courthouse ceiling: 1

• The number of times Andy shot the courthouse ceiling with Barney's pistol, thinking it was unloaded: 1

• The number of times Barney accidentally shot his pistol in the air: 2

• The number of times Barney accidentally shot something other than the courthouse ceiling or floor: 2

• The number of times Barney ripped his underwear trying to quick-draw: 1

• The number of windows and/or panes of glass broken by someone in all of the 249 episodes: 23

• The percentage of those broken by Ernest T. Bass in the five shows featuring him: 78 percent

OTIS CAMPBELL

· ·

AKA: EINSTEIN AND BIG CARD MAN

CREATED BY HAL SMITH

32 EPISODES

JAILED TWENTY-FOUR TIMES—TURNED AWAY ONCE

The character of Otis Campbell, introduced in "The Danny Thomas Show" pilot, was originally played by Frank Cady, best known for his role as Sam Drucker in "Petticoat Junction" and "Green Acres." Cady later appeared as Otis's Mount Pilot cellmate in Episode #145, "The Rehabilitation of Otis."

"I don't know how they happened to call me," said Hal Smith, "but they called my agent and said they'd like to read me for a part in "The Andy Griffith Show." It didn't seem to me that it would be a running part at the time."

Home away from home . . .

Smith went on to appear in thirty-two episodes of the show beginning with Episode #2, "The Manhunt," in 1960 and ending with Episode #204, "Otis, the Deputy," in 1966.

In Smith's opinion, the days of a series character like Otis Campbell are over. "I doubt a character like that would be allowed today," stated Smith. "Even then there was a bit of controversy. An account executive for one of our biggest sponsors was a confirmed alcoholic, and he kept trying to get me off the show. Andy stepped in and said, 'No way. He's part of it, and he's going to stay.' "

One for the road.

Since the character of Otis Campbell was based on the now sensitive social issue of substance abuse, updating Smith's role from the 1960s to the 1980s for "Return to Mayberry" presented a challenge.

"We really had a problem," Bullock recalled. "The town drunk, of course, wouldn't work anymore, so we thought about it and decided to make him an ex-drinker. We can dry him up and make him crazy about something else. So since we were putting him on the wagon, we figured we'd make him crazy about sugar. So we made him the ice cream man."

> "My experience in working with Andy was always a source of delight. He was easy to work with, and the atmosphere was always one of complete ease. If I remember correctly, I even had a slight crush on him."
>
> —JULIET PROWSE,
> actress/dancer

Well, he'd had a hard life.

In Episode #26, "The Inspector," Barney, wanting to fill a cell, went out and rounded up Otis, who was conveniently stewed. Barney happened to arrest Otis on his birthday. According to the candles on the cake Andy brought him, Otis was eight years old.

Those goats don't make good costars.

Today, the idea of a principal player in a hit show doing his own stunts would be out of the question. In the early 1960s, things were a little different, per Hal Smith:

In Episode #81, "The Loaded Goat," Otis comes into the courthouse after one of his benders to sleep things off in his usual cell. This time, however, the cell has been handed over to another inmate—a goat who had just snacked on a cache of dynamite. Otis enters after Barney and Andy have gone. The cell's back wall has been padded with Otis's mattress and a thin layer of hay lines the floor.

In the ensuing scene, Otis, thinking the liquor is playing tricks with his eyes, tries to climb into bed. He throws himself not once but twice against the mattress, which is fastened to the rear of the cell.

"What you see on the floor is all they had there . . . just that little bit of straw," Smith recalled. "I almost broke my back on that one. I took the fall myself. That was one take. I don't think I could've done another."

Breakfast is thrown in at no extra charge.

Ordinance 502 (The Otis Campbell Ordinance): Being intoxicated in a public place. Carries a $2 fine or twenty-four hours in jail.

A little hair of the dog.

To break the monotony of the everyday grind, witnessed in Episode #93, "Dogs, Dogs, Dogs," the Mayberry law officers and their staff were not above a little jailhouse tomfoolery.

"The hangover cure," Smith claimed, "that was for real. The egg yolk didn't break. Reggie, the propman, just gingerly stirred it and it was in there whole. They'd also loaded it up with hot sauce, so when I drank it, not only was I burning up with the hot sauce but that yolk got lodged in there and I nearly choked. We got that on one take, too."

I did, and I didn't, but I did.

One of the unique underlying qualities of "The Andy Griffith Show" was the way in which the scripts treated the characters. Two things were never an issue, right from the first episode: The characters must have their dignity and must always be dealt with honestly. No better example of this can be seen than in Episode #25, "A Plaque for Mayberry."

This episode, written by Ben Gershman and Leo Solomon, involved searching for and honoring the only remaining descendant of a local Revolutionary War hero. When the citizen turns out to be none other than Otis Campbell, the mayor and town council demand Andy tell Otis the ceremony is off. Andy, however, stands by Otis, and Otis steps forward to accept the plaque, sober and proud.

A man must make his family proud.

Hal Smith recalled this moment rather well. "My son, at the time, was about nine years old. He was sitting at home watching that show, and when I came in finally at the end, and they thought I was drunk, I looked over and the tears were rolling down his cheeks. Nine years old. That speaks for the appeal of that show."

That mayor was always very sensitive.

Strangely, the scene that Smith is referring to ends with the mayor offering a toast. Inappropriate as this might seem, it was the perfect tonic for a man with Otis's delicate condition. According to Smith, "The glasses were empty."

He was ahead of his time.

In "The Rehabilitation of Otis" Barney mentions he could hear the child within Otis crying out, "He'p me! He'p me!"

As a youth, he was endowed with good eyes and strong pinchin' fingers.

It was also in "A Plaque for Mayberry" that the audience was treated to its first lesson in modern law enforcement. "The sobriety test," as Smith remembered, "was also a lot of fun. I surprised Don on that one. When he said, 'All right, put your fingers together,' I just reached out and got his nose."

The Barney Fife, Peter Piper Nose Pinchin' Test for Drunks.

Step 1: – *Verbal coordination*
Subject asked to recite the tongue twister, "Peter Piper picked a peck of pickled peppers."
Result: Subject could say it . . . but Barney couldn't. (After working on it for four years, Barney finally got it right in Episode #138, "The Pageant.")

Step 2: – *Muscle Coordination*
Subject is asked to spread hands, close eyes, and bring his hands together touching the fingertips.
Result: Subject pinched Barney's nose between his fingers.

Step 3: – *Endurance*
Subject is asked to stand, lift his right foot, and, on command, start to hop.
Suggested command: "High-up!"
Result: Subject helped Deputy to a chair.

How dry I am.

Although Otis considered the confines of the Mayberry Courthouse friendly, in Episode #55, "Aunt Bee, the Warden," he found himself suddenly in less than hospitable surroundings.

The idea of placing a character in a situation that was pregnant with possibilities belonged to Andy Griffith. According to Hal Smith, "The idea for 'Aunt Bee, the Warden' was one of Andy's ideas. They were working on the script, and he thought it would be fun to send Otis to the Taylor house. The whole charm of that story worked because of that."

Once out of the jailhouse and into "The Rock," Smith turned in a brilliant performance as the happy but misplaced drunk. No sooner did he enter the Taylor household than he began exploring the comic possibilities. He surveyed his new surroundings, grabbed a vase filled with fresh flowers, and decided he needed a drink.

"The bit with the vase was an ad-lib. Things were kind of slowing down with the dialogue, so I thought, 'I'll just take a drink out of this vase.' Then we go upstairs, and I've got the vase—Andy tried to take it away from me, but I wouldn't let go. When he set me down on the bed, I just thought I'd go as far as I could with the gag. So I laid down and the water just spilled all over me. That was an ad-lib as well. They liked it and left it in."

And no more singing.

The same episode also featured the song "The Dipsy Doodle," an old favorite of Smith's. "I just started singing it," he said. "It seemed just right for Otis. I still remember it. It was a great old song. It went like this:

> *"The dipsy doodle is a thing to beware.*
> *The dipsy doodle will get in your hair.*
> *And if it gets you, then it couldn't be worse.*
> *The things you say will come out in reverse.*
> *Like, me love you,*
> *And you love I.*
> *That's the way the dipsy doodle works.*

"The tail end of it went:

> *Like the moon jumped over the cow, hey diddle,*
> *That's the way the dipsy doodle works."*

Smith continued, "Another ad-lib was when I was chopping wood at 'The Rock' out in Andy's front yard. Aunt Bee walks by, and I raise the ax to her. Andy was very good about things like that. It added to the fun. You felt like you were always contributing. He liked people to add whatever they could."

Food and water for my men and cows.

Of all his many memorable misadventures, Hal Smith said he would never forget the one in Episode #145, "The Rehabilitation of Otis." The script called for Otis to mount up and ride into town, but not on a horse. He came on a cow.

"That cow ... oh my God. I'll never forget that. I couldn't walk for two weeks. I used to ride horses, but that cow ... the way they're built, wide in the middle, and narrow at the front and back, I kept rocking back and forth. . . .

And I had to ride it up and down those steps. Once I fell off and Andy caught me. They had it on film, but they didn't keep it in."

Not so fast.

Directions to Rafe Hollister's still: Go out Route 22 past Waynesborough, Midville, Thorndyke, Upson, through Virginia, Pennsylvania, Ohio, then back through West Virginia, Kentucky, Tennessee, into Mayberry on Route 10 to Elm Street. 411 Elm Street. That's where Barney lives.

A good hourly wage, benefits, and all you can sniff.

In Episode #175, "Otis, the Artist," Otis is working as a glue dipper at the furniture factory.

. . . .

"There are very few shows where you love every character. I loved everyone on 'The Andy Griffith Show.' There's a special joy in being able to look at a situation where every character is delicious—Andy and the rest were just that. It gave me a feeling of overall warmth."

—MONTY HALL,
host-producer

. . . .

I'd give anything if I could just tell him "Fee, Fie, Fo, Fum" all over again.

Originally broadcast on December 12, 1966, Episode #204, "Otis, the Deputy," was Otis Campbell's swan song. He arrived drunk and was jailed in Mayberry for the final time. He was mentioned once more, in Episode #218, "Opie's Most Unforgettable Character." In that episode, it is claimed that Otis is doing his drinking in Mount Pilot.

Hal Smith died from a heart attack on January 28, 1994. He was seventy-seven years old.

ERNEST T. BASS

....

"HE'S A PESTILENCE, AND A PESTILENCE
WILL FIND YOU."
AKA: OLIVER GOSSAGE, KREE-TURE
CREATED BY HOWARD MORRIS
5 EPISODES

"What was I thinking? I don't know. It was just another job to me."

—HOWARD MORRIS

Didn't know you were creating royalty, did you?

Jim Fritzell and Everett Greenbaum devised one of the most outlandish characters ever to scream, jump, and cackle his way across the small screen. The name of this rather unique individual? Ernest T. Bass.

Out of 249 episodes of "The Andy Griffith Show," Ernest T. Bass was featured in only five. In those five episodes, the writers and Howard Morris, the man who portrayed Ernest T., created a legend. "Which is," in Morris's words, "a remarkable comment to make about any character in theatricaldom. And not a tribute to me, but to several other things—one has to be the insanity in the nation. I tell you, when I go South with this character— occasionally we get invited to appear down South at one of these fan conventions—I am treated like royalty."

Maybe he's the black sheep of the royal family.

"We were in Columbia, South Carolina, at this beautiful hotel for another of these conventions, and when we went in, I was in costume. I'm dressed as Ernest T., and we go in and they're having buffet. We're going to eat there. I said, 'Listen, I've gotta go to the john.' I go into the john and I come out and I'm walking through this incredible lobby, but I'm by myself, and a guy with a badge comes up, stops me, and says, 'Where you going?'

"I said, 'I'm going—you know . . .'

"He says, 'Get the hell out of this lobby.' And just as he's about to throw me out, the producer comes up and saves me. He says, 'You can't throw this guy out. This is Ernest T. Bass.' Well the guy turned white as a sheet."

This Aaron guy must be one smart cookie.

Even with the ingenious imagination of writers Fritzell and Greenbaum and the wild portrayal by Howard Morris, credit for the creation of this character again lies partially on a hunch of producer Aaron Ruben's.

"I had worked with Aaron Ruben previously on 'Your Show of Shows,' " Morris said. "The list of writers on that show you wouldn't believe. Aaron Ruben, Mel Brooks, Woody Allen—Carl Reiner was an actor who also contributed. A guy named Doc Simon—you probably know him better as Neil—he was there with his brother Danny. There was a guy named Joe Stein who wrote a little thing called *Fiddler on the Roof*. Larry Gelbart, who wrote 'M*A*S*H.' This was the quality of writers we had. We were all young kids. We were in our twenties and thirties, and we'd be in a room about this size, screaming and yelling all day. That was how we wrote the show. We'd scream and yell for an hour, and then we'd go and write the sketch."

In case you wonder who this be . . .

A common occurrence in television is for a producer to ask writers to develop a character for a specific actor. The role of Andy Taylor was specifically created with Andy Griffith in mind. In the case of Ernest T. Bass, however, the character was created with absolutely no actor in mind.

"Aaron called me," recalled Morris. "He said, 'Would you come and do this for us?' Aaron didn't know what to do with it, he told me. They'd invented this *thing*, and they thought he was kind of a big bumpkin. A big, lumbering, guy. So I read it, and something happened in me. I don't know what. Where is Ernest T. Bass in a little Jew from the Bronx? I came up and read this character for them, and at first I played him as a heavy. But me as a heavy? Howie Morris as a heavy? Had we played him as a heavy it wouldn't have been as funny."

It's me, it's me.

"I made up all the poetry," Morris said. "That was not written in. That was something I would write for each segment, and they said, 'Go ahead, do it, do it!' It worked."

It's Ernest T.

People were afraid of what Ernest T. might do next. The actors in the show played fear in their dealings with him. They never knew what he was going to do. How did he get out of jail? "That's for me to know an' you ta find out!"

Scary what you can find deep inside the psyche.

"Creatively I can't tell you where it came from," Morris commented, referring to his interpretation of E.T. "He must have been in there somewhere wanting to come out. But he didn't have to be in the hills. In New York, you'll find an Ernest T. on the corner of every street. They just took him and put him in this wonderful setting."

Irritatin', isn't it?

As an actor, Morris was trained differently than the other members of the cast. He took the typical rhythm of "Andy Griffith" and put a new spin on it.

"I came in to 'The Andy Griffith Show' cold. I didn't know anyone, just Aaron. And let me tell you, they were shocked! Andy, who's a wonderful man, was absolutely stunned. When they had to drag me out of Mrs. Wiley's, they had never done anything like that. I told Andy and Don, 'Really try to get me out, and I'm really going to stay in.' They didn't know what to do—my feet were hooking around doors . . . by the time they got me out of there we were all exhausted!"

And I'm strong.

Ernest T. claimed to be able to do eighteen chin-ups. He was the best rock thrower in the county, and he was saving up for a gold tooth, according to "Mountain Wedding."

By "Ernest T. Bass Joins the Army," E.T. has become a veritable Rocky Balboa, claiming to be able to chin himself twenty times—with only one hand!

Every concert is sold out.

" 'Ol' Esmariah?' That was an old hillbilly song. I just sang it. In fact, I still sing it. When I go on these appearances I break into that, and you'd think I was Garth Brooks."

> *"Old Esmariah,*
> *Jump in the fire,*
> *Fire too hot,*
> *Jump in the pot,*

Pot too black,
Jump in the crack,
Crack too high,
Jump in the sky,
Sky too blue,
Jump in canoe,
Canoe too shalla'
Jump in the talla',
Talla' too soft
Jump in the loft,
Loft's just right,
I'll stay all night . . . "

You ain't seen the last of Ernest T. Bass.

"For some reason this kind of character has a certain appeal. He's the kind of lunatic that Sam Kinison was, and not unlike this guy Kramer on 'Seinfeld,' who's brilliant by the way. It's this attitude they all had: 'Well, I belong here. What the hell are you doing?' "

Howard Morris continued. "Little kids come up to me and they say, 'Mr. Bass . . .' And I'll say, 'Hello, how are you?' They'll say, 'I'm just fine. How're you? When I grow up I want to be just like you.' That's some comment. I want to say, 'Are you kidding? He's a nut!' "

I'm your slave.

Even though it all took place over thirty years ago, Morris has an amazing recollection of the performances, quoting many of the lines, rhymes, and songs. Morris's final performance as Ernest T., however, remains a complete blank.

"I have no memory of 'Malcolm at the Crossroads.' I had hurt my back. I was in such pain that I couldn't do anything. But it had to be done. We were on a schedule, so the doctor fed me painkillers, and I was so out of it they had to feed me a line at a time. That's the kind of schedule we were on. It had to be done."

He keeps proving that he's the best rock thrower in the county.

Episode #94, "Mountain Wedding"

• First window broken by Ernest T. Bass: the Darling cabin's window. The weapon of choice? A rock, of course. Attached to the rock was a note declaring Ernest T.'s love for Charlene.

• Ernest T. breaks five more of the cabin's windows with rocks.

Episode #99, "Ernest T. Bass Joins the Army"

• Ernest T. breaks the courthouse front window with a rock, followed by:

A window at the induction center
A streetlight in front of Mrs. Mingus's house
Two panels out of Hanna Lou's greenhouse
A window at Rich Briar's hardware store
Two more courthouse windows
And the new window being carried over for the courthouse.
It wasn't actually Ernest T. who broke that window.
Barney broke it trying to protect it from Ernest T.

Episode #113, "My Fair Ernest T. Bass"

• Ernest T. throws a rock through the front window of Mrs. Wiley's.

Episode #133, "The Education of Ernest T. Bass"

• Ernest T. throws a rock through the courthouse window.

• Ernest T. throws a rock with a love note attached through Helen's front window. He is carted off to jail.

Episode #164, "Malcolm at the Crossroads"

• Not wanting to be wasteful, Ernest T. throws a perfectly good brick through an off-screen window after he is fired as a crossing guard.

• Total: 17 windows, one street lamp, and one window broken by proxy.

Just don't throw a rock through the lens.
In the midst of performing as Ernest T. Bass, Morris began a career as a director. "When I returned as a director—this guy who played Ernest T. could come back and direct? I think they were scared to death."

Morris recalled how Carl Reiner coaxed him to start directing: "We had a chat one day, and he said, 'Do you want to direct?' I said, 'Do I—do I what?' He said, 'I'll tell you what I'll do . . .' " The two of them went to Sheldon Leonard and received permission for Morris to hang around the lot for three months. He also had the freedom to do whatever he wanted.

"I went everywhere . . . on sets, I went into the editing rooms, story conferences, and then they gave me a show to direct. I was appalled. I did an episode of 'The Dick Van Dyke Show,' and it was a hit. So they brought me back for more." From there, Morris graduated to "The Andy Griffith Show."

"You weren't going to teach any of them how to act. Andy, Don, Frances, Howard, even Ron, they were all brilliant. You just had to turn them on and let them go."

"I almost gave up acting, but there was something in me that said, 'Wait a minute—get back in there.' "

Among his directing credits are the pilot episode for "Get Smart" and eight episodes of "The Andy Griffith Show." The episodes, all from the show's fifth season, were "Barney's Bloodhound," "Family Visit," "Aunt Bee's Romance," "Barney's Physical," "The Darling Baby," "Andy and Helen Have Their Day," "Otis Sues the County," and "Three Wishes for Opie."

"Every show I directed, it would go on the air and two minutes after the show ended, the phone would ring. It would be Andy. He'd be calling to say, 'Good job, good show.' "

If you put this in a play, nobody would believe it.

Ernest T. was not only a favorite of the television audience, he was also somewhat of a legend on the studio lot as well. "Sheldon always talked about my character as 'the most incredible comedy creation ever *perpendicularized*. I said, 'What the hell are you talking about?' He'd say, 'Ernest T. Bass— *unfathomable*.' "

Just another day working on a legend.

"The Andy Griffith Show" became such a legend because it offered a better time and place to society. Mayberry was a throwback for America. Similarly, the show was a different kind of experience for the actors and writers. "There was no ego to get in the way. It was incredible," Morris said. "Listen to what people say when they talk about the weak parts of the show. They'll say, 'Well, in the first five or six years . . . it was—whatever.' Think about that. The first five or six years. Wow. That's 150 to 180 shows. And then they did another 100. That's how good that show was. Sure it was weak at times. But at the same time it was so fantastic for so long! Wow."

Morris had nothing but high praise for the show. "Is there anything wrong?

Is there anything bad? I'll tell you, it was a phenomenon, and I came out of crazy variety—'Your Show of Shows.' It was nuts, and we dealt with each other's aberrant personalities all day long. That's what we made funny from— life experience. A bunch of crazy, screaming Jews in the room. This show, 'The Andy Griffith Show,' was like nothing else. It was a phenomenon. There were no Southerners, really. It wasn't about Southerners or the South. This was a show about human beings. And a nicer time in our country, which is really what people revere about it."

LYDIA
CROSSWAITHE

· ·

CREATED BY JOSIE LLOYD

2 EPISODES:

EPISODE #68, "BARNEY MENDS A BROKEN HEART"

EPISODE #147, "GOOBER AND THE ART OF LOVE"

HER NAME MEANT NATIVE OF LYDIA, BUT SHE

HAILED FROM GREENSBORO.

Dislikes.

• The outdoors. When she goes outdoors, Lydia gets herpes.

• The guitar. She does not mind the clarinet or the saxophone, but she hates the guitar.

• Chitchat. Ordinary conversation is acceptable, but she hates to chit-chat.

• Pretzels. They lay on her chest.

• Gambling. She does not gamble.

• Bowling. If she threw a ball, she would wind up in traction for a month.

• Car rides. Because she gets carsick, she prefers to ride with her head out the window like a dog.

- Dancing. She does not dance.

- Candy. She gets sick from too much of it.

Likes.

- None.

Separated at birth.

Lydia bore a remarkable resemblance to the lovely Juanita Pike. Juanita, the daughter of Mayor Pike, appeared in Episode #13, "Mayberry Goes Hollywood," and sang "Flow Gently Sweet Aft'n" at the reception for the Hollywood movie producer. She was seen again in Episode #20, "The Beauty Contest."

MR. SCHWUMP

....

CREATED BY UNKNOWN
9 EPISODES
NO LINES

But who was he?

Mr. Schwump made his Mayberry debut on the porch of Mrs. Wiley's house in Episode #113, "My Fair Ernest T. Bass." Everett Greenbaum, one of the people responsible for letting him loose in Mayberry, told how Mr. Schwump came to life. "We wanted to portray an unpleasant stag line. So we created this character that we wanted to look like he might pinch you when you went by. We never saw the actor until later, but he was brilliantly cast."

Beauty is in the eye of the beholder.

Howard Morris remembered Mr. Schwump well. "Mr. Schwump! The worst toupee you'll ever see in your life. And an expression on his face like a bloody cretin. Andy loved him. He befriended him. He loved the way he looked."

The life and times of Mr. Schwump.

Mr. Schwump only appeared in nine episodes of "The Andy Griffith Show." Although the character was memorable, the actor was never given credit for the role. The following is a brief description of Mr. Schwump's appearances in Mayberry.

• Episode #113, "My Fair Ernest T. Bass." Mr. Schwump stood on the porch with other members of the party following the attack by Ernest T. Bass. He was credited with trying to pinch him.

• Episode #133, "The Education of Ernest T. Bass." Mr. Schwump sat on the bench outside the courthouse with Andy.

• Episode #123, "The Fun Girls." Before going to the dance, Andy complained that he would not stand in a stag line with Old Man Schwump. Not only didn't Mr. Schwump get a line in this episode, he also didn't get a dance.

• Episode #141, "Otis Sues the County." Once again, Mr. Schwump sat on a bench with Andy.

• Episode #175, "Otis, the Artist." Mr. Schwump was seated in art class.

• Episode #203, "Only a Rose." Obviously a joiner, Mr. Schwump sat in the first row of the Garden Club meeting at the town hall.

• Episode #210, "Floyd's Barbershop." When everyone was loitering around the courthouse following the closing of Floyd's Barbershop, Mr. Schwump sat in Barney's old chair reading the paper.

• Episode #240, "Barney Hosts a Summit Meeting." Always at the center of the action, Mr. Schwump showed up at Andy's house to see the summit and get his picture taken.

• Episode #247, "Sam for Town Council." The consummate party animal, Mr. Schwump showed up at Andy's election party, waiting for the early returns.

MAYBERRY'S
MUSIC

....

"Earle Hagen was one of the major composers in series television. In the early days of television, he was a one-man training ground. People working for him were recognized around town and considered for other jobs first and foremost because they'd worked for Earle."

—HARRY LOJEWSKI,
retired vice president
of music at MGM/UA

Now's your chance to say how you feel.

"The music was superb," Jack Dodson said. "Most people never talk much about Earle Hagen. Though I've always wanted to, I have never had a chance to express to Hagen how brilliant I thought his work was."

That ain't just whistling "Dixie."

There is no TV theme more popular than the one musical director Earle Hagen wrote and produced for "The Andy Griffith Show." A talented musician and composer, Hagen scored well over 3,000 episodes for series, including "Gomer Pyle, U.S.M.C.," "That Girl," "The Mod Squad," "The Dick Van Dyke Show," and "Mike Hammer," to name just a few.

I like the whistling, but Barn pushed hard for "I'm Just a Vagabond Lover."

"It was just an idea," Hagen responded when asked about the genesis of that opening melody. "The whistling and the theme happened at the same time." Hagen's idea was to lay down a simple title. "I had done plenty of elaborate ones, but it seemed to me that the whistling would be endemic for Andy because he was that kind of character. He was the kind of guy who'd whistle something." How long did it take to create the theme? Hagen recalled, "I wrote the whole thing in about an hour." After that he went into the studio. "I hired a little rhythm combo—just a bass drum and guitar, and we did a demo the same day." The whistling was done on the demo, and later on the finished theme, by Hagen himself. "It was the first, and last, time I whistled anything."

Nobody could call Sheldon an interloper.

The theme is just one small part of what made "The Andy Griffith Show" a musical standout. Hagen, hired by Sheldon Leonard, was the man responsible for scoring each episode and overseeing the recording sessions. The idea of a musical director being allowed to operate for any length of time without supervision would not even be considered today. In the early days of television, more attention was paid to music because of that freedom from constant supervision. Hagen said, "In today's world, the network controls just about everything. In that era, the sponsors owned the shows, and they let the talent do what they thought was right."

In "The Andy Griffith Show" and other Sheldon Leonard series, Hagen was left alone to do what he did best. "I worked for Sheldon Leonard for over seventeen years," Hagen said. "Not once did he ever come into a recording session."

How about something from the light classics?

Another stroke from Hagen's musical brush involved the creation of musical themes that became signatures for the characters. "I had two for Barney," Hagen said. "One was 'The Lawman,' for when he was acting bigger than life, and the other one I guess you'd call 'The Twitchy Theme,' for when he was, well, being twitchy."

Sometimes it's harder to be bad.

His job, as Hagen put it, was "to let the show dictate the music." As good as he was, Hagen was sometimes asked to be bad. Episode #72, "The Mayberry Band," featured the town's musical marchers stumbling on their instruments.

Ironically, seasoned professionals were being paid to imitate rank amateurs; Hagen's responsibility was to make sure that the drama did not become melodrama.

Hagen explained, "You had to have really good musicians, and you had to tell them you wanted it to be bad but you didn't want it to be burlesque. We did an arrangement of 'The Stars and Stripes Forever' that was so funny that Andy, who was playing tuba, fell apart when we did the take. What made it funny wasn't only that the band didn't play it well, but one of the guys got a bar behind the rest and stayed there. Which is what probably would have really happened."

That's entertainment.

Two of the more prominent uses of music inside the show were Barney's harmonica playing and the Darlings.

The Darlings were the Dillards, a popular folk group in the 1960s who did their own arrangements. One member of the Darlings, however, was not a Dillard. Patriarch Briscoe Darling played his favorite instrument, the jug. Since there were no synthesizers in the 1960s, Hagen improvised. "We got a big bottle, and one of the guys blew across it."

The harmonica, "if it was important," Hagen said, was actually overdubbed by studio musician Tommy Morgan.

Once more for the orange and blue.

One other popular piece of music written by Hagen was the Mayberry Union High fight song. Used as the climax to a CBS special honoring "The Andy Griffith Show," Jack Dodson said it was the one moment of the special he will never forget. "I really loved getting up to sing the Mayberry High song. It's such a great song. You couldn't have a better high school song than that."

And dig this.

The inimitable "Bobby Fleet and His Band with a Beat" made several trips to Mayberry. This band, however, will not be cutting a reunion album. It was composed of actors playing roles, not instruments. "That was done in the studio by professionals, studio musicians," Hagen said. "The band members you saw on screen were character actors typed for the parts of the musicians, but they didn't play."

Is there anything he can't do?

One actor who was the genuine article was Andy Griffith. "He used to sing most of his numbers right on the stage," Hagen said. "Those numbers were often recorded live." Andy, who Hagen said is very knowledgeable about music, chose those numbers himself.

I'm a big bundle of singing talent.

Don Knotts shared memories of his musical skills: "Between takes we'd sing and harmonize, and we'd work it into the show. You'll see it at the beginning of some of the shows. One time I was playing around, and I hit a bad note. Andy just glanced at me, and we left it at that. One thing I liked about the show was we wouldn't lean on things like that. We'd do them and let them go."

" 'The Song Festers' was difficult to do because I had to intentionally sing off-key, and that's tough to do."

· ·

" 'The Andy Griffith Show'

was pure family

entertainment. It was a blend

of warmth, humor, and

simple Americana."

—STEVE GARVEY,

baseball player
· ·

Put a nickel in the jukebox.

Music was such an important part of the show. The following chart details the various musical compositions that were played during the series.

Mayberry's Musical Numbers

Song Title	Played by	Episode
"You Get a Line and I'll Get a Pole"	Andy on porch with guitar	#1
"Ridin' on That New River Train"	Andy and Jim Lindsey: guitar; Barney, Andy: duet	#3
"Jingle Bells"	Barney on harmonica	#11
"Flow Gently Sweet Aft'n"	Sung by Juanita Pike	#13
"Saxamania"	Saxophone by Floyd's son	#15
"I'm Just a Vagabond Lover"	Song Barney knew on the harmonica	#15
"Animal Crackers"	Song Barney knew on the harmonica	#15
"Finiculi, Finicula"	Song Barney knew on the harmonica	#15
"I Ain't Gonna Be Treated This'a Way"	Andy on guitar and vocals	#17
"Ain't Got Time to Kiss You Now"	Andy and The Country Boys	#19
"Honey, Oh Baby, Mine"	Andy and The Country Boys	#19
"Que Sarah, Sarah"	Song Barney knew on the harmonica	#19
"Seein' Nellie Home"	Andy on guitar; Andy, Ellie, Barn and Thel: vocals	#22
"Hail to Thee, Miss Mayberry"	Sung by Floyd (also written by Floyd)	#31
"Rock n' Roll Rosie from Raleigh"	Hit song by Jim Lindsey (referred to but not sung)	#31

Song Title	Played By	Episode
"Midnight Special" Variation	Lindsey and Andy on guitar; Andy: vocals	#31
"One for My Baby"	Sung by Barney after being compared to Sinatra	#35
"Sourwood Mountain"	Andy on guitar and vocals	#37
"John Henry"	Andy on guitar and vocals	#37
"Bringin' in the Sheaves"	Hummed by Barney to help Otis get to sleep	#47
"Juanita"	Sung by Barney to warm his vocal cords	#52
"It Was Mary"	Sung by Barney to taunt Andy	#52
"Honey, Oh Baby, Mine"	Andy on guitar; Andy and Barney: vocals	#54
"Spread a Little Sunshine Every Day"	Andy on guitar; Andy and Barney: vocals	#54
"Dig My Grave with a Silver Spade"	Andy on guitar and vocals	#54
"The Dipsy Doodle"	Sung by Otis Campbell	#55
"Seein' Nellie Home"	Andy on guitar; Andy, Barney, Thel, Mary: vocals	#59
"I Wish I Was an Apple"	Andy on guitar and vocals	#59
"La Cucaracha"	Barney on bongos	#59
"My Little Grey Home in the West"	Sung by Junior Hubacher in jail (makes the warden cry)	#63
"Down in the Valley"	Andy on guitar; Peg and Andy: vocals	#65
"The Stars and Stripes Forever"	The Mayberry Band with Bobby Fleet	#72
"Little Brown Church in the Vale"	Andy: guitar; Andy, Barn, Malcolm Tucker: vocals	#77
"Dear Old Donnegal"	Sung by Barney as cleaning lady in bank	#78
"Chattanooga Choo-Choo"	Played by Carl Benson's Wildcats at high school reunion	#82
"Tiko-Tiko, the Umbrella Man," and "Moon Over Manora"	Possible audition songs from the light classics	#83
"Believe Me if All Those Endearing Young Charms"	Sung by Barney and Rafe Hollister; Andy on guitar	#83
"Acapela"	Sung by Barney to tune of "La Cucaracha"	#83
"Look Down That Lonesome Road"	Rafe Hollister vocals; Andy Taylor: guitar	#83
"Ridin' on That New River Train"	Rafe Hollister vocals; Andy Taylor: guitar	#83
"Toot-Toot Tootsie"	Aunt Bee on piano; Opie and Bee: vocals	#87
"Chinatown"	Aunt Bee on piano; Ladies' Church Aid Club: vocals	#87
"Slimy River Bottom"	The Darlings (makes Charlene cry)	#88
"Dooley"	The Darlings	#88
"Dooley"	The Darlings	#94
"Never Hit Your Grandma with a Great Big Stick"	A song that makes Charlene Darling cry (not performed)	#94
"Dance Til Your Stockin's Are Hot And Ravely"	A song in the Darlings' repertoire (not performed)	#94
"Leanin' on the Ever-lastin' Arms"	The Darlings; Andy Taylor on guitar	#94
"Jump in the Pot"	Ernest T. Bass on gas can and vocals	#94
"Dirty Me, Dirty Me, I'm Disgusted with Myself"	A song that makes Briscoe Darling cry (not performed)	#96
"Doug's Tune"	Andy and the Darlings	#96
"Dan Tucker"	Andy and Opie on guitar and vocals	#96
"Low and Lonely Over You"	The Darlings—Briscoe: vocals	#96
"No 'Count Mule"	Sung by Gomer while getting ready for bed	#97
"I'm Sorry I Broke Your Heart, Mother"	Sung by Otis Campbell	#106
"The Marines' Hymn"	Sung by Gomer in courthouse and under bucket	#107
"We Will Not Sing"	Sung by the demonstrating ladies	#111
"Row, Row, Row Your Boat"	Sung by Barney to keep the ladies busy	#111

SONG TITLE	PLAYED BY	EPISODE
"We Shall Meet, but We Shall Miss Him"	Andy on guitar; Andy and Barney: vocals	#115
"Santa Lucia"	The Mayberry Choir (Barney as soloist)	#116
"Now Is the Month of May"	Barney (for Eleanora Poultice's voice class)	#116
"Santa Lucia"	Sung by Gomer while changing J. Master's tire	#116
"Shady Grove"	The Darlings—Charlene: vocals	#121
"Nothin' Could Be Finer than to Be in Carolina"	Earle Hagen's band	#123
"When the Saints Come Marching In"	Earle Hagen's band	#123
"John Jacob Jingle Heimer Smith"	Sung by the campers, Barn, Andy, and Gomer	#127
"It's Sylvia"	Sung by Leonard Blush, but interrupted by news	#128
"Hail to Thee, Miss Mayberry"	Sung by Floyd Lawson	#138
"There Is a Time for Love and Laughter"	The Darlings—Charlene: vocals	#139
"Evo Walker"	The Darlings	#139
"Sweet Adeline"	Sung by Barney and Otis while drunk in cell	#141
"Over Yonder"	Andy on guitar and vocals	#151
"Love Lifted Me"	Sung by the congregation at Sunday services	#174
"Bringin' in the Sheaves"	First song sung with the new organ	#174
"Some Enchanted Evening"	Sung by Clara for Mr. Robinson	#174
"Leanin' on the Everlastin' Arms"	Sung by the congregation with Mr. Robinson	#174
"The Gypsy Melody"	Sung by the Gypsies	#183
"Flora's Theme"	Background music that sounds like "A Summer Place"	#186
"Texarkana in the Morning"	Million-copy hit for Keevy Hazelton (not sung)	#189
"My Hometown" (words and music by Earle Hagen)	Written by Aunt Bee and Clara Edwards; sung with Keevy	#189
"In the Gloaming"	Sung by the Mayberry Barbershop Quartet	#191
"The Beautiful Isle of Make Believe"	Sung by the Mayberry Barbershop Quartet	#191
"Salty Dog"	Andy and The Darlings—Charlene: vocals	#193
"The Grass Is Greener over Yonder"	The Darlings	#193
"A Wandering Minstrel"	Sung by Floyd	#197
"I Wish I Was an Apple"	Andy on guitar and vocals out on the porch	#203
"Don't Tell Aunt Rosy"	Sung by Otis Campbell	#204
Andy on the porch with the guitar		#222
Opie plays guitar		#227
Opie plays guitar		#228
Opie becomes the new guitarist for "The Sound Committee"		#229
"Oh Grant Us the Evening Prayer"	Sung by the church choir	#238
"The Lord Be Gracious unto You"	Sung by the church choir wearing new robes	#238
"You and I"	Sung by Goober, Edith, Doris, Andy, and Sam	#249

MAYBERRY'S Q&A

· ·

MAYBE YOU KNOW THE ANSWERS, BUT DO YOU KNOW
THE QUESTIONS? SINCE GAMBLING WAS ILLEGAL IN
MAYBERRY, VALUES ARE IN JELLY BEANS.

The Answers . . .

LAW AND ORDER FOR 200.
According to a 1961 FBI survey, it was the lowest in the whole dad-blamed country.

LAW AND ORDER FOR 400.
This famous case was named for the chronic jaywalker whose tickets were repeatedly torn up by Sheriff Taylor.

LAW AND ORDER FOR 600.
Barney's body, when used correctly.

LAW AND ORDER FOR 800.
Contrary to what Andy said, this was Barney's self-proclaimed number-one job.

LAW AND ORDER FOR 1,000.
Maximum security.

MAYBERRY CRIME BOOK FOR 200.
The green things in Asa's gun belt.

MAYBERRY CRIME BOOK FOR 400.
The harm in helping Otis save face by making him a deputy.

MAYBERRY CRIME BOOK FOR 600.

After Miss Tillman reported an apple pie stolen from her window and Jess Crawford called in reporting a chicken thief, Barney declared this to be the condition of Mayberry.

MAYBERRY CRIME BOOK FOR 800.

In his left shirt pocket.

MAYBERRY CRIME BOOK FOR 1,000.

There oughta be a law against it—according to dry cleaner Fred Goss.

THE LEARN-A-MONTH CLUB FOR 200.

According to Johnnie Paul Jason, this item, when soaked in "stagnation" water, will become a snake.

THE LEARN-A-MONTH CLUB FOR 400.

Baked Alaska.

THE LEARN-A-MONTH CLUB FOR 600.

Some people want it and can't get it. Barney had it, and couldn't get rid of it.

THE LEARN-A-MONTH CLUB FOR 800.

If you ride into the wind with your mouth open and you put your tongue on the roof of your mouth, it's impossible to do this.

THE LEARN-A-MONTH CLUB FOR 1,000.

According to Warren, this foreign city is 90 percent women and all of them are beautiful.

ORDINARY PEOPLE FOR 200.

According to Opie, he walks around in trees, wears a shiny silver hat, has twelve extra hands that he wears on his belt, and jingles when he walks. Other than that, he's normal.

ORDINARY PEOPLE FOR 400.

She may be hot copy for the fifth grade, but uptown she don't mean a thing.

ORDINARY PEOPLE FOR 600.

His attributes included being able to do eighteen chin-ups, he was the best rock thrower in the county, and he was saving up for a gold tooth.

ORDINARY PEOPLE FOR 800.
He is a Chicken Coop Casanova.

ORDINARY PEOPLE FOR 1,000.
The half boy, as in one and a half underprivileged boys per square mile in Mayberry county.

HEALTH AND FITNESS FOR 200.
According to Johnnie Paul Jason, this was real good for the teeth.

HEALTH AND FITNESS FOR 400.
It's said eating burnt food will give you this.

HEALTH AND FITNESS FOR 600.
Members of this family could eat, and eat, and eat, and it would go right to muscle. Not to fat . . . to muscle.

HEALTH AND FITNESS FOR 800.
These are, in the words of Barney Fife, the two main requirements in becoming adept with the common slingshot.

HEALTH AND FITNESS FOR 1,000.
This, not the leg, is the true location of the petula obendala.

FOREIGN LANGUAGES AND CUISINE FOR 200.
This was Barney's failed attempt at a coded warning to Andy from O'Malley's Cabin.

FOREIGN LANGUAGES AND CUISINE FOR 400.
They twang Briscoe Darling's buds.

FOREIGN LANGUAGES AND CUISINE FOR 600.
Arf.

FOREIGN LANGUAGES AND CUISINE FOR 800.
Bugs, worms, and things.

FOREIGN LANGUAGES AND CUISINE FOR 1,000.
At the Naylens' anniversary party, they were found in potted plants, between magazine covers, and in the fireplace. James Masefield had three in his pocket when he went home.

The Questions . . .

LAW AND ORDER FOR 200.
What is the Mayberry crime rate?

LAW AND ORDER FOR 400.
What is the Emma Watson Case?

LAW AND ORDER FOR 600.
What is a weapon?

LAW AND ORDER FOR 800.
What is stalkin'?

LAW AND ORDER FOR 1,000.
What is the condition calling for one officer to be awake at all times?

MAYBERRY CRIME BOOK FOR 200.
What are bullets?

MAYBERRY CRIME BOOK FOR 400.
What is falsifyin'?

MAYBERRY CRIME BOOK FOR 600.
What is a regular reign of terror?

MAYBERRY CRIME BOOK FOR 800.
What is the place Barney keeps his bullet?

MAYBERRY CRIME BOOK FOR 1,000.
What is paper taffeta?

THE LEARN-A-MONTH CLUB FOR 200.
What is a horse hair?

THE LEARN-A-MONTH CLUB FOR 400.
What is the new dessert that's come out since it became a state?

THE LEARN-A-MONTH CLUB FOR 600.
What's an IQ?

THE LEARN-A-MONTH CLUB FOR 800.
What is pronounce words that start with the letter S?

THE LEARN-A-MONTH CLUB FOR 1,000.
What is Istanbul?

ORDINARY PEOPLE FOR 200.
Who is Mr. McBeevee?

ORDINARY PEOPLE FOR 400.
Who is Karen Folker?

ORDINARY PEOPLE FOR 600.
Who is Ernest T. Bass?

ORDINARY PEOPLE FOR 800.
Who is Orville Hendricks, the Taylors' butter and egg man?

ORDINARY PEOPLE FOR 1,000.
Who is Horatio?

HEALTH AND FITNESS FOR 200.
What is chewing tar?

HEALTH AND FITNESS FOR 400.
What is a good singing voice?

HEALTH AND FITNESS FOR 600.
Who are the Fifes?

HEALTH AND FITNESS FOR 800.
What are keen, sharp eyes and a strong set of pinchin' fingers?

HEALTH AND FITNESS FOR 1,000.
What is, in the brain?

FOREIGN LANGUAGES AND CUISINE FOR 200.
What is "Onvicts-kay ere-hay!" or pig Latin for "Convicts here"?

FOREIGN LANGUAGES AND CUISINE FOR 400.
What are pearly onions?

FOREIGN LANGUAGES AND CUISINE FOR 600.
What does Little Orphan Annie's dog Sandy say when he's agreeing with something she says?

FOREIGN LANGUAGES AND CUISINE FOR 800.
What is breakfast for Winkin', Blinkin', and Nod?

FOREIGN LANGUAGES AND CUISINE FOR 1,000.
What are Lillian's meatballs?

THE MAP

....

"Mayberry. Wherever that is, that's where I am."
                                    –HERBIE FAYE
                                    as bad guy
                                    Eddie Blake

"The map? That's something Aaron Ruben would know about."
                                    –SHELDON LEONARD

"The map? I never paid any attention to it."
                                    –AARON RUBEN

One of Mayberry's most visible set pieces was the map that hung behind Andy's courthouse desk. Though several different maps were used, the one that hung the longest did not appear until midway through the second season. That map made its debut in Episode #41, "Crime-free Mayberry."

Actress Aneta Corsaut:
"Of course, the map. I never looked at it."
Prior to Episode #41, several different maps were used. In Episode #15, "Those Gossipin' Men," there were two different road maps. One, a highway map of the California-Nevada border, remained through several shows. The other, a map of western Montana, disappeared after "Those Gossipin' Men." It was replaced in Episode #16, "Andy Saves Barney's Morale," with an upside-down map of Idaho.

Howard Morris:
"I looked at people, not at maps."
The map of Idaho hung upside down next to the same California-Nevada

map for several more episodes until someone finally turned it right side up in Episode #24, "The New Doctor."

Hal Smith:

"There was a map?"

Early in the second season, in Episodes #33 through #36, there was actually a map identifiable as a road map for the state of North Carolina. Mayberry was supposed to be located in North Carolina, so this was a step in the right direction. But by Episode #41, that map disappeared—never to be seen again.

Bill Idelson:

"Who cares?"

Everett Greenbaum:

"That's something I wouldn't know anything about."

Harvey Bullock:

"The map? Sure. It was a map of Silacongas, Arkansas. I'm lying. What else do you want to know?"

The map used most throughout the run of the series was left alone until Episode #73, "Lawman Barney," when it was turned upside down. The map remained in that position until the final season of the show. In Episode #228, "Tape Recorder," it was once again flipped to its original position. The map seemed to have a mind of its own because by Episode #231, "Andy's Investment," it had flipped back again. By the end of the episode, however, the map has turned again—and it stayed put for the remainder of the run of "The Andy Griffith Show."

George Lindsey:

"The map? I don't even know what you're talking about. In your town, if you went down to the courthouse all the time, would you know about the map? No. That will give you the key to the show. That's why these characters became real people. An actor may look at that map, but it's insignificant. It wasn't part of our lives. That's why the show was successful. We were those people. The audience believed we were those people and still do to this day."

SEPARATED
AT BIRTH

· ·

That stage was one of the happiest of all," Aaron Ruben said. "There were others that might have been as nice to work on, but ours was particularly warm and filled with good humor. People who did a guest shot would come in and express how sad they were that it was over."

Some, apparently, were so sad that they decided to sneak back for a return visit to "The Andy Griffith Show" under new identities.

I don't know your name, stranger.

In the 1960s, it was not unusual for an actor to play different roles in various episodes of a single series. Now, however, with audiences more attentive to players and their roles, an actor is usually considered ineligible to appear again in any other role on a given series, even if previously seen only for a brief moment.

· ·

"It's my most favorite show, ever! I've seen each episode at least fifteen times and I never get tired of it. This is actually from my mother-in-law, but I like the show very much, too."

—LORENZO MUSIC,
voice-actor

· ·

But your face is familiar.

Episode #12, "Ellie for Council," marked the first time the show used actors in multiple roles.

Frank Ferguson, who played Wilbur Pine, newlywed husband of Andy's old housekeeper, Rose, in Episode #1, "The New Housekeeper," appears as Sam in "Ellie for Council." Strangely, the actress who played his wife in this episode is the same one who played Rose in "The New Housekeeper." Perhaps Rose missed Mayberry so much that she decided to return with Wilbur. They must have been using assumed names in order not to upset Opie. Small towns can be that way sometimes.

Another dead ringer for Sam—and Wilbur—was storekeeper Charlie Foley, who appeared in two episodes: Episode #120, "Bargain Day," and Episode #152, "The Case of the Punch in the Nose."

If at first you don't succeed.

Stu Erwin did not display the same kind of devotion as Frank Ferguson. In Episode #5, "Opie's Charity," Erwin played a man who left Mayberry because he could not stand his wife Annabelle's manner. He returned to give their marriage another chance, but it must not have worked out. A mere seven episodes later, in "Ellie for Council," Erwin appears again. He's still married, but to another woman. He probably was exposed to too much city life during those seven episodes.

So much for pride.

Annabelle Silby (played by Lurene Tuttle) did not dare show her face in Mayberry for several years. But she did manage a return in Episode #117, "The Shoplifters." Unfortunately, the trauma that befell her in "Opie's Charity" caused her to sink so low that not only did she change her name, but she was also caught shoplifting in Weaver's Department Store.

The third time is always the charm.

There must have been something about Sam and Bess Muggins, played by Sam Edwards and Margaret Kerry, that Ol' Ben Weaver disliked. After making sure Sam stayed in jail in Episode #11, "Christmas Story," Ben ran him down again in Episode #28, "Andy Forecloses." Ben wanted Edwards and Kerry, this time posing as Lester and Helen Scobey, evicted from their Mayberry home. Finally shaking Ben, Sam Edwards changed his name to Tom Bedlow and returned in Episode #192, "The Lodge." Clearly, he had put his past behind him successfully since he was being accepted as a member of the Regal Order of the Golden Door to Good Fellowship.

I've got the perfect guy for the heavy.

Perennial tough-guy Allan Melvin made his debut on "The Andy Griffith Show" in Episode #50, "Jailbreak," playing Clarence "Doc" Malloy. Whenever the series needed a heavy, the producers turned to Melvin's stalwart mug. Melvin, an established character actor who portrayed regular characters in

"Gomer Pyle, U.S.M.C." and "Archie Bunker's Place," appeared on "The Andy Griffith Show" in eight different episodes playing eight different roles.

Twice cast as the good guy, Melvin returned in Episode #57, "Andy and Barney in the Big City," as Detective Bardolli and then as the Sergeant in Episode #99, "Ernest T. Bass Joins the Army."

With the exception of those two roles, Melvin was to play Mayberry's consummate bully. He appeared as Neil (Episode #73, "Lawman Barney"), Jake (Episode #90, "Barney's First Car"), the convict (Episode #118, "Andy's Vacation"), grocery boy Fred Plummer (Episode #135, "Barney's Uniform"), and Howard Sprague's nemesis, Clyde Plaunt (Episode #222, "Howard's Main Event").

And while we're on the subject.

Even a pestilence like Ernest T. Bass had a twin. Howard Morris appeared once as George, the TV repairman whom Barney ran out to Myers Lake in Episode #140, "Andy and Helen Have Their Day." In Episode #128, "Barney's Bloodhound," Morris contributed a voiceover as radio personality Leonard Blush.

A face only a mother could love.

He was Captain Barker, Captain Horton, the head T-man, and Inspector Rogers. Ken Lynch, who played the hard-nosed agent who once advised Andy to busy himself catching "chicken thieves and whatnot," was an actor born for these roles. His four appearances as lawmen came in Episode #2, "The Manhunt"; Episode #50, "Jailbreak"; Episode #102, "A Black Day for Mayberry"; and Episode #231, "Andy's Investment."

There's postage due, "I do," what's the difference?

Dub Taylor appeared as the Postmaster in Episode #3, "The Guitar Player," and then as the minister who married Charlene Darling and Dud Wash in Episode #94, "Mountain Wedding."

Wanna fight?

One woman who was a fan favorite on the show would have to be Fun Girl Jean "Daphne" Carson. First appearing in Episode #68, "Barney Mends a Broken Heart," Carson twice reprised the role of Daphne—in Episode #123, "The Fun Girls," and Episode #155, "The Arrest of the Fun Girls."

Later in the same season, as Naomi Connors in Episode #74, "Convicts at Large," Carson was seen hiding out at O'Malley's cabin.

She could tango, teach breathing, and make a great license plate.

Also featured in "Convicts at Large" was Reta Shaw, playing fellow escapee Big Maude Tyler, who eventually danced out of the cabin into waiting handcuffs. We never learned why she was headed toward Mayberry, but it may have been to meet with her lookalike. Voice teacher Eleanora Poultice (Episode #116, "The Song Festers") had a striking similarity to Big Maude.

Here's a headline you'll be seeing on the racks at the grocery.

Gilbert Jamel (Gavin MacLeod) was arrested for bank robbery by Sheriff Andy Taylor (Episode #150, "TV or Not TV"). MacLeod then went on to portray Bryan Bender—the actor who played none other than Andy Taylor in the Hollywood version of his life story, *Sheriff Without a Gun* (Episode #167, "The Taylors in Hollywood").

Is this a coincidence, or what?

Newspaper reporter Jean Boswell (Ruta Lee) posed as a college student to dig up enough dirt on the sheriff to put "Andy on Trial" (Episode #61). Lee later filled the role of actress Darlene Mason opposite actor Bryan Bender (MacLeod) in *Sheriff Without a Gun*.

If their agents were better, they could have played the deputies.

Lewis Charles played a convict in Episode #95, "The Big House"; the Miracle Salve Company owner in Episode #122, "A Deal Is a Deal"; and a crooked carnival worker in Episode #158, "Opie and the Carnival."

Actor Al Checco attempted to knock off the Mayberry Security Bank in Episode #78, "The Bank Job." Later, using the name Hennessey, he was lured back by a briefcase full of cash in Episode #149, "If I Had a Quarter Million Dollars."

· ·

"If only Mayberry could be real and the rest of us fictional, what a lovely world this would be."

—LARRY GELBART,
writer

· ·

He was good—but he was no Bryan Bender.

Without question, the most accomplished of all the actors who appeared in multiple roles would have to be Jack Nicholson. As Mr. Garland, the husband of the woman who left her baby on the courthouse steps, he was in a brief scene at the end of Episode #202, "Opie Finds a Baby." Nicholson then returned in the show's final season playing Marvin Jenkins, the accused, in Episode #223, "Aunt Bee, the Juror."

It's no wonder he was tired.

He was the sleepy security guard at the Mayberry Bank, the clerk at the Mayberry Hotel, the night watchman at Weaver's Department Store, a neighbor, the bank guard again, a veterinarian, and an M.D. Charles Thompson appeared in seven separate episodes beginning in the third season.

He can be seen in the following shows:

Episode #78, "The Bank Job"
Episode #102, "A Black Day for Mayberry"
Episode #117, "The Shoplifters"
Episode #131, "Barney's Physical"
Episode #150, "TV or Not TV"
Episode #214, "Goodbye, Dolly"
Episode #232, "Suppose Andy Gets Sick"

MAYBERRY
FOLKLORE

· ·

Although Andy Griffith was brought up in rural surroundings, nobody has claimed that "The Andy Griffith Show" was autobiographical to any great degree. Yet the show did try to be authentic, so it steeped its characters in the actual traditions and folklore of the South.

One of the resources drawn on by the writers was a six-volume work entitled *North Carolina Folklore,* a collection of popular beliefs and superstitions published by Duke University Press. "Aaron Ruben showed them to me," Bill Idelson said. "You could look through these and get all kinds of ideas, oddities, peculiarities of speech . . . Aaron had them all."

One example that was taken directly from *North Carolina Folklore* can be seen in Episode #50, "Jailbreak." Barney sneaks into the cell with Clarence "Doc" Malloy (Allan Melvin). Trying to convince Malloy that he is a hardened criminal, Barney fakes a jailbreak as part of his plan to catch Malloy's partner and recover the stolen money. As they step out of the cell, Malloy and Barney simultaneously say the phrase "So far, so good." Barney, forcing him to lock pinkie fingers with him, says "needles" while Malloy says "pins."

"That came from those books," Harvey Bullock admitted. "Aaron added it after reading of this superstition."

The following is a list of some of the common practices in the little town of Mayberry inspired by those volumes.

Episode #49, "The Jinx."

- It is bad luck to look over the left shoulder of a man playing checkers.

- According to Barney's grandmother's book *Signs, Omens, Portents and Charms to Ward Off Bad Luck,* rub the head of a redheaded man to insure good luck. If a man cannot be found, a boy will do.

Barney talks to the animals.

> *"Come fish come,*
> *come fish come,*
> *Sam's at the gate,*
> *with a frosted cake,*
> *come fish come.*
> *Fly away buzzard,*
> *fly away crow,*
> *way down South where the winds don't blow.*
> *Rub your nose,*
> *and give two winks,*
> *and save us from the awful jinx."*

Said while putting your right arm over your head, touching your left earlobe and closing your eyes.

> *"Wink'um pink'um, nodamus rex,*
> *protect us all from the man with the hex."*

Buzz Fluharte's scientific fact, or the biggest crock of nothing ever heard.

There are atmospheric rays that control bodily motions. If a person containing a negative gets between you and these rays, that person creates a static that jars any successful motion into an unsuccessful motion, thus jinxing you.

Episode #40, "Opie's Hobo Friend."

"Tuscarora," the word that the hobo Dave uttered to conjure up gumballs as if by magic, was a touch of magic from Bullock's past. "There's a Tuscarora Mountain as you come into Binghamton," Bullock's boyhood home. "It was funny, I'd always loved Tuscarora. It was a great word. It felt good."

Episode #64, "Opie's Rival."

During a ceremony to become blood brothers, Andy makes a speech honoring:

- Boojum Snark, spirit of the fire

- Brillin Trant, spirit of the water

- Robley Barch, spirit of the air

Episode #121, "Divorce Mountain Style."

• Divorce proceedings: Bury the beak of an owl, four tail feathers from a chicken hawk, a piece of bacon, and a broken comb under an oak tree and say an incantation over them. The items must stay buried until the new moon.

• Put a willow chip under a dog's head while it is dreaming, then put it under your own pillow and you will have the same dream.

• If a rider dressed in black, riding east to west on a white horse in the light of a full moon, passes a bridegroom, the bridegroom and the union are cursed.

• If a rider wears a ruby ring while on a horse, the horse will go mad.

Episode #142, "Three Wishes For Opie."

Count Iz Van Tileckie was the spirit Barney summoned from the lamp he bought at an auction. The count was a two-hundred-year-old spirit that granted Opie three wishes and Barney only one. Floyd offered the explanation that the count just liked kids better.

Opie's Three Wishes:

• A jackknife.
   The result was immediate. Andy came in with one right after Opie wished for it.

• A "B" in arithmetic.
   Helen gave him a "B" when maybe he deserved a "C." He was improving, and she wanted to give him some encouragement.

• Having Miss Crump as his sixth-grade teacher.
   Barney thought Opie was wishing that Andy would marry Helen. After clearing up his misunderstanding, Helen told Opie that his third wish, too, was granted. She had just found out that she was being transferred from the fifth to sixth grade.

Barney's Wish:

- A new fingerprint set.

  Moments after making the wish in the presence of Goober and Floyd in the back room of the courthouse, the door opened and the fingerprint set was carried in by a mysterious messenger. The messenger turned out to be Andy.

Helen's Wish:

- Helen also wished for the wedding.

  It was granted, eventually. Andy and Helen's marriage was announced in the "Mayberry After Midnite" column in the *Mayberry Gazette.* It would come true in the first episode of "Mayberry R.F.D.," but by then the whole business with the wishes had long been forgotten.

Episode #146, "The Lucky Letter."

Barney's Bad Luck:

- He runs his head into the courthouse door.

- He nicks himself shaving.

- He nearly walks in front of a truck that comes screeching to a halt—right on his foot.

- He runs into a car parked behind the squad car by going accidentally in reverse.

- He starts a fight with Thel over her plans to meet Edgar Coleman to repair hymn books.

- He gets his foot stuck in a bucket at the dump while searching for the chain letter that caused his grief.

Floyd's Good Fortune:

- First thing in the morning, a traveling fertilizer salesman gave him a $1 tip.

Goober's Good Fortune:

• Three flat tires had already been brought in that week.

Episode #193, "The Darling Fortune."

The Omen of the Owl:

• If you're lookin' for a bride an' you see an owl that day, the next female you see is sure to steal your heart away.

The Counteromen:

• A second owl in the daytime.

THE *INSIDE*
MAYBERRY
AWARDS

·······································

The Writers Guild Awards for Best Writing in a Comedy Series.
Each year the Writers Guild of America honors writers with awards for the best scripts. In the eight seasons of "The Andy Griffith Show," three episodes won awards for best writing in a comedy series.

1960–61
Episode #2, "The Manhunt"
Written by Jack Elinson and Charles Stewart

1962–63
Episode #90, "Barney's First Car"
Written by Jim Fritzell and Everett Greenbaum

1963–64
Episode #117, "The Shoplifters"
Written by Bill Idelson and Sam Bobrick

The Emmys.

1960–61: The Nominations are . . .
"THE ANDY GRIFFITH SHOW"
Outstanding Program Achievement in the Field of Humor

DON KNOTTS for Outstanding Performance in a Supporting Role by an Actor or Actress in a Series

And the winner is . . .
DON KNOTTS for Outstanding Performance in a Supporting Role by an Actor or Actress in a Series

1961–62: The Nominations are . . .
"THE ANDY GRIFFITH SHOW" for Outstanding Program Achievement in the Field of Humor

DON KNOTTS for Outstanding Performance in a Supporting Role by an Actor

And the winner is . . .
DON KNOTTS for Outstanding Performance in a Supporting Role by an Actor

1962–63: The Nominations are . . .
DON KNOTTS for Outstanding Performance in a Supporting Role by an Actor

Plaque, dated March 24, 1965, presented to Aaron Ruben upon his departure from "The Andy Griffith Show." It contained both badges, etched signatures from his stars and the inscription, "See we thought we'd put five on it because we worked with you five years."

And the winner is . . .
DON KNOTTS for Outstanding Performance in a Supporting Role by an Actor

1963–64: The Nominations are . . .
None.

1964–65: The Nominations are . . .
None.

1965–66: The Nominations are . . .
DON KNOTTS in Episode #176, "The Return of Barney Fife," for Outstanding Performance by an Actor in a Supporting Role in a Comedy

And the winner is . . .
DON KNOTTS in "The Return of Barney Fife," for Outstanding Performance by an Actor in a Supporting Role in a Comedy

1966–67: The Nominations are . . .
"THE ANDY GRIFFITH SHOW"
Outstanding Comedy Series

DON KNOTTS in Episode #212, "Barney Comes to Mayberry," for Outstanding Performance by an Actor in a Supporting Role in a Comedy

FRANCES BAVIER for Outstanding Performance by an Actress in a Supporting Role in a Comedy

And the winners are . . .
DON KNOTTS in "Barney Comes to Mayberry," for Outstanding Performance by an Actor in a Supporting Role in a Comedy

FRANCES BAVIER for Outstanding Performance by an Actress in a Supporting Role in a Comedy

1967–68: The Nominations are . . .
None

And now . . . The Emmas.

Named for chronic jaywalker and hypochondriac Emma Watson, the Emma Awards are presented by *Inside Mayberry* for all the outstanding achievements in "The Andy Griffith Show" that have thus far gone unrecognized in the field of television comedy.

For Best Eyebrows in a Television Series, the nominees are . . .
ANDY TAYLOR, in episodes #1–249

COUSIN VIRGIL, in the role of Barney's cousin, in Episode #62, "Cousin Virgil"

BILL MEDWIN, in the title role of Episode #60, "The Bookie Barber"

HOWARD SPRAGUE, in his role in Episode #217, "Big Brothers"

And the winner is . . .
BILL MEDWIN, "The Bookie Barber"

For Best Female Vocal, the nominees are . . .
PEGGY MCMILLAN for the song "Down in the Valley" in Episode #65, "Andy and Opie, Bachelors"

AUNT BEE for the song "Chinatown," sung while tipsy with the Ladies' Church Aid Club in Episode #87, "Aunt Bee's Medicine Man"

JUANITA PIKE for the song "Flow Gently Sweet Aft'n," sung at the reception for the producer in Episode #13, "Mayberry Goes Hollywood"

BERNARD P. FIFE for the song "Dear Old Donnegal," sung while dressed as the cleaning lady in Episode #78, "The Bank Job"

CHARLENE DARLING for the song "There Is a Time for Love and Laughter" in Episode #139, "The Darling Baby"

CLARA EDWARDS for the song "Some Enchanted Evening," sung to hook the Widower Robinson in Episode #174, "The Church Organ"

And the winner is . . .
PEGGY MCMILLAN, "Down in the Valley," "Andy and Opie, Bachelors"

For Best Entrance, the nominees are . . .

FLOYD LAWSON as Floyd Lawson Enterprises, descending the staircase in Episode #71, "Floyd, the Gay Deceiver"

ERNEST T. BASS as a lunatic with a shotgun in Episode #94, "Mountain Wedding"

MALCOLM MERRIWEATHER as a Britisher on a bicycle in Episode #89, "Andy's English Valet"

BERNARD P. FIFE as the proper gentleman using silent *ammenenies* in Episode #113, "My Fair Ernest T. Bass"

And the winner is . . . a tie!
FLOYD LAWSON in "Floyd, the Gay Deceiver"

And . . .
BERNARD P. FIFE in "My Fair Ernest T. Bass"

For Best Costume, the nominees are . . .
BERNARD P. FIFE as the bride of Dud Wash in Episode #94, "Mountain Wedding"

BERNARD P. FIFE as the cleaning lady in Episode #78, "The Bank Job"

BERNARD P. FIFE as the old lady gambler in Episode #60, "The Bookie Barber"

BERNARD P. FIFE as the hunting mannequin in Episode #117, "The Shop-lifters"

ERNEST T. BASS as Andy's cousin Oliver Gossage from Raleigh in Episode #113, "My Fair Ernest T. Bass"

HOWARD SPRAGUE in his hip bachelor outfit of madras jacket, new hat with a big feather, and black-and-white saddle shoes in Episode #217, "Big Brothers"

And the winner is . . .
HOWARD SPRAGUE in "Big Brothers"

For Best Performance in a Supportin' Role by an Animal, the nominees are . . .
DICKIE, THE BIRD in Episode #1, "The New Housekeeper"

BLACKIE, THE IMAGINARY HORSE in Episode #66, "Mr. McBeevee"

JIMMY, THE GOAT in Episode #81, "The Loaded Goat"

BO, THE ROOSTER in Episode #111, "Aunt Bee, the Crusader"

BARNEY'S BLOODHOUND, BLUE, in Episode #128, "Barney's Bloodhound"

OTIS'S COW in the role of OTIS'S HORSE in Episode #145, "The Rehabilitation of Otis"

OLD SAM, THE CARP in Episode #198, "Big Fish in a Small Town"

ERNEST T. BASS as himself in "My Fair Ernest T. Bass"

And the winner is . . .
BARNEY'S BLOODHOUND, BLUE, "Barney's Bloodhound," Howard Morris, director

For Best Actin' by Human Beings, the nominees are . . .
ANDY TAYLOR and BERNARD P. FIFE in the "Requiem for Otis" scene, Episode #115, "Hot Rod Otis"

BERNARD P. FIFE as Dr. U. T. Pendyke, D.V.M., Episode #122, "A Deal Is a Deal"

MALCOLM MERRIWEATHER as the drunken butler in Episode #124, "The Return of Malcolm Merriweather"

BERNARD P. FIFE as Nugatuck, Episode #138, "The Pageant"

AUNT BEE and OPIE TAYLOR, for acting natural as if nothing happened at dinner with Andy and Helen—after the news of Helen's arrest leaked out—in Episode #244, "Helen's Past"

And the winner is . . .
BERNARD P. FIFE, as Dr. U. T. Pendyke, D.V.M., "A Deal Is a Deal," Jeffrey Hayden, director

For Best Picture, the nominees are . . .
AUNT BEE'S glamour photo that hangs on the wall of the Taylor home in Episode #38, "Aunt Bee's Brief Encounter"

FLOYD'S photo on the front page of the *Mayberry Gazette* in Episode #71, "Floyd, the Gay Deceiver"

ANDY TAYLOR—the baby-in-the-buff photo—in Episode #41, "Crime-free Mayberry"

BARNEY'S crime photo, taken at the door of Wally's Filling Station in Episode #85, "The Great Filling Station Robbery"

BARNEY'S election poster photo that Floyd thought made him look as if he smelled something in Episode #148, "Barney Runs for Sheriff"

ANDY TAYLOR and DARLENE MASON in a publicity shot on Darlene's dressing-room sofa in Episode #168, "The Hollywood Party"

HELEN CRUMP being arrested in Kansas City—photo courtesy of the *Kansas City Chronicle*—in Episode #244, "Helen's Past"

And the winner is . . .
Barney's election poster photo in "Barney Runs for Sheriff"

Best Performance by a New Musical Group, the nominees are . . .
ANDY and THE COUNTRY BOYS singing "I Ain't Got Time to Kiss You Now" in Episode #19, "Mayberry on Record"

THE TAYLORS, featuring ANDY and OPIE singing "Dan Tucker" in Episode #96, "Briscoe Declares for Aunt Bee"

ANDY and THE DARLINGS, featuring CHARLENE DARLING singing "Salty Dog" in Episode #193, "The Darling Fortune"

THE DEMONSTRATORS, featuring BEATRICE TAYLOR, for their version of "We Shall Not Be Moved" in Episode #111, "Aunt Bee, the Crusader"

MEN BEHIND BARS, featuring OTIS CAMPBELL and BERNARD P. FIFE, on their recording of "Sweet Adeline" in Episode #141, "Otis Sues the County"

THE GYPSIES featuring JAMIE FARR for their original hit "Gypsy Melody" in Episode #183, "The Gypsies"

And the winner is . . .
MEN BEHIND BARS, featuring OTIS CAMPBELL and BERNARD P. FIFE

Best Musical Performance in the category of Rap, the nominees are . . .
ERNEST T. BASS for "Jump in the Pot"
   Ernest T. Bass: vocals and gas can from Episode #94, "Mountain Wedding"

THE YOUNG CAMPERS for "John Jacob Jingle Heimer Smith" from Episode #127, "Back to Nature"

BERNARD P. FIFE AND THE DEMONSTRATORS for "We Will Not Sing" From "Aunt Bee, the Crusader"

And the winner is . . .
ERNEST T. BASS for "Jump in the Pot"
   Ernest T. Bass: vocals and gas can from "Mountain Wedding"

Best Instrumental Performance . . . the nominees are . . .
BERNARD P. FIFE for "Jingle Bells" on harmonica
From Episode #11, "Christmas Story"

SON OF FLOYD for "Saxamania"
From Episode #15, "Those Gossipin' Men"

BERNARD P. FIFE for "La Cucaracha" on the bongos
From Episode #59, "Three's a Crowd"

THE DARLINGS for "Slimy River Bottom"
From Episode #88, "The Darlings Are Coming"

And the winner is . . .
THE DARLINGS for "Slimy River Bottom"
From "The Darlings Are Coming"

In the category of Best Male Vocal, the nominees are . . .
RAFE HOLLISTER and ANDY TAYLOR for "Look Down That Lonesome Road"
From Episode #83, "Rafe Hollister Sings"

OTIS CAMPBELL for "The Dipsy Doodle"
From Episode #55, "Aunt Bee, the Warden"

OTIS CAMPBELL for "I'm Sorry I Broke Your Heart, Mother"
From Episode #106, "Citizen's Arrest"

OTIS CAMPBELL for "Don't Tell Aunt Rosy"
From Episode #204, "Otis, the Deputy"

BRISCOE DARLING for "Low and Lonely over You"
From Episode #96, "Briscoe Declares for Aunt Bee"

GOMER PYLE for "No 'Count Mule"
From Episode #97, "Gomer, the House Guest"

GOMER PYLE for "The Marines' Hymn"
From Episode #107, "Gomer Pyle, U.S.M.C."

GOMER PYLE for "Santa Lucia"
From Episode #116, "The Song Festers"

BERNARD P. FIFE for "Now Is the Month of May"
From Episode #116, "The Song Festers"

LEONARD BLUSH for "It's Sylvia"
From Episode #128, "Barney's Bloodhound"

FLOYD LAWSON for "Hail to Thee, Miss Mayberry"
Words and music by Floyd Lawson from Episode #138, "The Pageant"

And the winner is . . .
OTIS CAMPBELL for "The Dipsy Doodle"
From "Aunt Bee, The Warden"

For Best Scream in a Comedy Series, the nominees are . . .
HARRIET, THE BANK TELLER
When she spots Barney walking across the street during a bank holdup in Episode #78, "The Bank Job"

HARRIET, THE BANK TELLER
After touching the vault door—after Gomer had tried to cut it with an acetylene torch in Episode #78, "The Bank Job"

AUNT BEE
When Gomer shoves a string of fish in front of her at the breakfast table in Episode #119, "Andy Saves Gomer"

And the winner is . . .
HARRIET, THE BANK TELLER
After touching the vault door—after Gomer had tried to cut it with an acetylene torch in Episode #78, "The Bank Job"

For Best Kiss in a Comedy Series, the nominees are . . .
ANDY AND SHARON DESPAIN in the garden outside the auditorium in Episode #82, "Class Reunion"

BARNEY AND THELMA LOU after Barney reclaims Thel from Jeff Pruitt in Episode #45, "The Farmer Takes a Wife"

ANDY TAYLOR AND HELEN CRUMP on Helen's sofa while Barney and Goober watch from the porch in Episode #147, "Goober and the Art of Love"

And the winners are . . .
BARNEY AND THELMA LOU

Betty Lynn as Thelma Lou.

In the category of Best Short Subject, the nominees are . . .
EARL HANSEN for the guy who hid in the trunk in Episode #85, "The Great Filling Station Robbery"

LEON, who appeared in Episode #49, "The Jinx"; Episode #78, "The Bank Job"; Episode #79, "One Punch Opie"; Episode #102, "A Black Day for Mayberry"; and Episode #117, "The Shoplifters"

And the winner is . . .
LEON

For Best Choreography, the nominees are . . .
BERNARD P. FIFE AND BIG MAUDE TYLER for the tango
From Episode #74, "Convicts at Large"

NATE BRACEY for the cha-cha
From Episode #82, "Class Reunion"

HELEN CRUMP for the schoolroom waltz
From Episode #132, "Opie Loves Helen"

GOMER PYLE for the fox-trot variations
From Episode #105, "A Date for Gomer"

HELEN CRUMP for the senior play
From Episode #197, "The Senior Play"

And the winner is . . .
GOMER PYLE for the fox-trot variations
From Episode #105, "A Date for Gomer"

Finally, the "Inside Mayberry" Award for the Worst Toupee Ever Worn in a
Comedy Series . . .
MR. SCHWUMP!

DON'T LOOK BACK

······································

"Gosh, would I like to see Goober and Floyd and Andy and all of them again ..."

—OLD SAM,
Episode #198,
"Big Fish in a Small Town"

Everybody associated with "The Andy Griffith Show" recognized the experience as one of the highlights of their careers. When the show passed into reruns, there was a collective feeling of sadness—both from the American public and the people who had worked so hard to create a television legend.

Aaron Ruben:

"I know this doesn't make good copy. How do you say to people that this was a group of people who all found each other at this particular time in their lives, and they all look back with such warmth and feeling—it was just a happy experience for everybody. Did I hate to go? Are you kidding? I wept. I realized then, as I do now, that it would never happen again. It was the best five years I had ever spent."

Howard Morris:

"You're talking about a bunch of guys who started as actors and writers in theater and radio, went to war, came back, and had to scramble again for work. Nothing exists anymore. It's all gone. It only exists in our minds. There was a turn-of-the-century English biographer who wrote, 'The best of our kind are but shadows.' That just makes me weep. I miss it."

Harvey Bullock:

"Leave it out there in the 'Never, Never Land' where it belongs."

Don Knotts:

"We were laughing all the time. If I didn't have to get up so early, I wouldn't have known I was going to work."

. . . .

"I still scan the TV channels, always hoping to catch an episode. My favorite one will always be 'Opie, the Birdman.' "

—CLINT BLACK, country music singer

. . . .

Farewell, adios, see you in the reruns.

"Now if there are no further questions, I will simply say, 'Congo bolo, bolo,' which means good night and thank you."
—Professor Hubert St. John, Episode #230, "Aunt Bee and the Lecturer"

"Carbolic acid, that's good-bye in any language."
—Roger Hanover, Episode #130, "Aunt Bee's Romance"

Collection of the authors

Aaron Ruben, producer of "The Andy Griffith Show" from 1961–1965.

"It's like the end of somethin', ain't it?"
—Goober, Episode #198, "Big Fish in a Small Town"

"Now you can cry."
—Andy Taylor, Episode #154, "Aunt Bee's Invisible Beau"

Everett Greenbaum:
"It was all made up!"

EPISODE GUIDE

···

SEASON 1, 32 EPISODES

Episode #1, "The New Housekeeper"
Original broadcast: October 3, 1960
In the premiere, Andy asks Aunt Bee to come to Mayberry and help raise his son, Opie, after Rose, their old housekeeper, marries and moves away. Opie refuses to accept Aunt Bee because her ways are different from those of Rose. Just as Aunt Bee has packed her bags and is about to leave the Taylor household, Opie stops Aunt Bee because he realizes *she* needs *him*.

Facts Known by Few:
Barney Fife was introduced as Andy's cousin, a fact that was later dropped.
Opie's bird, Dickie, did return. During the premiere season of "The Andy Griffith Show" there were several commercial segments scripted for the actors on the show. The first of these was used as a tag after the closing scene where Opie stops Aunt Bee from leaving. The commercial, written for Sanka Instant Coffee, was a scene between Andy and Opie in Opie's bedroom. Opie asks Andy why he thinks Dickie returned, and Andy tells him probably for some fine biscuits and gravy, and, of course, some good Sanka coffee.

Episode #2, "The Manhunt"
Original broadcast: October 10, 1960
Andy and Barney are the brunt of jokes by state troopers who come to Mayberry to capture an escaped convict. Andy is able to prove that he is not the country bumpkin the troopers think he is when he captures the convict himself by allowing him to steal his leaky fishing boat.

Facts Known by Few:
This episode, written by Jack Elinson and Charles Stewart, won the 1960 Writers Guild Award for best comedy writing in a series.

"The Manhunt" also marked the introduction of Otis Campbell, who was played by Hal Smith.

Episode #3, "Guitar Player"
Original broadcast: October 17, 1960

Andy helps local guitar player Jim Lindsey (James Best) find a job with "Bobby Fleet and His Band with a Beat." When Fleet's band arrives for a lunch stop in Mayberry, Andy arrests them for a parking violation and forces them to listen to Lindsey while jailed in the courthouse.

Episode #4, "Runaway Kid"
Original broadcast: November 7, 1960

Andy finds himself in a dilemma after teaching Opie a lesson about the importance of always keeping your word. Opie has made a sacred trust not to divulge that his new friend, George "Tex" Foley (Pat Rossen), is a runaway. Andy must grapple with violating Opie's trust or returning the boy to his family and explaining that there is always an exception to every rule.

Episode #5, "Opie's Charity"
Original broadcast: November 28, 1960

Andy is embarrassed when he mistakenly believes Opie has donated a total of 3 cents to the Underprivileged Children's Drive. Andy scolds Opie after learning he's saving money to buy his girlfriend a present. Later, Andy discovers Opie's true intentions: he is buying a present for an underprivileged girl, and the gift is a new winter coat.

Facts Known by Few:

As an early example of a television B story, this show about pride featured a subplot. Annabelle Silby (Lurene Tuttle), who told the town that her husband, Tom (Stu Erwin), had been killed in a car accident in Charlottesville, had some explaining to do when he returned to Mayberry alive and well. Annabelle had to admit that she told the story because she was too proud to admit that her husband had left her.

Episode #6, "Ellie Comes to Town"
Original broadcast: October 24, 1960

The first outsider to move to town, Ellie May Walker, Ph.G. (Pharmacy Gal), arrives to help her uncle at Walker's Drug Store. Before long she is faced with adapting to Mayberry ways after refusing to sell Emma Brand, the town hypochondriac, sugar pills.

Facts Known by Few:

After filming this episode, its broadcast was accelerated because the producers decided Andy needed a love interest.

This episode also features Barney's feeble attempt at memorizing and reciting the sheriff's rules.

Episode #7, "Irresistible Andy"

Original broadcast: October 31, 1960

Andy gets himself in his first jam with the opposite sex when he wrongly assumes Ellie is out to trap him as her husband. Andy tries to foil her plot when he sends three eligible Mayberry bachelors her way, but Opie helps Ellie uncover Andy's scheme.

Facts Known by Few:

Barney appeared here wearing the ol' salt and pepper for the very first time.

It was not intended to be a subliminal touch of humor, but Ellie plays out her seduction of Andy just under the ENLARGEMENT sign inside Walker's Drug.

Episode #8, "A Feud Is a Feud"

Original broadcast: December 5, 1960

Andy is caught in the middle of two feuding mountain families when one's son and the other's daughter show up at the Taylor house to be married. Andy brings the feud to an end by bluffing the heads of the families into settling the matter once and for all with a duel.

Facts Known by Few:

This episode included Andy's Romeo and Juliet monologue made famous during his career as a stand-up comedian.

Episode #9, "Andy, the Matchmaker"

Original broadcast: November 14, 1960

In the show's first try at finding a girl for Barney, the deputy is brought together with Miss Rosemary (Amzie Strickland) after Andy tricks him by deciding to declare for her himself.

Facts Known by Few:

Though the romance never bloomed, Amzie Strickland would pop up again in four other episodes playing different roles. She was probably waiting for a second chance at "The Barn."

Barney decides to resign for the first time because of a poem he thought Opie had chalked on a wall. Andy got Opie off the hook with the defense that Opie did not yet know how to write.

Episode #10, "Stranger in Town"

Original broadcast: December 26, 1960

Ed Sawyer, a mysterious stranger, arrives in Mayberry and puts the entire town on edge when he displays an eerie familiarity with the town's people, places, and things. Andy finally confronts Sawyer and learns that he is neither a foreign spy nor a spook, but only a man without a home.

Facts Known by Few:

Though it was not originally played by Howard McNear, this episode introduced the character of Floyd, the barber. The original Floyd (Walter Baldwin) was nearly blind and had an affinity for napping.

The gas station owner, first mentioned in this episode, was not Wally, but a man named George Safferly.

Episode #11, "Christmas Story"

Original broadcast: December 19, 1960

Andy and Barney keep the spirit of Christmas alive for Sam Muggins and his family after the town Scrooge, Ben Weaver, demands Andy keep Muggins incarcerated for running a still. After being accidentally inoculated with a little of the courthouse's Christmas spirit, Weaver comes around and manages to get himself arrested so he can bring gifts for all.

Facts Known by Few:

This episode was the only holiday story ever aired during the entire eight-year run of "The Andy Griffith Show."

This episode marked the first correspondence from the three Hubacher brothers, who sent a postcard that read MERRY CHRISTMAS FROM STATE PRISON.

One small problem with the story in this episode was with the mention that Ben Weaver's store sold "spirits." Mayberry was in a dry county.

Barney's new girlfriend, Hilda Mae, is mentioned for the first time in this episode.

Episode #12, "Ellie for Council"

Original broadcast: December 12, 1960

Ellie runs for office, breaking the Mayberry tradition of what had been an all-male town council. Once again, Andy learns a lesson from Opie when he hears his own antiwoman opinions parroted by his son. Realizing the error of his ways, Andy speaks in favor of Ellie, rallying the citizenry to her side.

Facts Known by Few:

An early TV editorial on feminism, this episode was an example of how "The Andy Griffith Show" went beyond its appearance of being only a rural show by using universal themes.

Episode #13, "Mayberry Goes Hollywood"

Original broadcast: January 2, 1961

A Hollywood producer visits Mayberry and, taken with the town's charm, decides to use it as the setting of a new film. The town members become screen-struck and busily go about giving Mayberry a face-lift, changing everything the producer liked. Just before the citizens are about to cut down a landmark oak tree, the producer stops them and tells them what Mayberry's appeal was to him: the townspeople's simple, honest, down-to-earth ways.

Facts Known by Few:

This show marked the first appearance of Howard McNear in the role of Floyd, the barber.

Episode #14, "The Horse Trader"

Original broadcast: January 9, 1961

Andy proves fallible when he cons a traveling antique dealer into buying the town's old cannon with a fabulously fictional story of the cannon's glorious past. Opie follows his father's example and cons a friend of his into trading roller skates for some "licorice seeds" that Opie got in a bad trade for his cap pistol. Andy, again seeing his own actions mirrored by his son, turns around and makes amends for his bad dealings.

Facts Known by Few:

Barney first shows his weakness for mixed drinks when he gets loaded on ice cream sodas at the drug store.

Episode #15, "Those Gossipin' Men"

Original broadcast: January 16, 1961

Aunt Bee teaches Andy a lesson after he ridicules the Mayberry women for being such terrible gossips. Bee sets a trap to prove the men are just as bad by planting the seed of a rumor that ends up leading most of the Mayberry males to the hotel room of a mild-mannered shoe salesman. The men are convinced he is a talent scout for the fictitious TV show "Manhattan Show Time."

Facts Known by Few:

Floyd is seen with his saxophone-playing son for the only time in the series. The idea of having a son was later dropped. His audition tune was "Saxamania."

Barney plays harmonica for the first time. His repertoire includes "I'm Just a Vagabond Lover," "Animal Crackers," and "Finiculi, Finicula."

Episode #16, "Andy Saves Barney's Morale"

Original broadcast: February 20, 1961

When Andy is called out of town, Barney gets his first chance as Actin' Sheriff of Mayberry and jails twenty citizens, including the bank president, Mayor Pike, and Aunt Bee. Andy returns and promptly dismisses all the prisoners. Barney is so discouraged that he threatens to quit, so Andy spreads the word that he may have to let Barney go. The citizens return, jail themselves, and demand they be tried as charged.

Facts Known by Few:

This show marked the first use of a flashback when Barney's new girlfriend, Hilda Mae, recounted her date with "The Barn" the night before.

Episode #17, "Alcohol and Old Lace"

Original broadcast: January 30, 1961

Based on an idea from a Broadway play, Andy and Barney run down moonshiners with the help of the Morrison sisters, Jennifer and Clara Belle. With more help from Opie, they discover that the Morrison sisters are themselves running a still—and running their competition out of business. When

Opie brings flowers back to the courthouse preserved in a Mason jar full of moon, Barney and Andy realize what is happening and go to destroy the still.

Facts Known by Few:

Jack Prince, later appearing several times as Rafe Hollister, makes his "Andy Griffith Show" debut as bootlegger Ben Sewell.

Since the Morrison sisters only sold their moonshine for celebrating holidays, the show mentioned many obscure celebrations, including Panama Canal Day, a reference to *Arsenic and Old Lace.*

Episode #18, "Andy, the Marriage Counselor"

Original broadcast: February 6, 1961

The battling Boones, husband and wife, are engaged in an ongoing battle royal. Andy decides to put an end to their bickering by putting them on a probationary program of daily niceties. His brilliant idea backfires when the Boones turn nasty toward the rest of the town. Finally, Andy gives in when he realizes the couple's way of expressing their love for each other is based on their freedom to fight.

Facts Known by Few:

Barney takes his first try at the martial arts in this show's opening scene when he demonstrates the new skill he's picked up right out of the book *The Art of Judo* by Professor Matsu Matto. The demonstration goes awry when Andy, as the attacker, insists on doing his part wrong.

Episode #19, "Mayberry on Record"

Original broadcast: February 13, 1961

Mr. Maxwell, an independent record producer, passes through Mayberry and records some of the local talent. After Barney, Floyd, and several other locals invest some money with Maxwell, Andy becomes suspicious. Having convinced the town they've been conned, Andy has to eat his words when Maxwell returns with the syndicate's first dividend check.

Episode #20, "The Beauty Contest"

Original broadcast: January 23, 1961

Andy finds himself the center of attention when chosen to judge the Founder's Day beauty contest. Everyone in town tries to "persuade" him to get behind his or her pick. His solution, at the last moment, is to award the honor to an older woman, Erma Bishop (Lillian Bronson), whose selfless work qualifies her as the woman who is most suited to wear the crown.

Facts Known by Few:

This episode featured Floyd's original composition, "Hail to Thee, Miss Mayberry."

This marked the first appearance of Josie Lloyd in the role of Mayor Pike's daughter, Josephine. She appeared in one more episode in the same role and in two others as Lydia Crosswaithe.

Episode #21, "Andy and the Gentleman Crook"

Original broadcast: February 27, 1961

The legendary con artist Gentleman Dan Caldwell (Dan Tobin) arrives for a stopover in the Mayberry jail and quickly beguiles Aunt Bee, Opie, and Barney with his charm and sophistication. When Barney is left alone to watch him, Caldwell reels him into his web, takes his gun, and manages to escape. Before he reaches the courthouse door, Andy walks in with Aunt Bee and Opie, who are able to see through Caldwell's charismatic veneer.

Facts Known by Few:

Barney misfires his gun for the first time, accidentally firing a shot into the courthouse floor. Andy feels sorry for him and gives him another bullet. Later in this episode, Andy, under the impression the gun is not loaded, fires Barney's bullet into the courthouse ceiling.

Episode #22, "Cyrano Andy"

Original broadcast: March 6, 1961

Andy is caught in the middle of a misunderstanding between Barney and Thelma Lou. The victim of Thel's scheme to make Barney jealous, Andy is cast as a rival for Thelma Lou's affections. Andy finally manages to work his way out of the mess and brings the two lovebirds back together.

Facts Known by Few:

This episode marked the debut of Betty Lynn in the role of Thelma Lou.

Episode #23, "Andy and Opie, Housekeepers"

Original broadcast: March 13, 1961

Aunt Bee leaves for Mount Pilot after Cousin Edgar calls to tell her Maude has taken ill. Within hours, the Taylor house has become a lion's den, and

Andy and Opie must enlist the help of Bee's friend Bertha (Hope Summers) to get it back in order before Bee returns. Andy realizes that Bee's feelings will be hurt if she thinks they don't need her and promptly dispatches Opie to mess the place up again. After discovering the newly made mess, Bee feels wanted again and all is well—until Bertha shows up.

Facts Known by Few:
Hope Summers debuts in this episode in the role of Bertha Edwards.

Episode #24, "The New Doctor"
Original broadcast: March 27, 1961
Barney convinces Andy that handsome, young Dr. Robert Benson (George Nader) is moving in on Ellie. Andy decides to act and steps between these "two people lost in a world of pills" to claim Ellie's hand. When he learns that Dr. Benson is actually about to be married to someone else, Andy is forced into a proposal. Ellie, though, turns him down.

Facts Known by Few:
This episode is known for its "checkup" scene in which Barney, trying to spy on Dr. Benson, ends up scared for his own life.

Episode #25, "A Plaque for Mayberry"
Original broadcast: April 3, 1961
After discovering the descendant of a local Revolutionary War hero sought for a commendation by the Women's Historical Society is none other than Otis Campbell, the mayor and town council pressure Andy to tell Otis he is no longer getting the award. Andy stands by his friend, and Otis comes through with flying colors.

Facts Known by Few:
This show includes Barney's "Peter Piper Nose-pinchin' Test for Drunks."

Episode #26, "The Inspector"
Original broadcast: April 10, 1961
The state inspector (Tod Andrews) visits the Mayberry jail to check on police procedures and is horrified at the lackadaisical approaches he finds. After threats to remove Andy from office, he accompanies him on a call to a local moonshiner (Jack Prince) and discovers Andy is more of a lawman than he had imagined.

Facts Known by Few:

Jack Prince makes his second appearance, this time as Luke Ranier.

Episode #27, "Ellie Saves a Female"

Original broadcast: April 17, 1961

Reprising the feminist theme, Ellie decides to liberate local farmer's daughter Francine Flint (Edris March) against the strong objections of her father. Andy finds peace by convincing Farmer Flint that you have a better chance of catching bees, or in this case an extra hand, by using honey.

Facts Known by Few:

Unofficially, this episode marked the beginning of the television make-over, when women received a beauty treatment and the audience saw the "before and after," a trend that would become very popular, especially on talk shows, in years to come.

Episode #28, "Andy Forecloses"

Original broadcast: April 24, 1961

Ben Weaver is up to his Scrooge-like tactics again; this time he is out to evict the Scoby family from their home. He is foiled by some of Andy's patented reverse psychology.

Facts Known by Few:

No, it's not déjà vu all over again. Though the character names were different, Lester and Helen Scoby were played by the same actors (Sam Edwards and Margaret Kerry) whom old Ben Weaver jailed in Episode #11, "Christmas Story."

This episode marked the first time we heard mention of "counter cutie" Juanita Beasley who, according to Barney, was the new waitress hired over at the Junction Café.

Episode #29, "Quiet Sam"

Original broadcast: May 1, 1961

Barney becomes suspicious of the odd habits of Sam, an unfamiliar farmer. Sam (William Schallert) is acting strangely because his wife is about to give birth to their first child and Sam has nobody to help him. With the local doctor unavailable, Andy and Barney come to the rescue. Andy winds up not only delivering the child but also baby-sitting Barney.

Facts Known by Few:

Here we find out about Barney's distinguished past as a member of the armed forces. Stationed across the "big pond" (Staten Island), Barney did his part to whip the dreaded Hun. There, as second in command, he and a corporal were in charge of more than 3,000 books in the PX library.

The writing team of Jim Fritzell and Everett Greenbaum wasted no time working in their "Andy Griffith Show" calling card. In this, their first episode, they managed to work in at least one rock. It was held by Floyd, who served as Barney's backup at the Sam Becker farm. The rock was the only weapon Floyd could bring because the Mrs. wouldn't let him take the stick.

Episode #30, "Barney Gets His Man"

Original broadcast: May 8, 1961

Barney accidentally nabs bad-guy bank robber Eddie Brooks (Barney Phillips) while issuing him a ticket for littering. Brooks tries to escape after spotting state troopers, but the troopers get their man—and Barney. Before Brooks is carted off, he makes a point of promising revenge on the bumbling deputy responsible for his capture. Brooks manages to escape and is last seen making a beeline to Mayberry. Andy orchestrates Brooks's recapture, tricking Barney into firing his gun (directly at Andy, by the way), which induces Brooks to surrender.

Facts Known by Few:

Barney's first surprise party was thrown in this episode. It was a harbinger of bad news.

Barney is in high form as the nervous deputy, drawing his gun first on Thelma Lou and then on a bunny rabbit. He also crams three pieces of chewing gum in his mouth and soon swallows them.

Episode #31, "The Guitar Player Returns"

Original broadcast: May 15, 1961

Hometown hero Jim Lindsey makes a flashy return, but the town soon suspects he is not the big star he appears to be. After Andy investigates, he learns Jim cannot pay his bills. Furthermore, a collection agent shows up in Mayberry to repossess Jim's new Mercedes. Andy takes matters into his own hands, calls in Bobby Fleet, and Bobby and Jim patch up their creative differences.

Facts Known by Few:

This show marked the farewell performance of Elinor Donahue (Ellie), who left without a grand send-off. She was neither mentioned nor heard from again. Some insiders believe she ran off with Bobby Fleet.

The show also included Barney giving his first police escort to a civilian. This one provided Jim Lindsey with safe passage from the courthouse to the Mayberry Hotel, three doors away.

Episode #32, "Bringing Up Opie"

Original broadcast: May 22, 1961

Opie is banned from the friendly confines of the Mayberry courthouse when Aunt Bee decides it is not an atmosphere conducive to the proper upbringing of a young boy. Andy goes along with Bee's wishes until Opie wanders off and turns up miles away in another town. After his return, Bee agrees that father and son are better off together than apart.

SEASON 2, 31 EPISODES

Episode #33, "Barney's Replacement"

Original broadcast: October 9, 1961

Barney's pride gets the best of him when Bob Rogers (Mark Miller), a book-smart rookie from the state attorney's office, is sent to Mayberry to get law-enforcement experience. Convinced Andy is out to replace him, Barney beats him to the punch and resigns to enter the business world as a door-to-door Miracle Sweep vacuum salesman. Andy tricks Barney into rejoining the force by showing him that Rogers does not have the mettle for the job.

Facts Known by Few:

Barney is placed under arrest for the first time when cited for a violation of the Green River Ordinance, an obscure law requiring a license in order to peddle merchandise door-to-door.

Episode #34, "Opie and the Bully"

Original broadcast: October 2, 1961

Andy learns Opie is being terrorized by a local bully (Terry Dickinson), who threatens him with pulverization until he gets Opie's lunch money. Andy decides to let Opie fight this battle on his own. Opie goes to face his nemesis, and Andy suffers as he waits for his son to return. Opie returns to the courthouse as the better man—he won the fight for his rights.

Facts Known by Few:

After this episode aired, the name Hotie Snitch became synonymous with the word bully.

This episode was chosen to lead off the second season because the producers wanted a father-son story for the season premiere.

Episode #35, "Andy and the Woman Speeder"

Original broadcast: October 16, 1961

Andy arrests beautiful big-city woman Elizabeth Crowley (Jean Hagen). By the time she reaches trial, Miss Crowley has used flattery and bribes to turn the witnesses for the prosecution—Opie, Barney, and Floyd—against Andy. After winning the case, Miss Crowley sees the error of her ways and promptly speeds out of town intentionally so Andy can arrest her again and allow her to pay the fine she deserved in the first place.

Facts Known by Few:

The bribe Opie received was a baseball autographed by the entire New York Yankees team. Though the year of the team was not mentioned, the show was filmed in October 1961. Assuming the ball was from the same season, some of the signatures on the ball would have been: Tony Kubek, Clete Boyer, Yogi Berra, Elston Howard, Bobby Richardson, Moose Skowron, Whitey Ford, Ralph Terry, Roger Maris, and Mickey Mantle.

Maris hit his world record sixty-one home runs in 1961, and the Yankees won the World Series (on October 9, exactly one week prior to this show's broadcast) beating the Cincinnati Reds in five games.

If Opie had kept that ball in good condition, he could have sold it at age thirty-five for at least $1,000. Who could blame Opie for switching to Miss Crowley's side? All Barney got was a compliment that he looked a lot like Frank Sinatra.

The ball was not the only valuable object in this episode. To make the cell a little more comfortable for a lady, the walls were hung with Degas prints.

Episode #36, "Barney on the Rebound"

Original broadcast: October 30, 1961

Barney's head is turned by lovely young newcomer Melissa Stevens (Beverly Tyler), who proves to be the more attractive half of a team of con artists out to trap naive young bachelors into breach-of-promise settlements. Andy saves the day by calling the bluff of Melissa's suspiciously young "father," George Stevens. In the middle of what the pair had hoped would be their payoff, Andy begins the wedding vows, and the two back off.

Facts Known by Few:

George Stevens was played by actor Jackie Coogan, who later went on to create the role of Uncle Fester in TV's "The Addams Family." Coogan, a former child star, inspired the "Coogan Law," which protects the interests of all child actors, including, of course, Ronnie Howard.

Episode #37, "The Perfect Female"

Original broadcast: November 27, 1961

Once again the feminist theme is brought to the fore when Thelma Lou arranges a blind date between her visiting cousin and the at-present-unattached Andy Taylor. To everyone's surprise, they hit it off, but the relationship collapses when Karen Moore (Gail Davis) takes up a shotgun and shows Andy that she is not the usual delicate female. After Andy gets a good dressing-down, he admits the error of his ways.

Facts Known by Few:

Andy's success at skeet shooting was no fluke. Andy Griffith and Lee Greenway (Andy's close friend and the show's makeup artist) were both avid shooters. Greenway, in fact, was an accomplished champion.

Episode #38, "Aunt Bee's Brief Encounter"

Original broadcast: December 4, 1961

Aunt Bee falls for traveling handyman Henry Wheeler (Edgar Buchanan). Andy soon realizes Wheeler is not as nice as he seems. So before things get out of hand, Andy explains patiently to Wheeler that he would not want his Aunt Bee hurt by any false promises. To emphasize the point, Andy holds the conversation on the porch while he cleans his shotgun. Wheeler prudently decides it is time to leave Mayberry.

Episode #39, "Mayberry Goes Bankrupt"

Original broadcast: October 23, 1961

Andy teaches Mayberry exactly what "love thy neighbor" means in this episode. Andy is forced to evict Frank Myers (Andy Clyde) from his home only to later discover that he holds a century-old bond that is originally believed to be worth $349,119.27. Since the Mayberry treasury holds just over $10,000, the mayor and town council scramble to keep Frank happy by renovating his run-down home. Later, the bond is discovered to be worthless because it was paid for with Confederate currency. Once again the town turns on the old man, but Andy is able to convince everyone that they have done something nice and should leave it at that.

Episode #40, "Opie's Hobo Friend"
Original broadcast: November 13, 1961

Opie becomes fascinated with David Browne (Buddy Ebsen), a vagrant hobo who uses his wits to live on the edge of the law. After realizing his son has taken a liking to the wily wanderer, Andy tries to find Dave some honest work. Andy's plan goes sour when Opie, at Dave's encouragement, is caught playing hooky. Andy then has a long talk with the hobo. Dave sees his side and arranges to get himself arrested in order to show Opie that he was not the man he thought him to be.

Facts Known by Few:
This is the first episode written by Harvey Bullock. Dave's magic word, "Tuscarora," was taken from Tuscarora Mountain—located in New York State, where Bullock was born and raised.

Episode #41, "Crime-free Mayberry"
Original broadcast: November 20, 1961

Two crooks posing as an FBI man and a photographer come to Mayberry to congratulate the Sheriff's Department for achieving a crime-free record. Andy gets suspicious after the supposed FBI agent allows his picture to be taken. When the pair crack the Mayberry Bank's vault, Andy is inside waiting for them—he had come in the back door. Always the gracious sheriff, Andy thanks them for opening the vault that had been locked for almost fifteen years after the combination was lost and the vault company had gone out of business.

Facts Known by Few:
This episode features a baby photo of Andy Taylor in the buff.

Episode #42, "The Clubmen"
Original broadcast: December 11, 1961

One of Andy's big-city fishing buddies invites him to join the Esquire Club, an exclusive Raleigh men's organization. Barney is also asked to join and he, of course, overreacts and alienates the entire group by trying too hard to fit in. Andy is offered membership, but Barney is not; Andy tells his fishing buddy that he must decline because he does not feel right joining a club that wouldn't let in his own best friend. Before Andy can break the news to Barney, Barney assumes Andy was the one rejected and sits down to write the club a scathing letter of rejection himself.

Facts Known by Few:

Andy had in fact joined a club that wouldn't allow Barney in once before. It was the Philomathian Literary Society (Episode #82, "Class Reunion"). Barney had been blackballed by Jack Egbert, and when he found out, he cried.

Episode #43, "The Pickle Story"

Original broadcast: December 18, 1961

It's canning time again, and Aunt Bee has put up another batch of pickles. After realizing the only thing they're good for is killing flies brave enough to land on them, Andy and Barney decide to substitute store-bought for her homemade and hand the originals to travelers passing through Mayberry. After the switch, the gherkins' popularity rises and Bee gets the grand notion to try the pickle contest in the county fair. Unfortunately, the perennial winner is Clara Johnson, Bee's best friend, and she has her heart set on winning her eleventh blue ribbon in a row. Andy and Barney have no choice but to destroy all eight jars before she can enter, so they eat night and day until the pickles are all gone. They do their work proudly, but Bee decides that since the boys liked them so much, she will make a double batch.

Episode #44, "Sheriff Barney"

Original broadcast: December 25, 1961

Barney gets an offer to become the sheriff of Greendale, and Andy tries to discourage him. Unsure how to handle the matter, Andy gets an idea from an innocent remark Opie makes during a courthouse game of checkers and decides to allow Barney to be sheriff of Mayberry for a day. Given the opportunity to get a taste of what the office of high sheriff entails, Barney understands that he is not up to the job, but the realization crushes him. Andy must now rebuild Barney's self-esteem, so he arranges for moonshiner Rafe Hollister, who has just turned himself in, to go out, find Barney, and surrender to him. Barney is so absorbed in self-pity, Hollister almost leaves from frustration, but Barney eventually gets his man.

Facts Known by Few:

Jack Prince makes his third appearance as a local moonshiner, but his first as Rafe Hollister.

Episode #45, "The Farmer Takes a Wife"

Original broadcast: January 1, 1962

One of Andy's old pals, Big Jeff Pruitt (Alan Hale), comes to Mayberry looking for a suitable woman to be his wife. Andy and Barney give him a hand, but Big Jeff just cannot find a woman who suits him. Finally, Big Jeff finds the perfect woman: Thelma Lou. Andy instructs Thel to accept Big Jeff's proposal and then go about trying to civilize him into being a city-dwelling house husband. That is more than the big farmer can abide, and he heads back for the hills and his old gal, Big Bertha, just as Barney comes to Thel's demanding Big Jeff either flee or fight.

Facts Known by Few:

One of the signature phrases Hale made famous as The Skipper in "Gilligan's Island" was first uttered on "The Andy Griffith Show" when he referred several times to none other than Barney Fife as "little buddy."

This show also contained the first utterance of one other famous phrase when Barney let go with his first "Nip it in the bud!"

Episode #46, "The Keeper of the Flame"

Original broadcast: January 8, 1962

Opie is accepted as a member of a secret society called The Wildcats after he takes a sacred oath never to reveal the club secrets. Given the job of Keeper of the Flame, Opie is fingered as the guilty party when the barn that the club meets in is burned to the ground. The fire was actually started by the barn's owner, farmer and moonshiner Jubell Foster (Everett Sloane). Not knowing this, Andy takes responsibility for the fire and is about to pay Foster for the value of the barn when Barney, having stumbled upon and unknowingly consumed some of Foster's moonshine, staggers out drunk.

Facts Known by Few:

At the time Aunt Bee discovers Opie's hidden matchbox containing the Sacred Candle, she is listening to a radio soap opera. Although the popularity of radio had faded when "The Andy Griffith Show" was airing, this reference was one of many anachronisms written into the show. Aaron Ruben commented, "We weren't writing about the sixties. We were really writing about the thirties."

This was the first time Barney got gassed.

Episode #47, "Bailey's Bad Boy"

Original broadcast: January 15, 1962

Rich kid Ronald Bailey (Bill Bixby) is jailed when he blatantly defies the law. As Bailey waits for his influential father to bail him out, Andy teaches him the lesson of self-responsibility. Bailey decides to stand on his own two feet and take care of his traffic violations himself. Mr. Bailey's bad boy takes his punishment like a man.

Episode #48, "The Manicurist"

Original broadcast: January 22, 1962

Shapely young Ellen Brown (Barbara Eden) pops into Mayberry in search of a friendly town where she can make a living as a manicurist. When she lays claim to a corner of Floyd's Barbershop, the men of Mayberry aren't quite sure how to act. It isn't long before they come around to liking the whole idea, and it's the wives who become less than enthusiastic.

Episode #49, "The Jinx"

Original broadcast: January 29, 1962

Barney gets the whole town on guard when he declares Henry Bennett (John Qualen) to be a jinx. No matter how Andy tries to convince the town otherwise, Bennett's mere presence seems to consistently coincide with disaster. Even Andy gives up after a drawing fixed in Bennett's favor fails, and, in a scene reminiscent of *It's a Wonderful Life,* he tells Bennett, now surrounded by a roomful of well-wishers, that any man with this many friends must be lucky.

Facts Known by Few:

"The Jinx" was possibly the only episode that left both Don Knotts and Andy Griffith unsatisfied. "Something about it just didn't quite grab us," Knotts said. "Usually after we saw a show on the air, Andy and I would talk the next day and we were always very happy with them. That one, we both felt, missed."

Episode #50, "Jailbreak"

Original broadcast: February 2, 1962

A team of convicts is on the loose, and the state police arrive ridiculing

Sheriff Taylor and his deputy. This time, Horton (Ken Lynch) asks Andy to busy himself with "catching chicken thieves and whatnot," while the big boys go about the business of running down other crooks. Andy cracks the case by focusing in on the smallest details: a trailer hitch and an offhand remark by the dry cleaner about a suit with dog hairs. This leads to the convict's accomplice, but only after Barney somehow manages to let the one convict they have captured escape.

Facts Known by Few:

Allan Melvin made the first of five appearances, this time as bad guy Clarence "Doc" Malloy. Melvin went on to play a drill sergeant in "Gomer Pyle, U.S.M.C." and later starred in "Archie Bunker's Place."

Harvey Bullock, writer of "Jailbreak," based the character of Goss, the dry cleaner, on an ear doctor he knew in New York. "He was an old guy who smoked constantly, and when he talked to you, this unfiltered cigarette would just bounce up and down like someone had glued it to his lower lip. By the time you left he'd be just covered with ash, like an extinct volcano or something. He always intrigued me. So when I came to Goss, a dry cleaner, I thought that might work as a nice ironic twist."

Episode #51, "A Medal for Opie"

Original broadcast: February 12, 1962

Opie has his heart set on winning a medal in the annual Sheriff's Boys' Day races. Under the tutelage of legendary fifty-yard-dash winner Barney Fife, Opie enters the races confident of a win. When the day is done, however, Opie comes up empty. Andy finds Opie sulking at home, and the two have a heart-to-heart about the value of good sportsmanship.

Facts Known by Few:

One of the memorable moments in this episode is Barney recounting to Andy his date the night before with Juanita. The two went to Mount Pilot for Chinese. Barney sprung for the $2.75 dinner for one. Barney, who had a bad history with foreign waiters, didn't have enough money left over for a tip, and on the way out the waiter called him something in Chinese. Barney didn't know what it was, but he had a feeling it was not nice.

Episode #52, "Barney and the Choir"

Original broadcast: February 19, 1962

When that awful sound coming from the Mayberry choir is narrowed down to Barney Fife, the members decide they must get rid of him. Since no one wants to tell Barney he's not welcome, they decide to change the location of their rehearsals, but Barney the bloodhound still manages to run them down. Finally, in one of the show's most memorable scenes, Andy fabricates a story about a supersensitive microphone that Barney is going to use for his solo. The mike is so sensitive that Barney doesn't even have to make a sound for it to pick up his voice.

Episode #53, "Guest of Honor"

Original broadcast: February 26, 1962

It's Founder's Day again, and this time the celebration centers on honoring the first visitor to town with the key to the city. Unfortunately, the first person to drive in is Sheldon Davis (Jay Novello), an expert pickpocket and petty thief. When Andy runs a check on him and finds the truth about their "Guest of Honor," he decides to keep the whole thing hush-hush and just keep a close eye on him until the day is over and he can safely be escorted out of town. On Barney's watch, of course, the scheme goes bad. Davis escapes with Barney's key ring—the one that holds the *real* keys to the city.

Episode #54, "The Merchant of Mayberry"

Original broadcast: March 5, 1962

Mean old Ben Weaver (Will Wright) goes on a rampage when Bert Miller (Sterling Holloway), a traveling salesman, stops in Mayberry. Weaver demands Miller be taken off the street for not complying with a Mayberry law that prohibits anyone from selling goods without a permanent structure. Andy, out to have a little fun, decides to settle the matter in his own way by helping Bert build a nice little stand in a vacant lot down the street, setting off a trade war between Bert's stand and Weaver's Department Store. Ben finally gives in and decides the best way to eliminate the competition is to put him to work in his own store.

Facts Known by Few:

In this episode Andy initiates a popular running gag by playing a prank on a napping Barney Fife. Andy catches Barney asleep on the bench in front of the courthouse. After gently depositing some lipstick shavings in Barney's hand, Andy tickles Barn's lip with a piece of straw. After Barney gets on a nice coat of paint, Andy sends him to deal with Joe Waters, who parked his truck too close to a fire hydrant. Joe moves, blowing Barney a kiss on the way.

Episode #55, "Aunt Bee, the Warden"

Original broadcast: March 12, 1962

The Gordon boys are brought in for moonshining, and when Otis arrives for his regular stay at the jail, there is no room at the inn. When the Gordons accuse Otis of turning them in, Andy has no choice but to take Otis home to let him sleep it off at the Taylor house. Come morning, Otis finds that he's been turned over to "Bloody Mary," aka Aunt Bee, who decides to rehabilitate Otis once and for all.

Facts Known by Few:

Otis sings "The Dipsy Doodle," a popular song he ad-libbed into the show.

The ending—which has been cut from most syndicated versions currently shown to allow more time for commercials—has the Gordons escaping from their cell using the metal craft set that Barney brought in to help rehabilitate the prisoners.

Episode #56, "The County Nurse"

Original broadcast: March 19, 1962

Mary Simpson (Julie Adams), the first of the county nurses, enlists Andy's help in getting Rafe Hollister to submit to a tetanus shot. Rafe refuses until Andy, using that ol' reverse psychology trick, gets Rafe to change his mind after he serenades him with a song that Andy plans to sing at Rafe's funeral.

Episode #57, "Andy and Barney in the Big City"

Original broadcast: March 26, 1962

Andy and Barney visit Raleigh, where Barney captures a man he believes to be a jewel thief. Barney winds up capturing the hotel detective with the help of the real jewel thief. Andy steps in just in time to cover Barney's bungle and make it appear as though Barney's work brought the real jewel thief to justice.

Facts Known by Few:

This is the only show in which Allan Melvin played the part of a good guy—Detective Bardolli.

Episode #58, "Wedding Bells for Aunt Bee"

Original broadcast: April 2, 1962

Clara (Hope Summers) convinces Aunt Bee that she's the reason Andy isn't getting married. In order not to feel that she is in the way, Bee invents an imaginary beau. Andy misunderstands and becomes convinced that Bee is serious about finding a husband. When Bee needs to produce a body, she grabs the first one handy—Fred Goss (Fred Sherman), the Mayberry dry cleaner. When Andy finally figures out what has transpired, he tells Bee that she is not in the way and is part of his family. Goss is happily sent back to the solvents and hangers.

Facts Known by Few:

This is the first episode in which Otis Campbell appears without being jailed for drunkenness. He was preparing for the event, however, by bringing his suit to leave in the cell for Sunday services following his Saturday night out.

Episode #59, "Three's a Crowd"

Original broadcast: April 9, 1962

Andy tries to romance the county nurse, Mary Simpson, but Barney constantly interrupts. Finally, Andy becomes exasperated and tells Barney that he wants to be alone—with Mary. Barney understands perfectly, and he gathers everyone together for the first of several false wedding announcements involving Andy and his current female love interest.

Facts Known by Few:

Mary Simpson was back again—sort of. Though the name was the same, the actress was different. This time she was a blonde, played by actress Sue Ane Langdon.

Episode #60, "The Bookie Barber"

Original broadcast: April 16, 1962

Floyd gets his chance at being the proprietor of a two-chair shop when semiretired barber Bill Medwin (Herb Vigran) arrives with a proposition of expansion. Floyd jumps at the chance since Medwin promises to supply the chair and the customers. As it turns out, the barber is a bookie, and Barney jumps in to bust the criminal.

Facts Known by Few:

This show includes Barney's famous "compelsion" complex speech. It was also the first show in which Barney wore a dress.

Episode #61, "Andy on Trial"

Original broadcast: April 23, 1962

J. Howard Jackson, a wealthy newspaperman, seeks revenge on Sheriff

Taylor after Andy tracks him down for failing to appear in Mayberry court for a traffic violation. Unwittingly, Barney becomes a key witness in Jackson's attempt to remove Andy from office, supplying female reporter Jean Boswell (Ruta Lee) with information that is eventually used as evidence against Andy. When Barney is called to the stand, he is able to dispel all doubts that Andy is an honest man of the law and a true public servant.

Facts Known by Few:

This episode concluded with one of the strongest dramatic moments during the entire series. The genius of Don Knotts is displayed in his speech from the witness chair when he defends Andy as a friend and professional. The depth of the characters shown here is a perfect example of why "The Andy Griffith Show" is considered one of TV's best. Barney's defense of his friend highlights the dramatic side of comedy.

The view outside J. Howard Jackson's office window is the Hollywood Hills. Andy apparently would go to any length to bring in his man.

Episode #62, "Cousin Virgil"
Original broadcast: April 30, 1962

Virgil (Michael J. Pollard), Barney's awkward cousin from New Jersey, visits Mayberry and immediately makes a mess of everything he touches. After Virgil has dumped a roast in Andy's lap, driven the squad car through his gate, and smashed a pane of glass while sweeping up around the courthouse, Andy tries to get him out of his hair by sending him to polish the cell keys. Virgil polishes the teeth right off of them, making it impossible to let Otis out when he's due to leave the cell. At his wit's end, Andy is shown a set of hand-carved wood figures that Virgil himself made. Andy realizes the best tonic for Virgil is a good dose of self-confidence and leaves him alone to remove the door of the cell.

Episode #63, "Deputy Otis"
Original broadcast: May 7, 1962

Andy helps his number-one prisoner save face when Otis learns his brother Ralph is coming to visit. Having told his brother he is a member of the Mayberry sheriff's office, Andy makes an exception and deputizes his favorite ward long enough to convince Ralph he's a member of Mayberry's finest. As it turns out, Ralph isn't any better a man than Otis, coming in drunk to lock himself in the Mayberry jail—just as he always does at home.

Facts Known by Few:

The third and final correspondence from the Hubacher brothers comes in this episode when they write on the occasion of their second anniversary in the state pen. They mention in the letter a song sung by Junior to commemorate the occasion: "My Little Grey Home in the West." It made the warden cry.

Amzie Strickland, who played Barney's first gal Miss Rosemary, returns in the role of Verlaine Campbell, Otis's sister-in-law. That gal got around.

SEASON 3, 32 EPISODES

Episode #64, "Opie's Rival"

Original broadcast: December 3, 1962

Everybody but Opie takes an immediate shine to Peggy McMillan (Joanna Moore), who makes her first appearance as the new county nurse. No one takes more notice than Andy. When he pays her a little too much attention, Opie becomes jealous and plays sick to keep his pa from going out on a date. Andy catches on and patches things up, and the three lives happily . . . for another few episodes.

Facts Known by Few:

Filmed first, this episode was the tenth to air during the third season.

Episode #65, "Andy and Opie, Bachelors"

Original broadcast: November 8, 1962

Aunt Bee goes to visit Aunt Louise, leaving Andy and Opie to get by on their own. County nurse Peggy McMillan is there to keep an eye on the boys. All is fine until Floyd plants the idea in Andy's head that Peggy might just be out to catch a husband. Once again, after getting himself into trouble with his girl, Andy realizes better, apologizes, and everybody lives happily . . . for another two episodes.

Facts Known by Few:

In this episode written by Jim Fritzell and Everett Greenbaum, Bee uses the word "underwear" twice before departing on the bus. Years later, when asked to record a monologue for *Return to Mayberry,* Bavier refused after reading a line Greenbaum wrote that included the word "underwear," stating she would not say "underwear," had never said "underwear," and would not say "underwear" now.

Episode #66, "Mr. McBeevee"

Original broadcast: October 1, 1962

Opie weaves the fabulous tale of Mr. McBeevee (Carl Swenson), a man who walks in the treetops, wears a silver hat, has twelve extra hands, blows smoke from his ears, and jingles when he walks as if he had rings on his fingers and bells on his toes. But other than those few quirks, Mr. McBeevee is normal. Andy and Barney laugh it off, but when Opie brings back a quarter he claims was given to him by his friend, Andy is forced to call the stories to a halt. Faced with the threat of a spanking, Opie is still unable to betray the existence of Mr. McBeevee. Andy may have to accept the unacceptable in the face of Opie's insistence. Later, when out for a walk, Andy happens past the very same tree Mr. McBeevee, a telephone linesman, is working in. Andy gets his own introduction to the man who walks in the trees and Opie is vindicated.

Facts Known by Few:

"Mr. McBeevee" was chosen to be the premiere of the 1962–63 season.

Episode #67, "Andy's Rich Girlfriend"

Original broadcast: October 8, 1962

After Peggy McMillan shows up in a brand-new T-bird, Andy learns she's the daughter of the "M" in R & M Grain Elevators. Andy, against Barney's advice, struggles to fit in with the wealthy class. Realizing finally that it's better to be himself and that the true value of a person lies beyond his bankbook, the two live happily . . . for one more episode.

Episode #68, "Barney Mends a Broken Heart"

Original broadcast: November 5, 1962

Andy shows up for a date with Peggy McMillan (Joanna Moore) only to learn her old friend Don has arrived unexpectedly. Andy departs angrily when Peggy breaks their date and then encounters more problems when Barney decides to make things better by fixing him up with another girl. Andy ends up getting himself punched in the eye, but manages to fix things up with Peggy, and they live happily—until the end of this episode—and then we never see her again.

Facts Known by Few:

This show, which included Barney's "therapetic" speech, also marked the debut of Jean Carson and Joyce Jameson as "The Fun Girls."

Josie Lloyd, who appeared twice before as Juanita Pike, makes her first appearance as Lydia Crosswaithe from Greensboro.

Episode #69, "Andy and the New Mayor"

Original broadcast: October 15, 1962

Mayor Stoner (Parley Baer) makes his first appearance and is nothing but trouble for the sheriff's office. He finally learns the lesson so many others have: Not all sheriffin' has to be done by the book.

First reason no one liked Mayor Stoner . . .

He was always on time.

Episode #70, "The Cow Thief"

Original broadcast: October 29, 1962

Andy's law-enforcement practices come into question when a local farmer complains of missing milk cows. Mayor Stoner goes over Andy's head and calls in "an interloper" from the state office to take over the investigation. Andy manages to save the day by capturing the thief without the help of the outsider. Andy discovers that the thefts were being covered up by putting shoes on the cows.

Facts Known by Few:

The idea for this episode came from a comment made by Andy Griffith when he innocently mentioned in a story conference a memory he had of a farmer back home who used to put shoes on his cow.

The phrase "Let's get busy," popularized by talk show host Arsenio Hall, was actually first used in this episode—by Mayor Stoner.

Episode #71, "Floyd, the Gay Deceiver"

Original broadcast: November 26, 1962

Floyd finds himself in a jam when a woman he's been corresponding with writes to say that she plans on paying him a visit in Mayberry. Floyd begs Andy for help, explaining that he has deceived his Lonely Hearts Club companion by leading her to believe that he is a wealthy businessman. Andy reluctantly agrees to help Floyd but in the process discovers that Madeline

Grayson (Doris Dowling) isn't quite what she claims either. Floyd's poisonous pen pal is actually a con artist who travels around bilking lonely old men out of their money.

Facts Known by Few:

According to Aaron Ruben, who wrote and produced this episode, Howard McNear, who played Floyd, was terribly afraid that this story would never work.

Episode #72, "The Mayberry Band"

Original broadcast: November 19, 1962

Mayor Stoner strikes again, revoking funds allocated for the Mayberry Band's annual trip to the state band competition. He changes his mind after the band performs a special concert for his benefit—with a little bit of help from Bobby Fleet and His Band with a Beat.

Episode #73, "Lawman Barney"

Original broadcast: November 12, 1962

A couple of truck farmers defy Barney when he asks them to pack up their produce elsewhere. Andy makes matters worse by telling them that Barney, better known as Crazy Gun Fife, is a coldhearted killer. The truck farmers fall for it at first, but return after learning the truth at the gas station. Barney is forced to face them on his own. He musters the courage and learns that the uniform he wears represents more than just one man.

Facts Known by Few:

Allan Melvin makes his second appearance—as Neil, the truck farmer.

Episode #74, "Convicts at Large"

Original broadcast: December 10, 1962

Barney and Floyd are held hostage by a gang of escaped female convicts who have been hiding in O'Malley's cabin outside of town. Andy, who spots Floyd in town buying groceries (with one of the female cons), thinks they have a little party going until O'Malley arrives back in town on the bus. Andy and O'Malley engineer a clever scheme and capture all but the ringleader, Big Maude, whom Barney manages to tango out the door and into the cuffs.

Facts Known by Few:

Big Maude, played by actress Reta Shaw, appeared again in the role of Eleanora Poultice. Naomi, another member of the gang, was played by "Fun Girl" Jean Carson.

Shortly after the filming of this episode, Howard McNear suffered a stroke, temporarily halting his career. He would return again to the role of Floyd Lawson in Episode #119, "Andy Saves Gomer."

Episode #75, "The Bed Jacket"

Original broadcast: December 17, 1962

Aunt Bee drops hints that she would like a lacy bed jacket for her upcoming birthday, but Andy doesn't catch on. After giving her a set of salt and pepper shakers and two cases of canning jars, Andy realizes he's let his aunt down and rushes back to the store. The bed jacket, however, has been sold to Mayor Stoner. Dragging him out of bed, Andy begs the mayor to make a trade. Knowing he has Andy over a barrel, Stoner asks for Andy's favorite fishing pole, "Eagle Eye Annie."

More Reasons no one liked Mayor Stoner

Reason #2: He wore a tie while fishin'.

Reason #3: He didn't know how to tie it: the thin end was always longer than the wide end.

Episode #76, "Barney and the Governor"

Original broadcast: January 7, 1963

Barney is goaded into ticketing the governor's car and mistakenly believes Andy is setting him up for a dressing-down by the governor. In fact, the governor is coming to Mayberry to give him a personal commendation for performing a job without showing favorites. In the midst of all the action, Otis secretly spikes the water tank, giving both Barney and Mayor Stoner a surprise snootful.

Reasons no one liked Mayor Stoner

Reason #4: He couldn't hold his liquor.

Facts Known by Few:

The role of the governor's chauffeur was played by Ron Howard's father, Rance.

Either the governor had a snootful himself when picking out his vanity plates or the Hubacher brothers had been transferred to the license-plate shop in the state penitentiary. The governor's plate read:

A 1 A

NOTH CAPOLNJA 62

Episode #77, "Man in a Hurry"

Original broadcast: January 14, 1963

Big-businessman Malcolm Tucker (Robert Emhardt) is stuck in Mayberry for the Sabbath when his car breaks down outside the city limits. He's soon driven to frustration when he finds there is no way to get anything done in this two-bit town until the following day. After finally getting Gomer's cousin Goober to fix his car, Tucker gives in to the mood and decides to stay the night.

Facts Known by Few:

This was the first episode filmed to feature Jim Nabors, even though he was in Episode #78, "The Bank Job," which originally aired earlier on Christmas Eve 1962.

Though cut from the original script, Gomer bragged to Tucker how not long ago Goober put a washing-machine motor on his bicycle and drove it all over town—until he was caught by his mother.

Episode #78, "The Bank Job"

Original broadcast: December 24, 1962

Barney gets in a snit over the lax security at the Mayberry Security Bank and decides to prove his point when he slips by the bank teller dressed as a cleaning lady and accidentally locks himself in the vault. Later he is redeemed when real crooks are caught in a failed attempt to rob the bank.

Episode #79, "One Punch Opie"

Original broadcast: December 31, 1962

A new kid moves to Mayberry and immediately starts leading Opie's friends down the path of ruin. Opie finally decides to stand up to him and realizes the boy is all talk.

Facts Known by Few:

This episode features Barney's famous "Last stop on the road to crime" speech in which he proves by locking himself in the cell that it is definitely no fun when that iron door clangs shut.

Episode #80, "High Noon in Mayberry"

Original broadcast: January 21, 1963

Andy receives a letter from ex-con Luke Comstock, whom he sent upriver after putting a bullet in his leg. The letter says that Luke will be paying the sheriff a visit in Mayberry. Barney jumps to the conclusion that he's coming for revenge (R-E-V-E-N-G) and with Gomer's and Otis's help he sets up a twenty-four-hour watch on Andy. As it turns out, Comstock is coming to pay Andy a long overdue thanks for turning his life around, but not before Barney manages to get "all tied up" in his work.

Facts Known by Few:

This is the one episode in which Andy revealed a handgun he kept hidden on top of the china cabinet in the dining room.

This episode also marked Gomer's first time in uniform as a deputy.

Episode #81, "The Loaded Goat"

Original broadcast: January 28, 1963

Cy Hudges (Bing Russell) brings his goat Jimmy to town for one day, and Jimmy gets himself "loaded" on a cache of dynamite. Faced with the menace of a goat who could go "blooie" at any moment, Andy and Barney have to figure a way of getting him out of town. Music soothes this savage goat, as he follows Barney out beyond the city limits while playing his harmonica.

Reasons no one liked Mayor Stoner

Reason #5: Nepotism. Mayberry only got a new underpass because the new highway would go right past a fillin' station owned by the Mayor's brother.

Facts Known by Few:

In 1963, prices at the barbershop were up. The sign on Floyd's wall read:

Flattops $2.00
Butch $2.00
Shampoo 75¢
Shave 50¢
Tonics 25¢ extra

Episode #82, "Class Reunion"

Original broadcast: February 4, 1963

Andy and Barney decide to organize their twentieth high school reunion, and all the excitement centers on the return of Andy's old flame Sharon DeSpain (Peggy McCay). It looks like the torch may be relit when Peggy shows up and she and Andy pick up right where they left off, in the garden outside. Both wonder what ever happened when it finally occurs to them both that what separated them in high school is what separates them now. Sharon wants the bright lights and big city, and Andy is happy to stay where he is.

Facts Known by Few:

This show contains the only scene in which Andy was photographed with a filtered lens. In the garden scene with Sharon DeSpain you can see the difference by watching for Andy's close-up right before the kiss.

Episode #83, "Rafe Hollister Sings"

Original broadcast: February 11, 1963

Rafe Hollister (Jack Prince) makes his singing debut when he decides to audition for an upcoming concert. Some of the locals are appalled after John Masters (Olan Soule) chooses Rafe for the solo performance. Andy stands by his man, and Rafe gets raves.

Episode #84, "Opie and the Spoiled Kid"

Original broadcast: February 18, 1963

Arnold Winkler (Ronnie Dapo) makes his first appearance as a rotten little kid who tries to teach Opie how to manipulate his parents by throwing well-rehearsed tantrums. After terrorizing Mayberry, Winkler's bike is impounded and Opie learns a better lesson when he sees Winkler's ways just don't wash.

Episode #85, "The Great Filling Station Robbery"

Original broadcast: February 25, 1963

Barney enters the electronics age when he decides to solve a mysterious string of robberies at Wally's Filling Station using modern police technology. Andy is more concerned with clearing the name of the young man who was given a fresh start with a job at the station and who is the chief suspect in the case.

Facts Known by Few:

This was the first episode in which Gomer said, "Shazaam!"

A sign can be seen on the face of the filling station displaying its hours: IF YOU NEED GAS, WALLY'S IS OPEN FROM 7 A.M. TO 7 P.M.

Episode #86, "Andy Discovers America"

Original broadcast: March 4, 1963

Opie misunderstands a comment Andy makes at the breakfast table and tells his new teacher, "*old* Miss Crump," that according to his pa, history doesn't matter. In this debut show for Aneta Corsaut in the role of Helen Crump, Helen lays down the law to Sheriff Taylor and Andy responds with his own methods of motivating Opie and his friends to study.

Facts Known by Few:

Who were the Mayberry Minute Men?

Opie, Whitey, Howie, Johnny Paul Jason, and, of course, Barney.

Anyone who didn't get in is British!

Episode #87, "Aunt Bee's Medicine Man"

Original broadcast: March 11, 1963

Aunt Bee falls under the spell of traveling medicine man Colonel Harvey (John Dehner), but it turns out that the spell is mostly alcohol induced. Andy comes home to find Bee and her lady friends half cocked on the colonel's elixir and has to run them all in. A few hours later he nabs the colonel himself for peddling liquor.

Facts Known by Few:

Aunt Bee tells the colonel their house address is 332 Maple street. Two other addresses were given during the run of the show: 14 Maple and 22 Elm. When trying to find the Taylor house, remember, Bee has been known to drink.

Episode #88, "The Darlings Are Coming"

Original broadcast: March 18, 1963

This episode introduced the Darling family. Led by Briscoe, the clan comes to town to meet the bus carrying Charlene's beloved PFC Dudley A. Wash (Hoke Howell). Though they tend to get themselves into trouble, Andy tries his best to look the other way.

Facts Known by Few:

The price of a single room, with bath, at the Mayberry Hotel in 1963 was $2.50. Without a bath it was $1.75.

The name of the Darling boy without much personality was Oether. No other names were mentioned until the family's final appearance.

Episode #89, "Andy's English Valet"

Original broadcast: March 25, 1963

The gentleman's gentleman, Malcolm Merriweather (Bernard Fox), passes through Mayberry on his American tour. Entering town with a bang, he manages to cause a truck accident and is forced to work off the damages as Andy's personal valet.

Facts Known by Few:

Harvey Bullock met Bernard Fox while working in England and encouraged him to come to the States. This episode was written with Fox in mind to service his style of comedy.

Episode #90, "Barney's First Car"

Original broadcast: April 1, 1963

April Fool's! Barney becomes "Mr. Independent Wheels" when he spends most of his savings ($300) on a used car—only to find he's been taken by a bunco ring led by mastermind Myrt Lesch (Ellen Corby). By coincidence, Andy and Barney nab the gang when the crooks mistakenly resteal the car, which they think has been abandoned on a country road.

Facts Known by Few:

Everett Greenbaum, who wrote this episode with partner Jim Fritzell, told how fond Andy and Don Knotts were of one scene in this show: "There were some scenes we wrote that Andy and Don would do at parties. The scene in which Barney tells Andy about buying the septic tank for his parents, they loved that. They would do it word for word . . . 'You're a good son, Barn.'"

Episode #91, "The Rivals"

Original broadcast: April 8, 1963

When Opie can't do anything to catch the eye of little Karen Burgess (Ronda Jeter), Thel steps in to cheer him up and ends up the object of Opie's affections. Barney suddenly finds he's the third wheel and demands Andy have a talk with the boy. Andy drives the point home, and Opie dumps Thel for Karen.

Facts Known by Few:

This episode includes the famous "snow-cone speech" in which Barney remembers that snobbish little Vickie Harmes.

Episode #92, "A Wife for Andy"

Original broadcast: April 15, 1963

Andy and Helen finally become an item, but not before Barney has his say. Determined to find Andy a wife, Barney parades every eligible female in town through Andy's living room. Andy, though, wants nothing to do with any of them ... until he meets Helen Crump. She, of course, doesn't meet with Barney's approval.

Facts Known by Few:

Andy's favorite dish: leg of lamb.

Andy's first date with Helen: to Mount Pilot for Chinese.

Episode #93, "Dogs, Dogs, Dogs"

Original broadcast: April 22, 1963

A state inspector is on his way to visit the Mayberry jailhouse in order to determine whether or not the sheriff's office needs additional funds. Before he arrives, Opie brings a stray dog in who is followed by another ten of his four-legged friends. Luckily, the inspector happens to raise dogs himself. He befriends the dog-loving sheriff and deputy and sees to it they get the money they need.

Facts Known by Few:

This episode is highlighted by Barney's classic giraffe speech. He also quotes Shakespeare.

Episode #94, "Mountain Wedding"

Original broadcast: April 29, 1963

Andy and Barney visit the Darlings to rid them of Ernest T. Bass, who has his mind set on marrying daughter Charlene. In the debut of Howard Morris in this classic role, Barney ends up the bride.

Facts Known by Few:

The wedding ceremony was performed by Dub Taylor as the preacher.

Episode #95, "The Big House"

Original broadcast: May 6, 1963

Two escapees are held temporarily in the Mayberry jail while the feds wait for their partners to arrive. Gomer is deputized to help Barney out, but between the two of them, the criminals manage to escape three times.

Facts Known by Few:

This episode features Barney's famous "Here at the rock" speech.

The diner serves corned beef and cabbage on Tuesdays.

SEASON 4, 32 EPISODES

Episode #96, "Briscoe Declares for Aunt Bee"

Original broadcast: October 28, 1963

Briscoe Darling falls under the impression that Aunt Bee is sweet on him, so he decides to court her with the intention of making her his bride. When he is finished courting, Briscoe kidnaps Bee and takes her back to the Darling cabin. Andy rescues her by convincing Bee to try to reform Briscoe. Bee's attempt to civilize the Darlings causes Briscoe to call off the engagement.

Facts Known by Few:

This episode features Aunt Bee reciting one of her favorite poems, "My Fading Flower of Forgotten Love" by Agnes Ellicot Strom.

Episode #97, "Gomer, the House Guest"

Original broadcast: November 4, 1963

Wally fires Gomer for talking too much and working too little, and since Gomer lives in the back room of the filling station, the firing is also an eviction. Andy offers to take Gomer in, which is when the trouble starts. Before long, the Taylor house has become Wally's West, as Gomer's customers line up for repairs in Andy's driveway. Andy is able to prove to Wally that Gomer is the reason many of his customers come in, so Wally hires him back and Andy's life returns to normal.

Episode #98, "The Haunted House"

Original broadcast: October 7, 1963

Opie loses his baseball in the old Rimshaw House and is scared off by what he thinks are ghosts. Andy sends Barney out to fetch the ball. Barney forces Gomer to come with him, and they are both scared away by what they, too, believe are ghosts. Andy takes the two of them to the house and discovers the true spook is a moonshiner who has rigged up the house to keep interlopers away. Shazaam!

Episode #99, "Ernest T. Bass Joins the Army"
Original broadcast: October 14, 1963
Don't sit down, Ernest T.'s back in town. Ernest T. wants to join the army to get a uniform that he can wear back to the hills to impress his lovely Romeena. When he is refused induction, E.T. goes on a window-breaking rampage. Andy and Barney haul him in, but the jail can't hold him. After Ernest T. tells Andy his reason for coming to town, Andy settles the whole matter by giving him one of Barney's genuine whiplash cord uniforms to take home.

Facts Known by Few:
A #2 Amber alert: One lawman must be awake at all times.
A window with a BAR sign painted on it can be seen after Barney breaks the new picture window that was headed for the courthouse. This set was also used in "The Untouchables."

Episode #100, "The Sermon for Today"
Original broadcast: October 21, 1963
A visiting minister from New York delivers a sermon encouraging the members of the Mayberry congregation to "slow down." Those who are still awake take the message so seriously they spend the Sabbath working themselves to exhaustion in order to arrange a concert in an effort to relax.

Facts Known by Few:
The Taylors attended The All Souls Church, the Reverend Hobart Tucker (William Keene), D.D.

Episode #101, "Opie, the Birdman"
Original broadcast: September 30, 1963
Opie accidentally kills a mother bird with his new slingshot and takes it upon himself to raise the orphaned baby birds. After adopting them with the names Winkin', Blinkin', and Nod, Opie faces the difficult task of setting them free.

Facts Known by Few:
Though filmed sixth, this episode was chosen as the premiere show of the 1963–64 season.

Opie's birdhouse, created by Harvey Bullock, writer of "Opie the Birdman."

Aunt Bee took her first shot at Chinese cooking with a recipe she'd seen in the paper: ham loaf and green beans, Chinese style.

Show highlight: Barney shows off his knowledge of bird talk.

Episode #102, "A Black Day for Mayberry"

Original broadcast: November 11, 1963

What's this show about? "One little hint . . . it's worth seven million dollars." A top-secret gold shipment from the Denver Mint to Fort Knox is scheduled to make a stop in Mayberry, and only Andy and Barney know about it. It turns out that those gossipin' men can't keep a secret and everybody in town knows about the gold. The top-secret shipment is greeted with a carnival-like reception and Barney almost blows another secret when he discovers the gold is gone! What Barney did not know was that, at the last minute, the real shipment was diverted and the truck was a decoy.

Facts Known by Few:

Ron Howard's father, Rance, makes another appearance in the opening scene, as the treasury agent waiting for Sheriff Taylor.

Episode #103, "Opie's Ill-gotten Gain"

Original broadcast: November 18, 1963

Opie surprises everyone with a report card of straight A's only to find out later, after Andy rewards him with a new bicycle, that the marks were a mistake. Afraid he's let his pa down, Opie decides to run away and join the navy.

Facts Known by Few:

This show contains the memorable scene in which Barney recites the Preamble to the Constitution.

Episode #104, "Up in Barney's Room"

Original broadcast: December 2, 1963

Barney is evicted from his room at Mrs. Mendelbright's boardinghouse after being caught violating her rules regarding cooking and high-wattage bulbs. With nowhere else to go, he moves in temporarily to the back room of the courthouse. When he goes back to beg for his room, he learns that Mrs. Mendelbright (Enid Markey) is about to sell her home in order to pool assets with her new boyfriend, Mr. Fields (J. Pat O'Malley), whom she plans to marry. Something about the whole deal doesn't smell right to Barney. Andy finds out Mr. Fields is a con man, and he and Barney save Mrs. Mendelbright from financial ruin.

Facts Known by Few:

Barney paid six dollars a week rent for his room, and what did he get? Heartaches!

The word "Security" was no longer part of the Mayberry Bank's name.

Episode #105, "A Date for Gomer"

Original broadcast: November 25, 1963

The big annual Chamber of Commerce dance is approaching, and Thelma Lou refuses to go with Barney unless he gets a date for her cousin Mary Grace Gossage (Mary Grace Canfield), who is visiting from out of town. Both Andy and Barney are about ready to give up when Gomer appears. Just when all seems right, Gomer jumps up and leaves Mary Grace. After the entire evening is ruined, the four return to Thel's to find Mary Grace and Gomer kicking out a jam and having the time of their lives. Gomer had just gone off to find her a corsage (pronounced core-saige).

Episode #106, "Citizen's Arrest"

Original broadcast: December 16, 1963

Barney resigns and spends five days in jail after Gomer turns the tables and places him under citizen's arrest for a U-turn violation. Once Gomer finds out how serious the matter has become, he reports a fictitious robbery at the filling station in the hopes of pressing Barney back into service.

Facts Known by Few:

A bit of Mayberry history is revealed in this episode when Andy finds a custody receipt in his files that he issued to Barney in August 1953 for his first revolver.

Episode #107, "Gomer Pyle, U.S.M.C."

Original broadcast: May 19, 1964

This episode, filmed as the spinoff for the new series by the same name, took Gomer out of Mayberry and into the marines. Andy tags along for his first day at boot camp, and, realizing how important it is for Gomer to succeed, plants an idea in the head of Drill Sergeant Carter (Frank Sutton) that Gomer

Asa (Charles Thompson) and Barney (Don Knotts) try to get the drop on a suspect in "The Shoplifters."

TAGSRWC Collection

is related to Marine General Lucis Pyle. Carter, thinking he's being tested, takes Gomer under his wing and is stuck with him from that point on.

Facts Known by Few:

The gate use for Camp Wilson was actually the Cahuenga gate at Desilu Studios.

This show aired as the final episode of the 1963–64 season.

Episode #108, "Opie and His Merry Men"

Original broadcast: December 30, 1963

Opie plays Robin Hood to his own Sherwood Forest gang and gets involved in stealing from the "rich" Mayberry citizens in order to feed a "poor" hobo (Douglas Fowley) whom the gang meet in the woods. Andy goes out to meet their new friend in order to prove to Opie and the others that Andy is a good sheriff and that the hobo has been taking advantage of the kids' good intentions.

Episode #109, "Barney and the Cave Rescue"

Original broadcast: January 6, 1964

Andy and Helen wander into a cave while on the town picnic and are trapped when the entryway collapses behind them. Barney discovers what has happened and organizes a rescue party. Andy and Helen manage to find a safe exit through a hidden opening on the far end of the cave. Hearing a report of the accident on the radio, he and Helen have to climb back in so Barney can rescue them, saving Barney from becoming the laughingstock of the town.

Episode #110, "Andy and Opie's Pal"

Original broadcast: January 13, 1964

Opie has a new best friend, Trey Bowden (David A. Bailey), but before long, friend becomes foe when Andy starts giving Trey some attention. Andy teaches the jealous Opie a lesson when he excludes Barney from their Saturday fishing date. When Opie sees how hurt Barney is, he learns the importance of sharing.

Episode #111, "Aunt Bee, the Crusader"

Original broadcast: January 20, 1964

Aunt Bee champions the cause of a small farmer who has been forced to sell his farm to make way for a new highway. When Bee leads a group of ladies in a demonstration, Andy and Barney head out to break up the protest and stumble over a group of six stills Farmer Frisbee has hidden away under the henhouse.

Episode #112, "Barney's Sidecar"
Original broadcast: January 27, 1964
Determined to nip the speeding on Highway 6 in the bud, Barney purchases a motorcycle and sidecar at a military surplus auction. With the town up in arms over Barney's new toy, Andy tricks Barney into donating the motorcycle to a museum.

Episode #113, "My Fair Ernest T. Bass"
Original broadcast: February 3, 1964
Andy tries to make a silk purse out of a sow's ear when he takes it upon himself to turn Ernest T. Bass into a presentable gentleman. The big test comes at Mrs. Wiley's weekly reception when Andy tries to pass him off as his cousin. Even Andy is surprised at E.T.'s progress when Mrs. Wiley places his accent as being definitely Back Bay Bostonian, but the whole scheme blows up when Bass smashes a vase over the head of a man who won't allow him to cut in for a dance with his chosen woman.

Facts Known by Few:
This marks the first appearance of Mr. Schwump.

Episode #114, "Prisoner of Love"
Original broadcast: February 10, 1964
Andy is taken in by the charms of a seductive female prisoner. Andy can't get the image of her out of his mind and returns to the courthouse just in time to prevent her escape.

Facts Known by Few:
This show contained the kinkiest line ever uttered in Mayberry: "You sheriff, me prisoner."

Episode #115, "Hot Rod Otis"
Original broadcast: February 17, 1964
Otis saves up to buy a used car and becomes the object of full-time surveillance by a worried Barney. After catching Otis leaving a party drunk, the sheriff and deputy play a trick on Otis in order to convince him to give up

the car. It works, but it wasn't necessary. When Otis wakes up, he reveals that he had already sold it.

Episode #116, "The Song Festers"

Original broadcast: February 24, 1964

John Masters (Olan Soule) discovers Gomer's singing voice and decides to give him the solo in the upcoming concert instead of Barney. When Gomer realizes how important the solo is to Barney he feigns laryngitis, and just before curtain, Andy has to talk Barney into going on. Gomer's trick is discovered when, in his excitement to see Barney, he forgets himself and speaks in a full voice. As a result, Barney refuses his charity, but Andy grabs both of them as the curtain goes up and the solo becomes a trio.

Facts Known by Few:

The number of seconds the choir held the note before Andy, Barney, and Gomer stepped up to sing: 26.

The strange and unexplained: Miss Poultice had a portrait of a Saint Bernard over her fireplace. Go figure.

Andy's wife at that time, Barbara Griffith, appears as a member of the choir.

Episode #117, "The Shoplifters"

Original broadcast: March 2, 1964

The strange disappearance of merchandise from Weaver's Department Store has the Mayberry sheriff's office on full alert. When all other tactics fail, Barney decides to go undercover as a store mannequin and he catches the thief.

Episode #118, "Andy's Vacation"

Original broadcast: March 9, 1964

Andy is at wit's end with being sheriff, so he takes a vacation. Leaving Barney and Gomer in charge, he soon realizes that he'll never get any rest at home so he goes camping for a week in the woods. Trouble finds him when a prisoner held temporarily in the Mayberry jail sneaks away from Barney and Gomer and ends up finding Andy's campfire. Andy recognizes the prison garb and nabs him. He even has to capture him a second time after Barney and Gomer let him go again.

Episode #119, "Andy Saves Gomer"

Original broadcast: March 16, 1964

Andy finds Gomer napping in the garage and snuffs out a small fire in a can full of oily rags. Gomer blows the whole incident out of proportion, and Andy must then deal with Gomer's indebtedness. Gomer offers himself to Andy as slave for life. Desperate to get rid of Gomer, Andy tries to find a way to even the score by staging his own life-threatening mishap. Gomer screws it up and Andy must save his life again—but this time he is able to manufacture a story to get Gomer off his back.

Facts Known by Few:
Howard McNear returns to the show following his stroke.

Episode #120, "Bargain Day"
Original broadcast: March 23, 1964
Diamond Jim's, a new butcher shop, opens and Bee heads there hunting for a bargain. She walks out with a side of chewy beef to put in her last "bargain" purchase—a freezer that she discovers doesn't work. Now stuck with a freezer full of thawing beef she must return to Foley for help, but even though Foley offers to store the contraband, Andy won't allow it and instead buys a brand-new freezer.

Episode #121, "Divorce Mountain Style"
Original broadcast: March 30, 1964
The Darlings return to arrange a mountain divorce for daughter Charlene. Andy gets involved and gets tagged to be the next husband. He decides to fight fire with fire when Barney discovers a way to curse the proposed union in a book on mountain folklore and superstition.

Facts Known by Few:
The idea of the book on folklore came from an actual book used by Aaron Ruben and several of his writers entitled *North Carolina Folklore, Popular Beliefs, and Superstitions,* published by the Duke University Press.

Episode #122, "A Deal Is a Deal"
Original broadcast: April 6, 1964
Opie and his pals get suckered into selling useless salve in order to win a pony. When one of the boys gives up and sends his salve back, he gets a letter from the Miracle Salve Company advising that he has been blacklisted. Barney and Gomer head to Mount Pilot to "fight fire with fire." Disguised as Dr. Pendyke, D.V.M., Barney fools the two Miracle Salve cons into buying all their salve back by convincing them it is a miracle cure for the mange. The

plan backfires when a truckload of it arrives at the Taylors' front door addressed to Opie Taylor, Sr., the name Gomer used as his alias.

Episode #123, "The Fun Girls"
Original broadcast: April 13, 1964

Andy and Barney are forced to work late doing inventory and end up saddled with "The Fun Girls" from Mount Pilot—Skippy (Joyce Jameson) and Daphne (Jean Carson). They end up in hot water when they are caught by Helen and Thelma Lou, who drop by for an unannounced visit. Now with no dates for the big dance, Barney decides they will take Skippy and Daphne, who dump our heroes for Gomer and his cousin Goober.

Facts Known by Few:

This was the only episode of the show in which Gomer and Goober appeared together. They would appear together again in the TV movie *Return to Mayberry.*

Episode #124, "The Return of Malcolm Merriweather"
Original broadcast: April 20, 1964

Bernard Fox reprises his role of Malcolm Merriweather when he passes through Mayberry and is enlisted to help at the Taylor house in order to give Aunt Bee a break from her regular workload. The plan backfires when Aunt Bee, feeling useless with nothing to do, becomes listless and takes to bed sick. Malcolm realizes what has happened and gets himself fired by pretending to be drunk on cooking sherry.

Episode #125, "The Rumor"
Original broadcast: April 27, 1964

Barney starts a rumor that Andy and Helen are about to be married when he spots Andy sneaking a kiss in the jewelry store where Helen is shopping for a gift for her niece. "Tight Lips" Barney Fife proceeds to alert the entire town, and Aunt Bee decides to redecorate Andy's room—to make it more appropriate for a bride. When Andy and Helen are brought by the house for the surprise, they surprise everyone with the truth. Barney is the goat again, but Andy quells the crowd by telling them he'll pay them all back and give Bee the room she has always wanted.

Facts Known by Few:

Appearing as an extra at the party is Ron Howard's father, Rance.

Episode #126, "Barney and Thelma Lou, Phfft!"

Original broadcast: May 4, 1964

Gomer drops the big bomb on Barney and Thel's romance when, giving her a ride to Mount Pilot, he slips and repeats something Barney said about having Thelma Lou wrapped around his little finger. Thel turns the tables and starts flirting with Gomer to make Barney jealous. Barney becomes fighting mad, but matters get worse when Thel slips and kisses Gomer on the cheek, which to Gomer is tantamount to a proposal. Andy finally steps in and clears the whole mess up by getting Barney to apologize and Thel to take the kiss back.

Episode #127, "Back to Nature"

Original broadcast: May 11, 1964

Andy takes Opie and his gang on a camping trip. Barney, who tells the boys he's a regular pioneer when it comes to the wilderness, manages to get lost in the woods with Gomer. Andy finds them and manages to trick Barney into finding his way back to camp, where he tells the tale of how he managed to ensnare, clean, and cook a wild pheasant.

SEASON 5, 32 EPISODES

Episode #128, "Barney's Bloodhound"

Original broadcast: October 26, 1964

Barney's latest addition to the force is Blue, a stray dog he attempts to train as a crime-fighting bloodhound. The whole scheme backfires when Barney leads Blue to a criminal and the dog likes the lawbreaker better than the law enforcer. Blue comes through eventually, but only by accident. Blue hates the sound of the dog whistle, so Andy tricks the convict into blowing it and Blue attacks the escapee. Andy and Barney are able to nab their man.

Facts Known by Few:

Howard Morris, who directed this episode, said of Blue: "He was one of the best actors I've ever worked with. He was so developed, very polished, and a wonderful dog. He's long dead now, I guess."

Morris made his directing debut with this episode. He also served as the voice of Leonard Blush, broadcasting from Radio WMPD, "The Voice of Mount Pilot."

Episode #129, "Family Visit"
Original broadcast: October 5, 1964

Aunt Bee invites her sister Nora (Maudie Prickett) and brother-in-law Ollie (James Westerfield) for a visit. They show up with their rotten kids, and Andy tries his best to act pleasantly. Ollie pushes Andy to the limit when, after keeping him awake all night, he insults a citizen and then takes the squad car fishing. Ollie hears a report of an escaped convict on the loose and then brags that he would like to get his hands on the crooks. Andy plots to call his bluff. Andy phones Ollie from the courthouse and tells him the criminal has been spotted near Mayberry. Andy says that he will pick up Ollie and take him on the manhunt. Within seconds, Ollie, Nora, and the kids are packed and gone.

Episode #130, "Aunt Bee's Romance"
Original broadcast: October 19, 1964

Aunt Bee gets a letter from her old beau, Roger Hanover (Wallace Ford), who informs her he will be passing through Mayberry and plans on paying her a visit. Bee is excited, but Andy and Opie soon become annoyed at Roger's bad jokes and gags. The real reason for Roger's visit is revealed when Roger hints to Andy that if he doesn't fork up over $400, he just might have himself a new uncle. Andy calls his bluff, and Roger backs off, packs his bags, and hits the road.

Facts Known by Few:

This show contains the memorable scene in which Andy and Floyd discuss the weather. A debate rages over who said, "Everyone talks about the weather, but no one does anything about it." Andy claims it was Mark Twain, but Floyd is convinced it was Calvin Coolidge.

Episode #131, "Barney's Physical"
Original broadcast: September 28, 1964

On Barney's fifth anniversary with the sheriff's department, Andy learns that Barney's job is in jeopardy when the state passes new height and weight requirements. Andy breaks the news to Barney, who loses his temper and decides to quit. Andy doesn't give in so fast. He gets Bee to fatten him up and uses a harness Asa was given by Doc Harvey to stretch him to meet the new standards. The stretch works, but Barney gets a severe case of the hiccups and can't eat a bite. Just when all looks lost, Andy gets the idea to add weight a different way—by giving Barney what looks like a log chain for his ID tag.

Facts Known by Few:
According to this episode:

• Barney joined the sheriff's office on May 16, 1959.

• Barney met Thelma Lou in 1960 at Wilton Blair's funeral.

Aaron Ruben, upon departing "The Andy Griffith Show," received a plaque that recalled this episode. Barney's watch had an engraving of "5" on it because, as Floyd said, he had been with the department five years. Aaron Ruben's plaque had a "5" on it, too.

This was the first episode written by Bob Ross, who later assumed producer duties from Aaron Ruben.

Episode #132, "Opie Loves Helen"

Original broadcast: September 21, 1964

When Opie's school dance partner doesn't show for class, Opie is paired with Miss Crump, who unknowingly waltzes her way into Opie's heart. Andy and Barney realize Opie has a crush when he tells them he wants to spend his entire savings of 74 cents on a gift. Only later do they discover exactly which girl has captured Opie's fancy. Barney discovers that Helen is the lucky gal while relaying a love poem to Opie for his sweetheart. Andy has a man-to-man chat with Opie, telling him that he's messing with his woman. Opie understands perfectly and backs off.

Episode #133, "The Education of Ernest T. Bass"

Original broadcast: October 12, 1964

Ernest T. is back in Mayberry to get his diploma. He is so determined that Andy convinces Helen to allow him to attend class. E.T. is so out of control, she has to slap him across the knuckles to get his attention. Helen's discipline causes Ernest T. to fall in love with Andy's girl. Exasperated, Andy explains to Ernest T. that he loves Helen because she represents his "motha figer." Once that's all sorted out, Andy manufactures a diploma that Ernest T. receives in a touching graduation ceremony.

Facts Known by Few:

After years of talking, Ernest T. Bass finally got his gold tooth. It didn't come from a dentist but from a sign painter. The tooth was gold leaf and only cost $1. You can't beat that.

Episode #134, "Man in the Middle"
Original broadcast: November 2, 1964

Barney and Thel break up and it appears for good. In an effort to console Barney, Andy gets in hot water when Barney misrepresents his words to Thel. The harder they try to work things out, the worse it gets.

Episode #135, "Barney's Uniform"
Original broadcast: November 11, 1964

On his way back from finding out that Old Man Goss has misplaced his ol' salt and pepper suit, Barney spots Fred Plummer sweeping litter into the street and tickets him. Plummer pays the ticket but vows revenge, threatening to get his money's worth the first time he catches Barney out of uniform. Andy learns of the threat and arranges for Mr. Izamoto (Barney's judo instructor) to dress up in Barney's ol' salt and pepper and teach Plummer a lesson by proxy.

Facts Known by Few:

Foley's Market had a sale on "Lil' Pigs," whole or half for 37 cents.

Episode #136, "Opie's Fortune"
Original broadcast: November 16, 1964

Opie finds a man's purse containing $50 cash. When he tells his pa, Andy puts it away for safekeeping, telling Opie if no one claims it within a certain time, the money is his. Opie's patience is rewarded, and he buys a new fishing pole. When Opie returns to the courthouse to show it off, Barney and Andy are gone, but the owner of the purse finally shows. Opie realizes he must give the money back and leaves to get the money together. Andy misunderstands Opie's intentions and thinks he is trying to keep the money. Andy scolds him but quickly has a change of heart when he realizes that Opie was trying to return the money to its rightful owner.

Episode #137, "Goodbye, Sheriff Taylor"
Original broadcast: November 23, 1964

Andy leaves Barney in charge when he goes to Raleigh to interview for another job. Barney immediately starts searching for new deputies. The only guys who show up are Judd, Goober, and Otis. By the time Andy returns, the whole town has practically been turned upside down. Barney tries to cover it up, but Floyd can't mind his tongue and spills the beans.

Facts Known by Few:

This show contains the memorable scene in which Barney, testing Otis's reflexes, tosses a tomato at him that lands flat against his chest.

This is also the only episode in which Otis appears and is not either drunk or jailed.

Episode #138, "The Pageant"

Original broadcast: November 30, 1964

The town prepares for a performance commemorating the Mayberry Centennial and begins to search for a woman to play the leading role. Aunt Bee thinks she's fit for the part, but when she auditions, she doesn't have the right stuff. Andy is faced with breaking the bad news to her, but he gets himself out of that jam by appealing to Bee's strong sense of responsibility for her family.

Episode #139, "The Darling Baby"

Original broadcast: December 7, 1964

The Darlings return to Mayberry searching for an appropriate husband for Charlene's newborn girl, Andilina. During a social call on the Taylors, Briscoe thinks Opie is the man for the job, so he tries to railroad Andy into a contract of marriage between his son and Briscoe's granddaughter. Andy spooks Briscoe by signing the contract with a pen loaded with disappearing ink. Believing there's witchery in the Taylor bloodline, Briscoe packs up his family and heads back to the hills.

Facts Known by Few:

This was the last script written by the team of Everett Greenbaum and Jim Fritzell, who left to write three films for Don Knotts and then went on to write many episodes of "M*A*S*H."

Andilina's dowry:

Eight-by-ten fixer-upper cottage on the back twenty. Needs roof and some fresh mud on the floor. Comes with cow and two acres of side hill with good, strong boulders.

Episode #140, "Andy and Helen Have Their Day"

Original broadcast: December 14, 1964

When Andy and Helen realize they are so busy they don't have time for each other, Barney decides to give them the gift of a day alone together. Promising to take care of all their chores, Barney sends them for a Saturday picnic at Myers Lake. It goes very well—for the first two minutes. Then Barney shows up with the first of many problems. Andy eventually gets hauled away by a game warden for fishing without a license. Andy calls Barney to ask him to bring money to a neighboring town's justice of the peace to pay the fine. Barney, of course, misunderstands the message and thinks Andy and Helen are about to tie the knot.

Facts Known by Few:

Howard Morris directed this episode and appeared as George, the TV repairman.

Episode #141, "Otis Sues the County"

Original broadcast: November 23, 1964

Otis falls while leaving the cell, and a lawyer is able to convince him to sue the county for damages. The whole matter ends when Otis remembers that the whole thing happened because he tripped over his own suit coat.

Facts Known by Few:

In this show, filmed following Howard McNear's recovering from a stroke, sound-effect footsteps are used to cover Floyd's entrance into the courthouse.

Episode #142, "Three Wishes for Opie"

Original broadcast: December 2, 1964

Barney gets Andy in trouble with Helen when he summons the two-hundred-year-old spirit of Count Iz Van Tileckie from a kit he bought at an auction and then spreads the rumor that the two are about to be married.

Episode #143, "Barney Fife, Realtor"

Original broadcast: January 4, 1965

Barney decides to moonlight by selling real estate, but his career is derailed after a huge four-way deal is foiled by the honesty of children.

Episode #144, "Goober Takes a Car Apart"

Original broadcast: January 11, 1965

Goober promises to mind the phone while Andy is away, but he gets tied up working on Gilly Walker's car. When both Andy and Gilly (Larry Hovis) demand he live up to his promises, Goober decides to kill two birds with one stone by taking Gilly's car apart, reassembling it in the sheriff's office, and working on it there. Andy returns just in time for the test run and blows his stack. Before Goober can get the car outside again, some state patrolmen show up and mistake Goober's project for a clever car safety exhibit.

Episode #145, "The Rehabilitation of Otis"

Original broadcast: January 18, 1965

Barney decides to reform Otis and ends up running him out of Mayberry to do his drinking in Mount Pilot. The lawmen miss Otis so much they take a trip to the neighboring jail to beg him to come home.

Facts Known by Few:

Barney, way ahead of everybody when it comes to psychology, identified the "child within" syndrome in this episode, commenting that he could hear "the child within Otis crying out for help: 'Help me! Help me!' "

Episode #146, "The Lucky Letter"

Original broadcast: January 25, 1965

Barney receives a chain letter, and even though he insists he is not superstitious—just cautious—Andy shames him into tossing the letter in the trash. As soon as he does so, Barney is caught in a run of bad luck. With the police officers' pistol qualification upcoming, Andy realizes Barney has psyched himself out and needs help. Andy illustrates the ridiculous nature of the situation by bringing in Goober with another copy of the letter. Barney gets the point: Only a boob like Goober would believe in a chain letter. Andy brings a little insurance to the qualification in the form of Thelma Lou. That's all the luck Barney needs. With his woman there to impress, Barney fires a perfect score.

Facts Known by Few:

Barney received his letter from Floyd, who also sent one to Goober. Goober sent them to Gomer and his Aunt Floy.

Episode #147, "Goober and the Art of Love"

Original broadcast: February 1, 1965

Andy and Barney tire of Goober being the fifth wheel on their dates and try to fix him up with a girl of his own. They fix him up with Thel's cousin Lydia Crosswaithe (Josie Lloyd). Barney gives Goober a lesson in romance by eavesdropping on Andy while he is having a romantic evening at Helen's. In the end, Goober gets a girl and Andy and Barney have not one but two people to tag along on their evenings out.

Facts Known by Few:
Lydia Crosswaithe's house number, in case you want to drop by, is 598.

Episode #148, "Barney Runs for Sheriff"
Original broadcast: February 8, 1965

When he gets a job offer that would take him away to South America, Andy convinces Barney to run for sheriff. The offer falls through, but the election goes on. Turning ugly, Barney challenges Andy to a debate and accuses him of malfeasance. The examples he cites are typical Taylor oversights, such as allowing jaywalking, failing to have emergency equipment such as tear gas and submachine guns, and refusing to carry a sidearm. Andy readily admits he is guilty, but Barney backs off, endorsing Andy as the man for the job.

Episode #149, "If I Had a Quarter Million Dollars"
Original broadcast: February 15, 1965

While chasing off a hobo, Barney stumbles over a briefcase loaded with $250,000 in cash. When he and Andy find the money is from a bank robbery, Barney goes undercover to catch the thief. Barney openly flashes money around town as a lure for the crook. Unfortunately, the crook tricks Barney into believing he is an FBI agent on the same case and manages to get the money back during a stakeout. Andy arrives in time with the real federal agent and captures the criminal.

Episode #150, "TV or Not TV"
Original broadcast: March 1, 1965

An article on Andy entitled "Sheriff Without a Gun" appears in *Law and Order* magazine, drawing attention from an alleged Hollywood movie company. The movie company is just a front for a gang of robbers who want to pull a heist. The gang is caught in the act when Andy shows up at a "rehearsal" of a bank robbery. Andy doesn't fall for the scheme and hauls them to jail.

Facts Known by Few:
Some of the names Barney calls his gun: Old Roscoe, Old Persuader, and Old Blue Steel Baby.

Episode #151, "Guest in the House"

Original broadcast: March 8, 1965

Gloria (Jan Shutan), the daughter of a close friend of Aunt Bee's, pays the Taylors a visit after having a bad experience with her boyfriend back home. When she arrives, Andy is shocked at how attractive Gloria is, which makes Helen jealous. The matter is resolved when Gloria's beau comes to fetch her.

Facts Known by Few:

Another kinky moment in Mayberry history: Gloria plays "I'm the secretary and you're the boss" with Andy.

Episode #152, "The Case of the Punch in the Nose"

Original broadcast: March 15, 1965

Barney reopens an old case that involved Charley Foley (Frank Ferguson) charging Floyd with assault. The incident happened so long ago that nobody recalls how the whole thing began. Barney manages to refresh everyone's memory by staging a reenactment that is so close to the actual event it starts another frenzy of nose punching. Andy gets all those involved to talk out their problems, and it works. Barney discovers that the papers on the case still aren't officially closed, and he goes to the barbershop. He returns with a bloody nose.

Facts Known by Few:

Who threw punches?

Floyd punched Charley Foley.

Charley Foley punched Goober.

Otis punched Floyd. (Otis and Foley were kin.)

Goober punched Gilly Walker.

Opie punched Johnnie Paul Jason, Foley's nephew.

Lamar Tuttle, Floyd's cousin, punched Otis.

Betty Ann was punched by . . . someone. We don't know who.

And finally Barney was punched by Floyd or Foley.

The original case was handled nineteen years ago by Sheriff Poindexter.

Episode #153, "Opie's Newspaper"

Original broadcast: March 22, 1965

Opie takes his cue from the adults and spices up a penny newspaper he and his friend Howie publish with gossip he's overheard. When Barney and the

Taylors get a look at the new issue, they have to scramble to collect the copies before they are read by the rest of the town.

Facts Known by Few:

Barney once wrote a sports column in the Central High School paper called "Pick-ups and Splashes from Floor and Pool." Actually, the column ran just once. According to Barney, it was killed for being too controversial.

Episode #154, "Aunt Bee's Invisible Beau"

Original broadcast: March 29, 1965

Convinced Andy is worried about her, Aunt Bee fabricates a story linking herself romantically with Orville Hendricks (Woodrow Chamblis), the egg man. Barney learns that Orville, a regular "Chicken Coop Casanova," is married. Andy goes to talk to Orville, who is shocked by the accusation. Bee admits the reason for her transgression, and Andy shows her that she is loved at home.

Facts Known by Few:

In the second half of this episode Andy is seated on the sofa reading a newspaper. The paper is an actual copy of Griffith's hometown journal from Mount Airy, North Carolina.

Episode #155, "The Arrest of the Fun Girls"

Original broadcast: April 5, 1965

Skippy and Daphne pay a return visit to Mayberry and get themselves pulled in intentionally for speeding and reckless driving. Andy and Barney try to get them out of town quietly so that Helen and Thelma Lou don't see them. Nothing about these ladies is quiet, and the boys barely escape with their hides. All returns to normal.

Facts Known by Few:

Morelli's Monday-night special: creamed chicken. It's not bad if you like your main dish concealed in a heavy sauce.

Episode #156, "The Luck of Newton Monroe"

Original broadcast: April 12, 1965

Andy runs in Newton Monroe (Don Rickles), a traveling salesman, for operating a shop from the trunk of his car. When he realizes Monroe is a man down on himself and his luck, Andy tries to build his self-esteem. Monroe makes a mess of every job Andy gives him. Andy sees the horrible job he has done painting Andy's front porch, so Andy repaints it himself but convinces Monroe it was his handiwork. Monroe realizes that he's not inept—he's "ept." Monroe gives up being a traveling salesman to become a painter.

Episode #157, "Opie Flunks Arithmetic"

Original broadcast: April 19, 1965

When Opie does poorly in math, Andy overreacts and lords it over his son with an iron hand. Helen finally advises Andy that all work and no play is not the solution. Andy allows Opie to relax, enjoy himself, and be the best he can be.

Episode #158, "Opie and the Carnival"

Original broadcast: April 26, 1965

The carnival comes to town and takes Opie for a ride. Opie blows the money he saved for Andy's birthday present trying to win an electric razor in the carnival's sharpshooting game. The game is rigged, however. Andy finds out and sets out to do some fixing of his own. Andy cleans the shelves of prizes and then flashes his badge. He advises the pair of hucksters that when Opie comes to try again, he better walk away with a razor. Opie does win the razor, on his own.

Facts Known by Few:

Andy's prizes: two toasters, an ashtray, a carved figurine, an electric coffee percolator, an electric can opener, and a genuine ceramic cat from the Orient.

Lewis Charles and Billy Halop, playing the roles of Pete and Charlie, the two crooked hucksters, played crooks in Episode #95, "The Big House."

Halop was also known for his role in "The Dead End Kids" films of the 1930s and 1940s.

Episode #159, "Banjo-playing Deputy"

Original broadcast: May 3, 1965

Andy, struggling to find work for Jerry Miller (Jerry Van Dyke), a one-man band who has lost his job with a traveling carnival, hires him as a part-time deputy. After realizing he's too incompetent to fill Barney's shoes, he decides to let him go. Before he can give Jerry the bad news, the musician-turned-lawman busts some of his former pals who were responsible for a string of purse snatchings.

SEASON 6, 30 EPISODES

Episode #160, "Aunt Bee, the Swinger"
Original broadcast: October 4, 1965

U.S. Congressman John Canfield (Charlie Ruggles) retires to live in Mayberry and takes an interest in Aunt Bee. The two go on a date and immediately begin behaving as if they both just bathed in the fountain of youth. The spring in their steps soon gets sprung when they both realize each has been trying to impress the other by pretending to be full of youthful pep.

Facts Known by Few:

From the *Mayberry Gazette* column "Little Known Facts Known by Few": "If you eat too much polar bear liver, it'll kill you."

Episode #161, "Opie's Job"
Original broadcast: September 13, 1965

Opie competes with Billy Crenshaw (John Bangert) for a job as box boy at Foley's Market and, after a weeklong trial, wins the position. Opie learns Billy wanted the job to help pay family medical bills, so he cleverly gets himself fired by telling Foley he'd rather be playing baseball. When Andy finds out secondhand that Opie didn't want to work he scolds him and then, hearing his explanation, realizes his son has become a man.

Facts Known by Few:

The market job paid 75 cents an hour ... small potatoes for a guy like Goober, who was earning a wage of $1.50.

This was the premiere show of the 1965–66 fall season.

Episode #162, "The Bazaar"
Original broadcast: October 11, 1965

Jack Burns debuts as Deputy Warren Ferguson and doesn't waste any time getting himself in a jam when he arrests eleven bingo-playing church ladies for gambling. Andy urges him to drop the charges, but Warren will not budge until Andy makes his point by tricking Warren into a bet. Once Warren bites, Andy nabs him for the same offense, and Warren, in turn, comes around to Andy's way of thinking.

Facts Known by Few:

Jack Burns used a variation of "Nip it in the bud" in this episode. Warren was part of "The Andy Griffith Show" for this season, as a transition from Barney. Aneta Corsaut believed one reason why Warren never worked was the writers may have subconsciously still been writing for Don Knotts: "There was something about Jack that didn't translate well to this show. The urban edge that worked so well when he was teamed with Avery Schreiber didn't work the same way on this show. When you look back at the shows he did, I think you'll see that he was funny, but again, it was a problem of fitting into the chemistry of the show."

Episode #163, "Andy's Rival"

Original broadcast: September 20, 1965

Helen is visited by Frank Smith (Charles Aidman), a handsome teacher who proves to be a Renaissance man. Even though Smith is there only on scholastic business, Andy becomes jealous. Helen soon is so busy working on a project with Smith that she has to break dates with Andy, who loses his temper and confronts her. Helen tells Andy that she, too, has a career and sometimes must work hard to get ahead. Seems that Andy learned something from the teacher.

Facts Known by Few:

Things Frank knows about: History, architecture, throwing a curveball, classical guitar, and botany.

Things Andy knows about: How to make a wonderful fruit punch and how to play the guitar with feeling.

Frank also knew a pretty good trick he didn't mention: making a guitar pick magically disappear on close-ups of the guitar.

Helen's house number: 895.

Episode #164, "Malcolm at the Crossroads"

Original broadcast: September 27, 1965

Bernard Fox makes his third and final appearance as Malcolm Merriweather when he takes the job of crossing guard from Ernest T. Bass, also in his final appearance. E.T. vows revenge and challenges Malcolm to a fight. Knowing Malcolm won't stand a chance, Goober tries to teach him how to fight. Just when it looks like curtains, Andy tricks Ernest T. by mentioning Malcolm is part Irish, and Ernest T., part Irish himself, takes his new friend to his bosom, patching up the whole mess.

Facts Known by Few:
The price of Ernest T.'s planned honeymoon: $12. Tents cost money.

Episode #165, "Aunt Bee on TV"
Original broadcast: November 15, 1965

Aunt Bee wins many great prizes on the game show "Win or Lose," but loses her friends when she can't stop talking about all the wonderful new things she owns. The whole matter is settled when an agent from the IRS arrives looking for his cut of the booty. Bee then has to give up the prizes and, realizing how she has annoyed her friends, makes up with them.

Facts Known by Few:
The Taylors' chauffeur was named John. (That was his stage name. His real name was Bob.)

Episode #166, "Off to Hollywood"
Original broadcast: October 25, 1965

Andy receives a $1,000 check from the Belmont Film Studio for the rights to his story, "Sheriff Without a Gun." After entertaining all the things they could do with the money, Andy is talked into taking the family to Hollywood to see the filming.

Facts Known by Few:
Movie stars mentioned: John Wayne, Elvis Presley, and Fabian.

Episode #167, "The Taylors in Hollywood"
Original broadcast: November 1, 1965

The Taylors get their first taste of Hollywood when they arrive to see the filming of *Sheriff Without a Gun* but are unhappy with the way they are portrayed in the Hollywood version of Andy's story. Aunt Bee is especially annoyed until she sees her role is being played by a young, attractive blonde.

Facts Known by Few:
The studio gate shown in this episode was the same gate used in Episode #107, "Gomer Pyle, U.S.M.C."

Yes, that's Gavin MacLeod as Bryan Bender, Hollywood's version of Andy Taylor.

Episode #168, "The Hollywood Party"

Original broadcast: November 8, 1965

Helen becomes jealous of Andy's relationship with *Sheriff Without a Gun* starlet Darlene Mason (Ruta Lee) when she sees publicity photos of the two in Mason's dressing room.

Facts Known by Few:

It seems every time Andy goes out to dinner in a big city someone tries to get him to eat a snail. The third time must have been the charm because, after three invitations in six years, Andy accepts and tries one. He didn't like it.

Episode #169, "A Warning from Warren"

Original broadcast: October 15, 1965

Warren believes he has psychic powers that warn him of impending danger. He tries to stop Andy and Helen from going on a picnic, but the couple ignore Warren's warning. Warren refuses to give up and makes his own prophecy come true by dumping Andy and Helen in the drink when he overturns their rowboat.

Episode #170, "A Man's Best Friend"

Original broadcast: November 29, 1965

Opie and his friend Tommy (Michael Petit) play a trick on Goober by placing a tiny transmitter under the collar of Goober's dog Spot. The boys trick Goober into thinking that Spot talks, and Goober wastes no time making a fool of himself. When Andy explains to Goober what the boys have done, the two adults teach the kids a lesson with a dose of their own medicine.

Facts Known by Few:

Spot, named so by Goober because he had no spots, was the same dog named Blue from Episode #128, "Barney's Bloodhound."

Though it went unexplained, Wally's had changed from "Acme" brand gasoline to "Premium."

Episode #171, "Aunt Bee Takes a Job"

Original broadcast: December 6, 1965

Aunt Bee takes part-time work as the receptionist for a new print shop in Mayberry that Andy discovers is a front for counterfeiters. Andy busts the two cons just before they flee town, and Bee returns to the Taylor household to once again keep her house in order.

Episode #172, "The Cannon"

Original broadcast: November 22, 1965

It's Founder's Day again, and this time Mayberry plays host to a mobile museum that becomes the target of thieves. Just as the crooks are about to make their getaway, their escape is thwarted by Warren when he manages to get the old ornamental cannon working and blast the crooks' station wagon.

Episode #173, "Girl-shy"

Original broadcast: December 20, 1965

Warren turns out to be a sleepwalker because, after starting to snooze during an "International Secret Agent F-45" film on TV, he turns into an aggressive womanizer. The object of his affections happens to be Helen. Andy, unable to figure out what is going on, is forced to fire Warren, but hires him back when he realizes what has happened.

Episode #174, "The Church Organ"

Original broadcast: December 13, 1965

Clara pleads for a new organ for the church, and Andy gets the locals to pledge money to buy one from a local farmer. The only problem is that nobody honors his or her pledge. Just when buying the organ appears hopeless, Clara plays a seductive song for the widower who is selling it and the man decides to donate it to the church.

Facts Known by Few:

Farmer Harlan Robinson (Woodrow Chamblis) was the same egg man with whom Bee had her imaginary romance in Episode #154, "Aunt Bee's Invisible Beau."

Episode #175, "Otis, the Artist"

Original broadcast: January 3, 1966

Warren takes a try at reforming Otis by getting him interested in mosaic art. Otis gives it a try, but his work turns out to be as bad as his former habit. He finally does do a nice mosaic, but only after priming the pump with liquor.

Episode #176, "The Return of Barney Fife"

Original broadcast: January 10, 1966

Barney pays a return visit from his palatial suite at the Raleigh YMCA to attend his high school class reunion. This time, the talk of romance centers on him and Thelma Lou. Barney, however, is crushed to learn that she's now married. Trying to drown his sorrows in the fruit punch, Barney finally rallies back after he meets another classmate who professes an admiration for the former Mayberry lawman.

Facts Known by Few:
Barney was bringing in 95 "big ones" a week in his new job as Detective . . . $125 on Christmas.

Episode #177, "The Legend of Barney Fife"
Original broadcast: January 17, 1966
Barney returns to Mayberry and gets a big ego boost when he learns he is the idol of his replacement, Warren. Barney gets as much mileage out of his legendary feats as possible before the news breaks that an escaped convict is headed to Mayberry. Warren naturally thinks Barney will want to join them on the hunt, so Barney has no choice but to go. Andy steps in and makes Barney appear to be the hero—saving Barney's pride and Warren's fantasy.

Episode #178, "Lost and Found"
Original broadcast: January 24, 1966
Bee files a claim to collect insurance for the loss of a rare piece of jewelry. After getting the money, she spends it, then finds the missing piece.

Facts Known by Few:
The insurance agent was played by Jack Dodson, who would return to the show as a regular, playing Howard Sprague.

Episode #179, "Wyatt Earp"
Original broadcast: January 31, 1966
A traveling huckster (Pat Hingle) passes through Mayberry with a man he claims to be Clarence Earp, the grandnephew of Wyatt Earp. Clarence puts on a show, living up to his name by bullying everyone in his path. Then, when Andy realizes Opie is impressed with the showman's belief that "a man who can fight is a man who is right," steps in and offends Clarence, who challenges him to a duel. Andy wins by choosing a book as his weapon, proving Clarence is an impostor by checking the Earp family tree.

Episode #180, "Aunt Bee Learns to Drive"
Original broadcast: February 7, 1966
Aunt Bee becomes "Miss Independent Wheels" when she buys a car

from Goober and then must learn to drive. She breaks her promise to Andy not to drive on her learner's permit without a licensed driver accompanying her and backs into a tree. Lightning strikes twice when Andy comes home and accidentally backs into Bee's car, causing him to think he's the one who dented it.

Episode #181, "Look, Pa, I'm Dancing"
Original broadcast: February 14, 1966

An upcoming school dance has Opie worried he will make a fool of himself by dancing. Andy and Helen bring him around when the two of them get up and dance themselves. Opie figures he couldn't do any worse, so he asks a girl to dance.

Episode #182, "Eat Your Heart Out"
Original broadcast: February 28, 1966

Andy finds himself stuck in the middle between Goober and Flora (Alberta Nelson), the new waitress at the diner. When Flora takes more of a liking to Andy than Goober, Andy must find a way to put her off his scent and onto Goober's.

Episode #183, "The Gypsies"
Original broadcast: February 21, 1966

Andy runs a band of gypsies out of Mayberry, and in return they curse the town with a drought. When the curse comes true, the whole town starts to believe them. It turns out, however, that the gypsies' magic powers are only in being able to operate a shortwave radio that gives them a jump on the weather conditions.

Facts Known by Few:

Sylvio the gypsy is played by Jamie Farr, who went on to play Klinger in "M*A*S*H."

Episode #184, "A Baby in the House"
Original broadcast: March 7, 1966

Aunt Bee is asked to baby-sit for relatives while they go away for the weekend. Bee gets upset when each time she picks up the infant it starts to cry. The baby cries because Bee is nervous when she picks it up. After a while, Bee is worried that the baby is sick, so she forgets to be nervous, holds the baby, and it does not cry.

Episode #185, "The County Clerk"

Original broadcast: March 14, 1966

Jack Dodson makes his debut as the mild-mannered county clerk, Howard Sprague. In this episode, Howard, with the help of Andy and Helen, makes his first attempt to get out from under his mother's thumb. She doesn't give in easily, faking sickness when she learns he plans to go out on a date.

Episode #186, "Goober's Replacement"

Original broadcast: March 28, 1966

Goober's girlfriend Flora Mallerby (Alberta Nelson) offers to fill in for Goober at the filling station while Goober goes on a fishing trip. When Wally realizes that Flora can bring in the customers with her feminine charms, Goober returns to find he's out of a job. Andy intercedes, talks some sense into Flora and Wally, and Goober gets reinstated as Mayberry's top pump boy.

Episode #187, "The Foster Lady"

Original broadcast: March 21, 1966

Because of her natural, honest way, Bee is hired to represent Foster Furniture Polish in its new television advertising campaign. When the commercial is shot, Bee is so nervous in front of the camera she comes off completely false. The ad is canceled, and Bee returns to her normal life at home.

Facts Known by Few:

The crew shooting the commercial contained several members of the actual show's crew.

Episode #188, "The Battle of Mayberry"

Original broadcast: April 4, 1966

Opie gets himself in hot water when he enters an essay contest by writing a paper on the historic Battle of Mayberry, a famous fight between the settlers and the Indians that established the town of Mayberry. After interviewing many descendants of the people involved, Opie learns that the battle was nothing more than a misunderstanding caused by too much liquor. The only casualties were one scrawny cow, three deer, and one mule that was mistaken for a deer.

Episode #189, "A Singer in Town"

Original broadcast: April 11, 1966

Fictional pop singing star Keevy Hazelton (Jesse Peason) stops for a fishing vacation and ends up doing a cover of a song written by Bee and Clara on his weekly television show. Visiting the set, the two senior songwriters are upset at what Keevy has done to their song, and when they protest, Keevy performs it as they intended. The lines light up at the studio, and the song is a big hit.

Facts Known by Few:

The words and music to "My Hometown" were written by "Andy Griffith Show" musical director Earle Hagen.

Keevy was either the first known "air" guitarist or the worst person to ever pretend he was playing guitar on TV. If his hands even made it near the strings of the guitar, it was surely by accident.

SEASON 7, 30 EPISODES

Episode #190, "Opie's Girlfriend"
Original broadcast: September 12, 1966

Opie is asked to entertain Helen's visiting niece Cynthia (Mary Ann Durkin), who is athletically superior in every way to Opie. Opie takes a licking in football, then ends up with a black eye after starting a fight. Surprisingly, Helen suggests that Cynthia pretend to be impressed with Opie's machismo. Cynthia even throws a bowling match so that Opie can regain his male pride.

Episode #191, "The Barbershop Quartet"
Original broadcast: September 26, 1966

Howard gets laryngitis right before the big Mount Pilot Sheriff's Annual Barbershop Quartet Sing-off. Desperate for a tenor, Andy discovers that Jeff Nelson (Hamilton Camp), his current prisoner, may be the most gifted singer to come to Mayberry since Gomer left town. Andy decides to take a chance on his prisoner, who has a rabbit's urge to run. Andy regrets his decision when the prisoner escapes through the backstage bathroom window. He returns, however, after meeting a hobo who praises Sheriff Taylor, and Andy's quartet wins over rival Sheriff Wilson.

Episode #192, "The Lodge"
Original broadcast: September 19, 1966

Andy puts Howard up for membership in the Regal Order of the Golden

Door to Good Fellowship, a private Mayberry men's club. When the members vote, Goober blackballs him, thinking he is doing Howard a favor. As it turns out, Goober was told by Howard's domineering mother that Howard's father came to a ruinous end because of a weakness he had for card playing. When Goober learns that Howard's mother was lying, the club votes again and Howard is elected unanimously.

Episode #193, "The Darling Fortune"
Original broadcast: October 17, 1966

The Darlings pay their final visit to Mayberry. They are carrying $300 each and are looking for brides for the boys. They cannot find a suitable female and are just about to head back for the hills when they see the "omen of the owl," a sign that means the next female they see will steal their hearts away. Moments later, Helen shows up, and Andy has to convince the Darlings that Helen is not for them.

Facts Known by Few:
The Darling boys were finally named.

On guitar: Rodney
On mandolin: Dean
On the bass: Mitch
On banjo: Doug

Episode #194, "Aunt Bee's Crowning Glory"
Original broadcast: October 10, 1966

Aunt Bee is the talk of Mayberry when she buys a blond wig and becomes the sudden object of the new minister's attentions. Bee is then faced with the dilemma of letting the minister know that she is not as she appears. She removes the wig permanently when she realizes that everyone loves her for herself, not for her hair.

Episode #195, "The Ball Game"
Original broadcast: October 3, 1966

When Early Gilly takes ill, Andy takes over as umpire for the big Mayberry Little League game against Mount Pilot. The game is decided by a call at the plate when Opie slides into home and is called out by his father. The crowd erupts, and Andy gets an earful from town critics, who believe it was a bad

Aneta Corsaut

Frances Bavier and Aneta Corsaut on the set of "The Ball Game."

call. He's forgiven when Howard's column in the *Mayberry Gazette*'s sports page praises him for doing his best and for sticking by his decision. Helen has a snapshot of the play at the plate that shows Opie was indeed safe. She shows the photo to Aunt Bee and then rips it up, nipping the whole matter in the bud.

Episode #196, "Goober Makes History"

Original broadcast: December 19, 1966

Goober returns from a hunting trip sporting a beard and becomes convinced he is more intelligent. He grows into such an insufferable bore that no one can stand to be around him. When he realizes this, he shaves off the beard and decides to be himself again.

Episode #197, "The Senior Play"

Original broadcast: November 14, 1966

Helen directs the seniors in a musical revue that is censored by her old-fashioned school principal, who claims the revue is a flagrant display that highlights the problems America is facing with today's youth. Helen does not appreciate the pressure, so she makes her point by revamping the show to feature a 1920s, flapper-style theme. She proves that the youth of today are no different than the youth of yesteryear.

Episode #198, "A Big Fish in a Small Town"
Original broadcast: November 28, 1966

Howard talks his way into going fishing on opening day of the season. He ends up landing the legend of the lake, "Old Sam," a rare silver carp. Much to Howard's surprise, he realizes that by catching the fish he effectively broke the spirit of the town. He retrieves the rare carp from its new home in the state aquarium and returns it to the lake.

Facts Known by Few:
According to Jack Dodson, this was one of his favorite episodes.

Episode #199, "Mind over Matter"
Original broadcast: October 31, 1966

Goober becomes stricken with a psychosomatic case of whiplash and ends up being a pain in Andy's neck when the Taylors allow him to move into Andy's room until he is better. Goober catches Andy trying to trick him into realizing he's fine by trying to get him to raise his arms to catch a football. Goober gets so upset at the attempted trick that he throws his arms in the air, telling Andy he knows he can't raise them that high. Andy gets Goober to see that he can—it's a miracle.

Episode #200, "Politics Begins at Home"
Original broadcast: November 7, 1966

Howard and Aunt Bee square off in a race for town council. Howard, clearly more qualified, gets his due when Bee realizes during a debate that he is the person for the job.

Episode #201, "A New Doctor in Town"
Original broadcast: December 26, 1966

A sporty young doctor, Thomas Peterson (William Christopher), wheels into town and has a difficult time earning Mayberry's respect. When Andy learns Opie needs his tonsils taken out, he faces his own doubts and hands Opie over to the new doctor. Opie returns from surgery alive and well, and the doctor wins acceptance.

Fact Known by Few:

William Christopher later played Father Mulcahy in TV's long-running "M*A*S*H."

Episode #202, "Opie Finds a Baby"

Original broadcast: November 21, 1966

Opie and his friend Arnold (Sheldon Golomb) find an abandoned baby on the steps of the courthouse. They want to save it from the orphanage, so they start searching for a home for it. Andy realizes what's going on just as the baby's parents arrive to reclaim their child.

Facts Known by Few:

The father of the baby is played by Jack Nicholson.

Episode #203, "Only a Rose"

Original broadcast: December 5, 1966

Aunt Bee finally has a rose that she believes will beat even the contest entry of her rival and best friend, Clara Johnson. Her hopes are dashed when Opie hits the rose with a football. Disappointed, she watches Clara win at the flower show. But she gets a surprise when Clara turns the prize over to Bee after seeing a photo of her rose.

Episode #204, "Otis, the Deputy"

Original broadcast: December 12, 1966

When Andy is held hostage by an escaped convict, Howard and Otis come to the rescue. Howard foils Andy's escape and gets both of them captured, leaving their fate in Otis's hands. Even though he is drunk, Otis somehow manages to stumble through to rescue them.

Facts Known by Few:

Otis arrives drunk for the last time.

Episode #205, "Don't Miss a Good Bet"

Original broadcast: January 2, 1967

George Jones (Roger Perry) comes to Mayberry with a get-rich-quick scheme. He lures Goober, Floyd, Helen, and even Aunt Bee as investors in his treasure-hunting scheme. Andy warns them, but even he gets taken in by the wily prospector, who ends up skipping town with all the dough.

Facts Known by Few:
Floyd is named after his uncle on his mother's side of the family.

Episode #206, "Dinner at Eight"
Original broadcast: January 9, 1967
With Aunt Bee off visiting relatives and Opie away on a Scout trip, Andy is home alone. He is ready to spend a relaxing evening when Goober arrives to keep him company. He insists on making his special spaghetti recipe. Andy gives in, eats heartily, and then is reminded by Goober of an invitation to Howard's for dinner. Andy goes to see Howard, who did not actually invite Andy at all. They still whip up some spaghetti and eat, but then Andy realizes dinner was at Helen's. He rushes over, but he is in hot water for being late so he must endure another dinner of spaghetti.

Facts Known by Few:
Opie was a member of Boy Scout Troop 44.

Episode #207, "Andy's Old Girlfriend"
Original broadcast: January 30, 1967
Andy is in trouble when his old girlfriend Alice Harper (Joanna McNeil) returns to Mayberry. Helen becomes jealous, but Andy patches things up by telling her that she is the only woman he loves.

Episode #208, "The Statue"
Original broadcast: February 20, 1967
The Mayberry Civic Improvement Committee entertains ideas on how to spend the $1,200 it has in its treasury. The members decide to erect a statue to the town's greatest benefactor, Seth Taylor, Andy's great-great-grandfather. After the monument is built, Andy learns that Seth was nothing more than a selfish swindler. There is a bright side, however: if it wasn't for Seth's profiteering, Mayberry might have become a busy, crime-ridden place like Mount Pilot.

Facts Known by Few:
Mayberry's population in 1967: 1,800 citizens.

Episode #209, "Aunt Bee's Restaurant"
Original broadcast: February 6, 1967
For an investment of $400, Aunt Bee buys into the local Canton Palace.

After taking in upwards of $80 on opening night, Bee decides to turn her back on prosperity and returns to cook and care only for her family.

Episode #210, "Floyd's Barbershop"
Original broadcast: February 13, 1967

Howard Sprague buys the building that houses Floyd's Barbershop. He passes on the expense of ownership by raising Floyd's rent. After twenty-eight years in the same location, Floyd decides to pack his scissors and move on. When the barbershop crowd ends up loafing around the courthouse, Andy coaxes Floyd and Howard to reach a compromise. Floyd is reinstalled as barber of Mayberry.

Facts Known by Few:

Floyd's rent was raised from $50 to $65 per month. The compromise split the difference and set the rent at $57.50.

Episode #211, "A Visit to Barney Fife"
Original broadcast: January 16, 1967

Andy pays Barney a visit on his new beat in Raleigh and learns that Barney is in danger of losing his job. Andy gives him a boost by solving a string of grocery-store robberies. The gang of crooks turns out to be the family that rents Barney his room. Andy makes certain Barney gets credit for the arrests, which allows him to keep his job.

Episode #212, "Barney Comes to Mayberry"
Original broadcast: January 23, 1967

Barney pays a visit to Mayberry and happens to be on the same train with Teena Andrews, a local girl returning for the premiere of her new Hollywood film. When Teena's publicity man learns she used to date Barney when she was known as the homely Irene Flogg, he arranges for the former deputy to escort her to the premiere. Barney thinks he has sparked a new romance, but learns that Teena is married.

Facts Known by Few:

According to Barney, whether or not to wear a fedora with a tuxedo or to drink red wine were both matters of taste.

Episode #213, "Helen, the Authoress"
Original broadcast: February 27, 1967

Helen sells a children's book that she has written. She takes Andy to visit the Virginia publisher who bought the book. Helen's editor suggests she change her name to Helen Alexian Dubois. Andy becomes jealous when Helen's time is consumed by her writing and work with the editor. He comes to his senses, though, when he realizes he's feeling threatened by Helen's success.

Episode #214, "Goodbye, Dolly"

Original broadcast: March 6, 1967

Opie is asked to care for Dolly, the horse that pulled Walt Simpson's dairy truck. When she refuses to eat, Opie worries that it is his fault. Walt and Opie realize that Dolly is lonely for her old job, so Walt ties her to his new truck and continues to make his rounds with her.

Episode #215, "Opie's Piano Lesson"

Original broadcast: March 13, 1967

Opie talks Andy into letting him take piano lessons. Suddenly, the lessons conflict with football practice. Trying to do both, Opie gets caught when his friend Arnold sits in as a proxy for his half hour on the ivories while Opie quarterbacks the team. The matter is solved when Coach Flip Conroy (Rockne Tarrington) drops by and tells Opie he can do both. To illustrate his point, Conroy, an ex-New York Giant, sits down and plays a classical work on the piano.

Facts Known by Few:

This was the only episode featuring an African-American in a speaking role.

Episode #216, "Howard, the Comedian"

Original broadcast: March 20, 1967

Howard tries his hand at stand-up when he does a set on "Colonel Tim's Talent Time," a local amateur television showcase. He's a big hit, but he hurts his friends by including their names in his act. He is forgiven when the others realize Howard's fame has rubbed off on them—so they supply him with new material.

Facts Known by Few:

A CBS "eye" logo appeared on one of the cameras at the local TV station that broadcast "Colonel Tim's Talent Time."

The "Talent Time" theme was the same as "The Andy Griffith Show" theme.

Episode #217, "Big Brothers"

Original broadcast: March 27, 1967

Howard takes on the responsibility of being the Big Brother to a local teen, but ends up getting duped by the boy when Howard falls for the boy's older sister, Betty. Andy catches Howard at the Mount Pilot dance hall where Betty works, and Howard must admit his foolishness.

Episode #218, "Opie's Most Unforgettable Character"

Original broadcast: April 3, 1967

Andy puffs up with pride when he learns Opie has chosen him as the subject of a school essay on his "Most Unforgettable Character." Arnold selects his own father as the subject of his paper. Both boys receive the same grade—"F." Andy is dismayed, but not nearly as much as when he learns that Opie has written a second paper about Arnold's father that earned an "A." When Andy discovers that Arnold's second paper, which also garnered an "A", was about Andy, he realizes that Opie was too close to him to write anything of interest.

Episode #219, "Goober's Contest"

Original broadcast: April 10, 1967

Ernie Gilly's "Line Up For Loot" promotion causes a drop in business at Goober's gas station. Goober decides to hold his own contest. He makes an error at the printer and accidentally gives away a coupon worth $200. Floyd ends up with the mistaken prize and demands satisfaction. Since Goober can't pay, Andy must jail him for fraud. It is only a ruse, of course, because as soon as Floyd sees what happened, he demands that his friend be released.

Facts Known by Few:

Joe the printer was played by actor-director Rob Reiner.

SEASON 8, 30 EPISODES

Episode #220, "Opie's First Love"

Original broadcast: September 11, 1967

Arnold throws a swinging, "stag or drag" thirteenth birthday party, and

Opie goes from "drag" to "stag" when Mary Alice Carter (Suzanne Cupito) cancels her date with him after accepting the invitation of cool guy Fred Simpson (David Alan Bailey). Opie is dejected and decides not to go, but takes Andy's advice and goes alone with the intention of having the best time ever. Mary Alice, who gets dumped by Fred, sees Opie having fun and apologizes for standing him up.

Facts Known by Few:

The young actor who played the role of Arnold Bailey changed his name between the seventh and eighth seasons from Sheldon Golomb to Sheldon Collins.

Episode #221, "Goober, the Executive"
Original broadcast: December 25, 1967
After working for Wally for eleven and three-quarter years, Goober buys the station and faces the problems that come with ownership. He becomes so worried and preoccupied that he forgets to order gasoline. Taking advice from Opie, he makes up his mind to trust his own judgment and things fall into order.

Facts Known by Few:

The road map in Goober's garage, which can be seen when Opie and Goober have their talk, is actually a map of Southern California turned upside down.

Episode #222, "Howard's Main Event"
Original broadcast: September 16, 1967
Howard falls for Millie Hutchins (Arlene Golonka), the new woman at the bakery. He summons up the courage to ask her out, and he is rewarded with a wonderful evening. A relationship blossoms, and Howard is ecstatic—until he finds out Millie's old boyfriend is none other than Clyde Plaunt (Allan Melvin).

Episode #223, "Aunt Bee, the Juror"
Original broadcast: September 23, 1967
Aunt Bee is called for jury duty and ends up chosen to sit for a case involving a department-store burglary. On the surface it appears to be an open-and-shut case, but the accused, Marvin Jenkins (Jack Nicholson), insists on his innocence. The entire jury, except Aunt Bee, is convinced of Marvin's guilt. In the end, Andy catches the real criminal, who is attending the trial.

Episode #224, "Howard, the Bowler"
Original broadcast: September 18, 1967

Howard is one frame away from bowling a perfect game when the power in the alley fails and the match has to be suspended until the following night. Howard nearly psyches himself out, but returns to bowl three more strikes, recording the first perfect game in the history of Mayberry bowling.

Facts Known by Few:
The odds against someone bowling a perfect game were stated to be 348,000 to 1.

Episode #225, "Opie Steps Up in Class"
Original broadcast: October 9, 1967

Opie makes friends with the son of a wealthy family. When Andy attends a father-son get-together at the family's home, he catches himself doing just what he told Opie not to do: putting on airs.

Facts Known by Few:
According to Aaron Ruben, one problem shooting "The Andy Griffith Show" in California was caused by the presence of palm trees. "We were constantly adjusting camera angles to keep them out of frame," Ruben said. He missed a few in this episode. As Aunt Bee drives up to the Hollanders, several palm trees are seen on the right side of the frame.

Episode #226, "Andy's Trip to Raleigh"
Original broadcast: October 2, 1967

Andy drives to Raleigh to go over a deposition with lawyer Leigh Drake (Whitney Blake), who, he is surprised to find, is a beautiful young lady. Conducting business poolside, Andy gets a terrible sunburn and must make up a lie to cover himself with Helen by telling her he got it changing a flat tire. He is caught in his lie when the lovely attorney shows up in Mayberry.

Episode #227, "A Trip to Mexico"
Original broadcast: September 25, 1967

Aunt Bee wins a trip to Mexico and takes her two closest friends, Clara and Myrtle, with her. By the time they return, the threesome are no longer speaking. Andy gets all three women together to look at the photos from the trip. The good memories outweigh the bad, and the ladies forget their differences and make up.

Episode #228, "Tape Recorder"

Original broadcast: October 20, 1967

Opie and Arnold bug one of the jail cells with a new tape recorder and end up taping information that leads to the whereabouts of money stolen from a bank in Raleigh. When Opie takes the information to his father, Andy refuses to listen, telling Opie it would be a violation of the law. In the end, Andy manages to solve the case on his own without violating anybody's rights.

Episode #229, "Opie's Group"

Original broadcast: November 6, 1967

Opie joins a local rock group as the new guitar player. Before long his grades suffer and Clara, Opie's former piano instructor, speaks to him about his priorities. Clara becomes the band manager in exchange for Opie's promise to pay more attention to schoolwork.

Facts Known by Few:

Andy's suggestion for the band's name: The Young Swingers.

Episode #230, "Aunt Bee and the Lecturer"

Original broadcast: November 13, 1967

Aunt Bee catches the eye of Professor Hubert St. John (Edward Andrews), a visiting lecturer who soon expresses interest in marrying Bee. Bee declines when she realizes that his interest in her is mainly due to the remarkable similarities she possesses to his first wife.

Episode #231, "Andy's Investment"

Original broadcast: November 20, 1967

Andy opens a laundromat to help earn money for Opie's college education. The business soon monopolizes his time, so Andy decides to sell.

Episode #232, "Suppose Andy Gets Sick"

Original broadcast: December 11, 1967

The town is near martial law when the Police Emergency Committee—made up of Goober, Emmett, and Howard—forms after Andy succumbs to the flu and must take several days of bed rest. Goober sets a record, issuing fourteen tickets in one day. When he's not writing tickets, he is bothering Andy. Fed up with the constant annoyance, Andy drags himself out of bed and back to work.

Episode #233, "Howard and Millie"

Original broadcast: November 27, 1967

Howard and Millie decide to tie the knot and ask Andy and Helen to be best man and maid of honor. The four travel to Millie's home in West Virginia for the wedding, but by the time they arrive, the couple have second thoughts and the wedding is off.

Episode #234, "Aunt Bee's Cousin"

Original broadcast: December 4, 1967

Aunt Bee prepares for a visit from her globe-trotting cousin Bradford (Jack Albertson). Andy sees him arrive hobo-style, hopping out of a freight car. Andy tries to protect both Bee's feelings and her pocketbook by convincing Bradford to leave before Bee discovers the truth.

Episode #235, "Howard's New Life"

Original broadcast: December 18, 1967

Howard throws caution to the wind, leaves Mayberry, and moves to a Caribbean paradise. Renting a shack on the beach, he realizes that island life is not for him and returns to rediscover his true pot of gold in his old hometown.

Facts Known by Few:

The voice of the travelogue narrator at the beginning of the show belongs to writer Bill Idelson.

Episode #236, "Emmett's Brother-in-Law"

Original broadcast: January 8, 1968

Dub Taylor plays the role of an obnoxious insurance salesman who tries to help his sister (Mary Lansing) by getting her husband, Emmett, involved in insurance. Emmett tries, but his heart isn't in it. Emmett returns to his true love—his fix-it shop. His wife finds him there late one night, trying to coax an appliance back to life.

Episode #237, "The Mayberry Chef"

Original broadcast: January 1, 1968

Aunt Bee gets her own cooking show on local WZAZ-TV, Channel 12, Silver City. She sees that her outside interests conflict with her first priority—her family—so she gives up the show for her boys.

Episode #238, "The Church Benefactors"

Original broadcast: January 22, 1968

The church members struggle with the choice of how $500 endowed to the church should be spent. The choice comes down to new choir robes or the repair of the church foundation. Just after the Reverend Tucker decides in favor of spending the money on repairs, Howard comes in with a compromise that allows for both.

Episode #239, "Opie's Drugstore Job"

Original broadcast: January 15, 1968

Opie takes a job at the drugstore to earn money to buy a new electric guitar. The model of responsibility, Opie is left alone to watch the store and accidentally breaks a display bottle of expensive perfume. Afraid he's let down his boss, Mr. Crawford (Robert Simon), Opie gets Arnold to buy a replacement. He then learns that the display bottle was not filled with perfume, but only colored water.

Episode #240, "Barney Hosts a Summit Meeting"

Original broadcast: January 28, 1968

Barney is sent to Mayberry to arrange accommodations for an upcoming U.S.–Soviet summit. When Barney fails to secure a suitable home, Andy volunteers his. The meeting starts off badly—the quarters are cramped, the neighbors are bothersome—and all looks lost when both sides end up at the kitchen table for a midnight meeting over Aunt Bee's cold fried chicken. The result is a huge success, and Barney earns another feather in his fedora.

Facts Known by Few:

This was Don Knotts's final appearance on "The Andy Griffith Show." His performance won him his fifth and final Emmy.

Episode #241, "Mayberry R.F.D."

Original broadcast: April 1, 1968

This episode features Ken Berry in the role of gentleman farmer Sam Jones. It aired as the final episode of "The Andy Griffith Show" and was used as the spinoff for the series of the same name. The story centered around Sam hiring an immigrant Italian family to work the farm. The family finds it difficult to adapt to its new surroundings.

Episode #242, "Goober Goes to an Auto Show"

Original broadcast: February 5, 1968

Goober meets an old friend who appears successful. Goober tells the friend lies about his own wealth, but discovers his friend has also lied about the same thing. Andy goads Goober into coming clean, but Goober thinks better of it and leaves quietly, saving his friend from embarrassment.

Episode #243, "Aunt Bee's Big Moment"

Original broadcast: February 12, 1968

Aunt Bee decides her life needs a little more excitement, so she enrolls in flying lessons. After facing her fears, she solos successfully and decides to give up the sky for her place in the home.

Episode #244, "Helen's Past"

Original broadcast: February 19, 1968

Helen is dragged before the school board when word of a prior arrest is leaked by none other than Andy. Helen defends herself by stating that her prior arrest came while investigating organized crime for her college journalism thesis. Cleared of all charges, Helen is reinstated.

Episode #245, "Emmett's Anniversary"

Original broadcast: February 26, 1968

In a quandary over what to get his wife, Martha (Mary Lansing), for their anniversary, Emmett decides to buy her the fur she's always wanted. Trying to save a few dollars, he goes to Mount Pilot to see Flora's friend in the fur business. While Emmett is sneaking off with Flora, he is spotted by his wife, who thinks he is having an affair. Andy spills the beans to save Emmett's hide, but the plot thickens when Emmett decides against the mink and, with Martha expecting a fur, he returns with a bathrobe. He and Andy do some fancy talking, and Emmett rushes back to Mount Pilot to buy the fur.

Episode #246, "The Wedding"

Original broadcast: March 4, 1968

Howard is finally free when his domineering mother (Mabel Albertson) remarries. Left with the house, Howard goes wild, turning it into a swinging bachelor pad. He throws a party, but only he, Goober, Emmett, Andy, and Helen attend.

Facts Known by Few:

The price of impressionistic art: $10 to $15.

The price of regular art (clowns and apples and stuff): $5 or $7.

Episode #247, "Sam for Town Council"

Original broadcast: March 11, 1968

It's Sam Jones (Ken Berry) vs. Emmett Clark (Paul Hartman) in a showdown for the town council seat vacated by Herb Bradshaw. Emmett proves to be a wily campaigner, but honest Sam prevails.

Facts Known by Few:

Sam won by 405 votes.

Episode #248, "Opie and Mike"

Original broadcast: March 18, 1968

Opie comes to the aid of Sam's son, Mike (Buddy Foster), when he's bullied by Edgar Watson (Russell Schulman). Opie plays buddy to Mike until he spots the new girl in town, Heather Campbell (Diane Quinn).

Episode #249, "A Girl for Goober"

Original broadcast: March 25, 1968

A misunderstanding occurs when Goober applies to a computer dating service. Filling in queries about the number of books he reads monthly, Goober answers thirty. This is true—if comic books count. As far as painting is concerned, he enjoys it. He once painted a barn. As a result, Goober is paired with Dr. Edith Gibson (Nancy Malone). Even with Goober's new hairstyle, Edith sees through his veneer and they realize the date was a mistake. The two manage to become fast friends over Morelli's famous pounded steak (pounded right on the premises). Dr. Gibson sees a special quality in Goober.

THE MAYBERRY CHRONICLE

···

The following three charts chronicle "The Andy Griffith Show."
The first chart, "Mayberry's Characters," tells which actors appeared in each
episode. The abbreviations used are as follows:

A.G.	Andy Griffith
D.K.	Don Knotts
F.B.	Frances Bavier
R.H.	Ron Howard
H.Mc.	Howard McNear
H.S.	Hal Smith
E.D.	Elinor Donahue
B.L.	Betty Lynn
A.C.	Aneta Corsaut
J.N.	Jim Nabors
G.L.	George Lindsey
J.D.	Jack Dodson
P.H.	Paul Hartman

The second chart, "Series Totals," displays the number of episodes that
each of the regulars appeared in during the course of the show's eight-year
run.

The third chart, "Writers and Directors," lists the author and director of
each episode.

MAYBERRY'S CHARACTERS
THE FIRST SEASON

EPS.	TITLE	AIR DATE	A.G.	D.K.	F.B.	R.H.	H.Mc.	H.S.	E.D.	B.L.	A.C.	J.N.
#1	The New Housekeeper	10/3/60	•	•	•	•						
#2	The Manhunt	10/10/60	•	•	•	•		•				
#3	Guitar Player	10/17/60	•	•	•	•						
#4	Runaway Kid	11/7/60	•	•	•	•						
#5	Opie's Charity	10/28/60	•		•	•						
#6	Ellie Comes to Town	10/24/60	•	•	•	•			•			
#7	Irresistible Andy	10/31/60	•	•	•	•			•			
#8	A Feud Is a Feud	12/5/60	•		•	•						
#9	Andy, the Matchmaker	11/14/60	•	•		•			•			
#10	Stranger in Town	12/26/60	•	•		•						
#11	Christmas Story	12/19/60	•	•	•	•			•			
#12	Ellie for Council	12/12/60	•	•	•	•		•	•			
#13	Mayberry Goes Hollywood	1/2/61	•	•	•	•	•					
#14	The Horse Trader	1/9/61	•	•		•			•			
#15	Those Gossipin' Men	1/16/91	•	•	•	•	•					
#16	Andy Saves Barney's Morale	2/20/61	•	•	•	•	•	•				
#17	Alcohol and Old Lace	1/30/61	•	•			•	•				
#18	Andy, the Marriage Counselor	2/13/61	•	•	•	•						
#19	Mayberry on Record	2/13/61	•	•		•	•		•			
#20	The Beauty Contest	1/23/61	•		•	•	•		•			
#21	Andy and the Gentleman Crook	2/27/61	•	•	•	•		•				
#22	Cyrano Andy	3/6/61	•	•					•	•		
#23	Andy and Opie, Housekeepers	3/13/61	•		•	•						
#24	The New Doctor	3/27/61	•	•	•	•			•			
#25	A Plaque for Mayberry	4/3/61	•	•		•		•				
#26	The Inspector	4/10/61	•	•		•		•				
#27	Ellie Saves a Female	4/17/61	•	•		•			•			
#28	Andy Forecloses	4/24/61	•	•	•	•						
#29	Quiet Sam	5/1/61	•	•	•		•	•				
#30	Barney Gets His Man	5/8/61	•	•		•				•		
#31	The Guitar Player Returns	5/15/61	•	•	•	•	•		•			
#32	Bringing Up Opie	5/22/61	•	•	•	•		•				
			32	28	22	29	8	9	12	2	0	0

MAYBERRY'S CHARACTERS
THE SECOND SEASON

EPS.	TITLE	AIR DATE	A.G.	D.K.	F.B.	R.H.	H.Mc.	H.S.	B.L.	A.C.	J.N.	G.L.
#33	Barney's Replacement	10/9/61	•	•		•			•			
#34	Opie and the Bully	10/2/61	•	•		•						
#35	Andy and the Woman Speeder	10/16/61	•	•	•	•	•					
#36	Barney on the Rebound	10/30/61	•	•		•			•			
#37	The Perfect Female	11/27/61	•	•	•	•			•			
#38	Aunt Bee's Brief Encounter	12/4/61	•		•	•						
#39	Mayberry Goes Bankrupt	10/23/61	•		•	•						
#40	Opie's Hobo Friend	11/13/61	•	•	•	•						
#41	Crime-free Mayberry	11/20/61	•	•			•	•				
#42	The Clubmen	12/11/61	•	•	•	•	•					
#43	The Pickle Story	12/18/61	•	•	•	•						
#44	Sheriff Barney	12/25/61	•	•	•			•				
#45	The Farmer Takes a Wife	1/1/62	•	•	•				•			
#46	The Keeper of the Flame	1/8/62	•	•	•	•						
#47	Bailey's Bad Boy	1/15/62	•	•	•	•		•				
#48	The Manicurist	1/22/62	•	•			•					
#49	The Jinx	1/29/62	•	•	•	•	•					
#50	Jailbreak	2/5/62	•	•		•	•					
#51	A Medal for Opie	2/12/62	•	•	•	•						
#52	Barney and the Choir	2/19/62	•	•	•	•			•			
#53	Guest of Honor	2/26/62	•	•			•					
#54	The Merchant of Mayberry	3/5/62	•	•	•	•						
#55	Aunt Bee, the Warden	3/12/62	•	•	•			•				
#56	The County Nurse	3/19/62	•	•								
#57	Andy and Barney in the Big City	3/26/62	•	•	•	•						
#58	Wedding Bells for Aunt Bee	4/2/62	•		•	•		•				
#59	Three's a Crowd	4/9/62	•	•	•				•			
#60	The Bookie Barber	4/16/62	•	•	•	•						
#61	Andy on Trial	4/23/62	•	•				•				
#62	Cousin Virgil	4/30/62	•	•		•		•				
#63	Deputy Otis	5/7/62	•	•				•				
			31	28	20	21	7	8	6	0	0	0

MAYBERRY'S CHARACTERS

THE THIRD SEASON

EPS.	TITLE	AIR DATE	A.G.	D.K.	F.B.	R.H.	H.Mc.	H.S.	B.L.	A.C.	J.N.	G.L.
#64	Opie's Rival	12/3/62	•		•	•						
#65	Andy and Opie, Bachelors	11/8/62	•		•	•	•					
#66	Mr. McBeevee	10/1/62	•	•	•	•						
#67	Andy's Rich Girlfriend	10/8/62	•	•	•				•			
#68	Barney Mends a Broken Heart	11/5/62	•	•	•	•			•			
#69	Andy and the New Mayor	10/15/62	•	•		•						
#70	The Cow Thief	10/29/62	•	•		•						
#71	Floyd, the Gay Deceiver	11/26/62	•		•	•	•					
#72	The Mayberry Band	11/19/62	•	•		•	•					
#73	Lawman Barney	11/12/62	•	•			•					
#74	Convicts at Large	12/10/62	•	•			•					
#75	The Bed Jacket	12/17/62	•		•	•						
#76	Barney and the Governor	1/7/63	•	•				•				
#77	Man in a Hurry	1/14/63	•	•	•	•					•	
#78	The Bank Job	12/24/62	•	•							•	
#79	One Punch Opie	12/31/62	•	•	•	•						
#80	High Noon in Mayberry	1/21/63	•	•	•	•		•			•	
#81	The Loaded Goat	1/28/63	•	•		•		•				
#82	Class Reunion	2/4/63	•	•								
#83	Rafe Hollister Sings	2/11/63	•	•		•						
#84	Opie and the Spoiled Kid	2/18/63	•	•		•						
#85	The Great Filling Station Robbery	2/25/63	•	•		•					•	
#86	Andy Discovers America	3/4/63	•	•	•	•				•		
#87	Aunt Bee's Medicine Man	3/11/63	•	•	•	•						
#88	The Darlings Are Coming	3/18/63	•									
#89	Andy's English Valet	3/25/63	•	•	•	•						
#90	Barney's First Car	4/1/63	•	•	•	•			•		•	
#91	The Rivals	4/8/63	•	•	•				•			
#92	A Wife for Andy	4/15/63	•	•	•	•			•	•		
#93	Dogs, Dogs, Dogs	4/22/63	•	•		•		•				
#94	Mountain Wedding	5/6/63	•	•								
#95	The Big House	5/6/63	•	•							•	
			32	27	16	22	5	4	5	2	6	0

MAYBERRY'S CHARACTERS

THE FOURTH SEASON

EPS.	TITLE	AIR DATE	A.G.	D.K.	F.B.	R.H.	H.Mc.	H.S.	B.L.	A.C.	J.N.	G.L.
#96	Briscoe Declares for Aunt Bee	10/28/63	•		•	•						
#97	Gomer the House Guest	11/4/63	•		•	•					•	
#98	The Haunted House	10/7/63	•	•		•		•			•	
#99	Ernest T. Bass Joins the Army	10/14/63	•	•								
#100	The Sermon for Today	10/21/63	•	•	•	•					•	
#101	Opie the Birdman	9/30/63	•	•	•	•						
#102	A Black Day for Mayberry	11/11/63	•	•	•	•					•	
#103	Opie's Ill-gotten Gain	11/18/63	•	•	•	•				•		
#104	Up in Barney's Room	12/2/63	•	•					•			
#105	A Date for Gomer	11/25/63	•	•	•	•			•	•	•	
#106	Citizen's Arrest	12/16/63	•	•	•	•		•			•	
#107	Gomer Pyle, U.S.M.C.	5/19/64	•								•	
#108	Opie and His Merry Men	12/30/63	•	•	•	•						
#109	Barney and the Cave Rescue	1/6/64	•	•		•			•	•	•	
#110	Andy and Opie's Pal	1/13/64	•	•	•	•						
#111	Aunt Bee, the Crusader	1/20/64	•	•	•	•		•				
#112	Barney's Sidecar	1/27/64	•	•	•	•						
#113	My Fair Ernest T. Bass	2/3/64	•	•	•	•						
#114	Prisoner of Love	2/10/64	•	•	•			•				
#115	Hot Rod Otis	2/17/64	•	•				•				
#116	The Song Festers	2/24/64	•	•	•						•	
#117	The Shoplifters	3/2/64	•	•	•	•						
#118	Andy's Vacation	3/9/64	•	•	•						•	
#119	Andy Saves Gomer	3/16/64	•		•	•	•				•	
#120	Bargain Day	3/23/64	•		•	•					•	
#121	Divorce Mountain Style	3/30/64	•	•			•					
#122	A Deal Is a Deal	4/6/64	•	•	•	•					•	
#123	The Fun Girls	4/13/64	•	•	•				•	•	•	•
#124	The Return of Malcolm Merriweather	4/20/64	•	•	•	•						
#125	The Rumor	4/27/64	•	•	•	•	•		•	•	•	
#126	Barney and Thelma Lou, Phfft!	5/4/64	•	•					•		•	
#127	Back to Nature	5/11/64	•	•		•	•				•	
			32	27	23	22	4	5	6	5	17	1

MAYBERRY'S CHARACTERS
THE FIFTH SEASON

EPS.	TITLE	AIR DATE	A.G.	D.K.	F.B.	R.H.	H.Mc.	H.S.	B.L.	A.C.	J.N.	G.L.
#128	Barney's Bloodhound	10/26/64	•	•			•					
#129	Family Visit	10/5/64	•		•	•	•					
#130	Aunt Bee's Romance	10/19/64	•		•	•	•					
#131	Barney's Physical	10/28/64	•	•	•	•	•			•		
#132	Opie Loves Helen	9/21/64	•	•	•	•				•		
#133	The Education of Ernest T. Bass	10/12/64	•	•		•				•		
#134	Man in the Middle	11/2/64	•	•					•	•		
#135	Barney's Uniform	11/9/64	•	•	•							
#136	Opie's Fortune	11/16/64	•	•	•	•						
#137	Goodbye, Sheriff Taylor	11/23/64	•	•	•		•	•				•
#138	The Pageant	11/30/64	•	•	•	•						
#139	The Darling Baby	12/7/64	•	•	•	•						
#140	Andy and Helen Have Their Day	12/14/64	•	•	•					•		•
#141	Otis Sues the County	12/28/64	•	•			•	•				
#142	Three Wishes for Opie	12/21/64	•	•		•	•			•		•
#143	Barney Fife, Realtor	1/4/65	•	•	•	•						
#144	Goober Takes a Car Apart	1/11/65	•		•		•					•
#145	The Rehabilitation of Otis	1/18/65	•	•			•	•				
#146	The Lucky Letter	1/25/65	•	•		•	•		•			•
#147	Goober and the Art of Love	2/1/65	•	•					•	•		•
#148	Barney Runs for Sheriff	2/8/65	•	•	•	•	•		•	•		•
#149	If I Had a Quarter Million Dollars	2/15/65	•	•			•					•
#150	TV or Not TV	3/1/65	•	•	•	•	•					•
#151	Guest in the House	3/8/65	•		•	•	•			•		•
#152	The Case of the Punch in the Nose	3/15/65	•	•	•	•	•					•
#153	Opie's Newspaper	3/22/65	•	•	•	•						
#154	Aunt Bee's Invisible Beau	3/29/65	•	•	•	•				•		
#155	The Arrest of the Fun Girls	4/5/65	•	•	•			•	•	•		
#156	The Luck of Newton Monroe	4/12/65	•	•			•					•
#157	Opie Flunks Arithmetic	4/19/65	•	•	•	•				•		
#158	Opie and the Carnival	4/26/65	•		•	•				•		•
#159	Banjo-playing Deputy	5/3/65	•		•	•	•					
			32	26	22	21	17	4	6	12	0	13

MAYBERRY'S CHARACTERS

THE SIXTH SEASON

EPS.	TITLE	AIR DATE	A.G.	D.K.	F.B.	R.H.	H.Mc.	H.S.	A.C.	B.L.	G.L.	J.D.
#160	Aunt Bee, the Swinger	10/4/65	•		•	•	•		•			
#161	Opie's Job	9/13/65	•		•	•	•				•	
#162	The Bazaar	10/11/65	•		•	•					•	
#163	Andy's Rival	9/20/65	•		•	•			•		•	
#164	Malcolm at the Crossroads	9/27/65	•				•				•	
#165	Aunt Bee on TV	11/15/65	•		•	•	•		•		•	
#166	Off to Hollywood	10/25/65	•		•	•	•		•		•	
#167	Taylors in Hollywood	11/1/65	•		•	•						
#168	The Hollywood Party	11/8/65	•		•	•			•			
#169	A Warning from Warren	10/15/65	•				•		•		•	
#170	A Man's Best Friend	11/29/65	•		•	•	•		•			
#171	Aunt Bee Takes a Job	12/6/65	•		•							
#172	The Cannon	11/22/65	•		•		•				•	
#173	Girl-shy	12/20/65	•		•				•		•	
#174	The Church Organ	12/13/65	•		•	•	•					
#175	Otis, the Artist	1/3/66	•		•	•		•			•	
#176	The Return of Barney Fife	1/10/66	•	•	•				•	•		
#177	The Legend of Barney Fife	1/17/66	•	•	•		•				•	
#178	Lost and Found	1/24/66	•		•	•						•
#179	Wyatt Earp	1/31/66	•			•	•					
#180	Aunt Bee Learns to Drive	2/7/66	•		•	•	•		•		•	
#181	Look, Pa, I'm Dancing	2/14/66	•		•	•	•		•		•	
#182	Eat Your Heart Out	2/28/66	•				•		•		•	
#183	The Gypsies	2/21/66	•		•				•		•	
#184	A Baby in the House	3/7/66	•		•				•		•	
#185	The County Clerk	3/14/66	•		•				•			•
#186	Goober's Replacement	3/28/66	•		•	•					•	
#187	The Foster Lady	3/21/66	•		•	•	•				•	
#188	The Battle of Mayberry	4/4/66	•		•	•	•		•		•	
#189	A Singer in Town	4/11/66	•		•	•	•				•	
			30	2	24	22	18	1	15	1	22	2

MAYBERRY'S CHARACTERS
THE SEVENTH SEASON

EPS.	TITLE	AIR DATE	A.G.	D.K.	F.B.	R.H.	H.Mc.	H.S.	A.C.	G.L.	J.D.
#190	Opie's Girlfriend	9/12/66	•		•	•	•		•	•	
#191	The Barbershop Quartet	9/26/66	•		•	•	•				•
#192	The Lodge	9/19/66	•		•		•			•	•
#193	The Darling Fortune	10/17/66	•		•				•	•	
#194	Aunt Bee's Crowning Glory	10/10/66	•		•	•	•		•		
#195	The Ball Game	10/3/66	•		•	•	•		•	•	•
#196	Goober Makes History	12/19/66	•		•	•	•		•	•	•
#197	The Senior Play	11/14/66	•				•		•	•	
#198	Big Fish in a Small Town	11/28/66	•			•	•			•	•
#199	Mind over Matter	10/31/66	•		•	•	•		•		
#200	Politics Begins at Home	11/7/66	•		•	•	•			•	•
#201	A New Doctor in Town	12/26/66	•		•	•	•		•		
#202	Opie Finds a Baby	11/21/66	•		•	•			•	•	
#203	Only a Rose	12/5/66	•		•	•	•				
#204	Otis, the Deputy	12/12/66	•					•			•
#205	Don't Miss a Good Bet	1/2/67	•		•	•	•		•	•	
#206	Dinner at Eight	1/9/67	•		•	•			•	•	
#207	Andy's Old Girlfriend	1/30/67	•						•		•
#208	The Statue	2/20/67	•		•		•			•	•
#209	Aunt Bee's Restaurant	2/2/67	•		•				•	•	
#210	Floyd's Barbershop	2/13/67	•		•	•	•			•	•
#211	A Visit to Barney Fife	1/16/67	•	•							
#212	Barney Comes to Mayberry	1/23/67	•	•	•						
#213	Helen, the Authoress	2/27/67	•				•		•	•	•
#214	Goodbye, Dolly	3/6/67	•		•	•				•	•
#215	Opie's Piano Lesson	3/13/67	•		•	•					
#216	Howard, the Comedian	3/20/67	•		•	•	•			•	•
#217	Big Brothers	3/27/67	•				•			•	•
#218	Opie's Most Unforgettable Character	4/3/67	•		•	•			•	•	•
#219	Goober's Contest	4/10/67	•				•			•	
			30	2	26	24	23	1	17	26	19

MAYBERRY'S CHARACTERS
THE EIGHTH SEASON

EPS.	TITLE	AIR DATE	A.G.	D.K.	F.B.	R.H.	A.C.	G.L.	J.D.	P.H.
#220	Opie's First Love	9/11/67	•		•	•		•		
#221	Goober, the Executive	12/25/67	•			•		•		•
#222	Howard's Main Event	10/16/67	•				•	•	•	
#223	Aunt Bee, the Juror	10/23/67	•		•	•		•		
#224	Howard, the Bowler	9/18/67	•		•		•	•	•	•
#225	Opie Steps Up in Class	10/9/67	•		•	•			•	•
#226	Andy's Trip to Raleigh	10/2/67	•				•	•	•	•
#227	A Trip of Mexico	9/25/67	•		•	•	•		•	•
#228	Tape Recorder	10/20/67	•		•	•		•		
#229	Opie's Group	11/6/67	•		•	•		•		•
#230	Aunt Bee and the Lecturer	11/13/67	•		•	•	•	•	•	
#231	Andy's Investment	11/20/67	•		•	•	•			
#232	Suppose Andy Gets Sick	12/11/67	•		•	•		•	•	•
#233	Howard and Millie	11/27/67	•		•		•	•	•	
#234	Aunt Bee's Cousin	12/4/67	•		•	•	•	•	•	•
#235	Howard's New Life	12/18/67	•		•	•		•	•	•
#236	Emmett's Brother-In-Law	1/8/68	•				•		•	•
#237	The Mayberry Chef	1/1/68	•		•	•		•		
#238	The Church Benefactor	1/22/68	•		•	•	•		•	•
#239	Opie's Drugstore Job	1/15/68	•			•		•	•	
#240	Barney Hosts a Summit Meeting	1/28/68	•	•	•			•		
#241	Mayberry, R.F.D.	4/1/68	•		•		•	•	•	•
#242	Goober Goes to an Auto Show	2/5/68	•		•	•		•		
#243	Aunt Bee's Big Moment	2/12/68	•		•	•	•	•	•	•
#244	Helen's Past	2/19/68	•		•	•	•	•	•	
#245	Emmett's Anniversary	2/26/68	•			•		•		•
#246	The Wedding	3/4/68	•				•	•	•	•
#247	Sam for Town Council	3/11/68	•		•	•	•	•	•	•
#248	Opie and Mike	3/18/68	•		•	•		•		
#249	A Girl for Goober	3/25/68	•			•	•	•		
			30	1	22	22	16	25	19	17

SERIES TOTALS

Eps.	Years	Andy Griffith	Don Knotts	Frances Bavier	Ron Howard	Howard McNear	Hal Smith	Betty Lynn	Aneta Corsaut	Jim Nabors	George Lindsey	Jack Dodson	Paul Hartman	Elinor Donahue
249	8	249	141	171	177	78	32	26	64	23	82	39	17	12

WRITERS AND DIRECTORS

THE FIRST SEASON

Eps	Air Date	Title	Written By	Directed By
#1	10/3/60	The New Housekeeper	Jack Elinson and Charles Stewart	Sheldon Leonard
#2	10/10/60	The Manhunt	Jack Elinson and Charles Stewart	Don Weis
#3	10/17/60	Guitar Player	Jack Elinson and Charles Stewart	Don Weis
#4	11/7/60	Runaway Kid	Arthur Stander	Don Weis
#5	11/28/60	Opie's Charity	Arthur Stander	Don Weis
#6	10/24/60	Ellie Comes to Town	Jack Elinson and Charles Stewart	Don Weis
#7	10/31/60	Irresistible Andy	David Adler	Don Weis
#8	12/5/60	A Feud is a Feud	David Adler	Don Weis
#9	11/14/60	Andy, the Matchmaker	Arthur Stander	Don Weis
#10	12/26/60	Stranger in Town	Arthur Stander	Don Weis
#11	12/19/60	Christmas Story	David Adler	Bob Sweeney
#12	12/12/60	Ellie for Council	Jack Elinson and Charles Stewart	Bob Sweeney
#13	1/2/61	Mayberry Goes Hollywood	Benedict Freedman and John Fenton Murray	Bob Sweeney
#14	1/9/61	The Horse Trader	Jack Elinson and Charles Stewart	Bob Sweeney
#15	1/16/61	Those Gossipin' Men	Jack Elinson and Charles Stewart	Bob Sweeney
#16	2/20/61	Andy Saves Barney's Morale	David Adler	Bob Sweeney
#17	1/30/61	Alcohol and Old Lace	Jack Elinson and Charles Stewart	Gene Reynolds
#18	2/6/61	Andy, the Marriage Counselor	David Adler	Gene Reynolds
#19	2/13/61	Mayberry on Record	Benedict Freedman and John Fenton Murray	Gene Reynolds
#20	1/23/61	The Beauty Contest	Jack Elinson and Charles Stewart	Bob Sweeney
#21	2/27/61	Andy and The Gentleman Crook	Ben Gershman and Leo Solomon	Bob Sweeney
#22	3/6/61	Cyrano Andy	Jack Elinson and Charles Stewart	Bob Sweeney
#23	3/13/61	Andy and Opie, Housekeepers	David Adler	Bob Sweeney
#24	3/27/61	The New Doctor	Jack Elinson and Charles Stewart	Bob Sweeney
#25	4/3/61	A Plaque for Mayberry	Ben Gershman and Leo Solomon	Bob Sweeney
#26	4/10/61	The Inspector	Jack Elinson and Charles Stewart	Bob Sweeney
#27	4/17/61	Ellie Saves a Female	David Adler	Bob Sweeney
#28	4/24/61	Andy Forecloses	Ben Gershman and Leo Solomon	Bob Sweeney
#29	5/1/61	Quiet Sam	Jim Fritzell and Everett Greenbaum	Bob Sweeney
#30	5/8/61	Barney Gets His Man	Ben Gershman and Leo Solomon	Bob Sweeney
#31	5/15/61	The Guitar Player Returns	Jack Elinson and Charles Stewart	Bob Sweeney
#32	5/22/61	Bringing Up Opie	Jack Elinson and Charles Stewart	Bob Sweeney

WRITERS AND DIRECTORS
THE SECOND SEASON

Eps	Air Date	Title	Written By	Directed By
#33	10/9/61	Barney's Replacement	Jack Elinson and Charles Stewart	Bob Sweeney
#34	10/2/61	Opie and the Bully	David Adler	Bob Sweeney
#35	10/16/61	Andy and the Woman Speeder	Jack Elinson and Charles Stewart	Bob Sweeney
#36	10/30/61	Barney on the Rebound	Jack Elinson and Charles Stewart	Bob Sweeney
#37	11/27/61	The Perfect Female	Jack Elinson and Charles Stewart	Bob Sweeney
#38	12/4/61	Aunt Bee's Brief Encounter	Ben Gershman and Leo Solomon	Bob Sweeney
#39	10/23/61	Mayberry Goes Bankrupt	Jack Elinson and Charles Stewart	Bob Sweeney
#40	11/13/61	Opie's Hobo Friend	Harvey Bullock	Bob Sweeney
#41	11/20/61	Crime-free Mayberry	Paul Henning	Bob Sweeney
#42	12/11/61	The Clubmen	Fred Fox and Iz Elinson	Bob Sweeney
#43	12/18/61	The Pickle Story	Harvey Bullock	Bob Sweeney
#44	12/25/61	Sheriff Barney	Ben Gershman and Leo Solomon	Bob Sweeney
#45	1/1/62	The Farmer Takes a Wife	Jack Elinson and Charles Stewart	Bob Sweeney
#46	1/8/62	The Keeper of the Flame	Jack Elinson and Charles Stewart	Bob Sweeney
#47	1/15/62	Bailey's Bad Boy	Ben Gershman and Leo Solomon	Bob Sweeney
#48	1/22/62	The Manicurist	Jack Elinson and Charles Stewart	Bob Sweeney
#49	1/29/62	The Jinx	Jack Elinson and Charles Stewart	Bob Sweeney
#50	2/5/62	Jailbreak	Harvey Bullock	Bob Sweeney
#51	2/12/62	A Medal for Opie	David Adler	Bob Sweeney
#52	2/19/62	Barney and the Choir	Jack Elinson and Charles Stewart	Bob Sweeney
#53	2/26/62	Guest of Honor	Jack Elinson and Charles Stewart	Bob Sweeney
#54	3/5/62	The Merchant of Mayberry	Ben Gershman and Leo Solomon	Bob Sweeney
#55	3/12/62	Aunt Bee, the Warden	Jack Elinson and Charles Stewart	Bob Sweeney
#56	3/19/62	The County Nurse	Jack Elinson and Charles Stewart	Bob Sweeney
#57	3/26/62	Andy and Barney in the Big City	Harvey Bullock	Bob Sweeney
#58	4/2/62	Wedding Bells for Aunt Bee	Harvey Bullock	Bob Sweeney
#59	4/9/62	Three's a Crowd	Jack Elinson and Charles Stewart	Bob Sweeney
#60	4/16/92	The Bookie Barber	Ray Saffian Allen and Harvey Bullock	Bob Sweeney
#61	4/23/62	Andy on Trial	Jack Elinson and Charles Stewart	Bob Sweeney
#62	4/30/62	Cousin Virgil	Phillip Shukin and Johnny Greene	Bob Sweeney
#63	5/7/62	Deputy Otis	Fred Fox and Iz Elinson	Bob Sweeney

WRITERS AND DIRECTORS
THE THIRD SEASON

Eps	Air Date	Title	Written By	Directed By
#64	12/3/62	Opie's Rival	Sid Morse	Bob Sweeney
#65	11/8/62	Andy and Opie, Bachelors	Jim Fritzell and Everett Greenbaum	Bob Sweeney
#66	10/1/62	Mr. McBeevee	Ray Saffian Allen and Harvey Bullock	Bob Sweeney
#67	10/8/62	Andy's Rich Girlfriend	Jim Fritzell and Everett Greenbaum	Bob Sweeney
#68	11/5/62	Barney Mends a Broken Heart	Aaron Ruben	Bob Sweeney
#69	10/15/62	Andy and the New Mayor	Ray Saffian Allen and Harvey Bullock	Bob Sweeney
#70	10/29/62	The Cow Thief	Ray Saffian Allen and Harvey Bullock	Bob Sweeney
#71	11/26/62	Floyd, the Gay Deceiver	Aaron Ruben	Bob Sweeney
#72	11/19/62	The Mayberry Band	Jim Fritzell and Everett Greenbaum	Bob Sweeney
#73	11/12/62	Lawman Barney	Aaron Ruben	Bob Sweeney
#74	12/10/62	Convicts at Large	Jim Fritzell and Everett Greenbaum	Bob Sweeney
#75	12/17/62	The Bed Jacket	Ray Saffian Allen and Harvey Bullock	Bob Sweeney
#76	1/7/63	Barney and the Governor	Bill Freedman and Henry Sharp	Bob Sweeney
#77	1/14/63	Man in a Hurry	Jim Fritzell and Everett Greenbaum	Bob Sweeney
#78	12/24/62	The Bank Job	Jim Fritzell and Everett Greenbaum	Bob Sweeney
#79	12/31/62	One Punch Opie	Harvey Bullock	Bob Sweeney
#80	1/21/63	High Noon in Mayberry	Jim Fritzell and Everett Greenbaum	Bob Sweeney
#81	1/28/63	The Loaded Goat	Harvey Bullock	Bob Sweeney
#82	2/4/63	Class Reunion	Jim Fritzell and Everett Greenbaum	Charles Irving
#83	2/11/63	Rafe Hollister Sings	Harvey Bullock	Charles Irving
#84	2/18/63	Opie and the Spoiled Kid	Jim Fritzell and Everett Greenbaum	Bob Sweeney
#85	2/25/63	The Great Filling Station Robbery	Harvey Bullock	Bob Sweeney
#86	3/4/63	Andy Discovers America	John Whedon	Bob Sweeney
#87	3/11/63	Aunt Bee's Medicine Man	John Whedon	Bob Sweeney
#88	3/18/63	The Darlings Are Coming	Jim Fritzell and Everett Greenbaum	Bob Sweeney
#89	3/25/63	Andy's English Valet	Harvey Bullock	Bob Sweeney
#90	4/1/63	Barney's First Car	Jim Fritzell and Everett Greenbaum	Bob Sweeney
#91	4/8/63	The Rivals	Harvey Bullock	Bob Sweeney
#92	4/15/63	A Wife for Andy	Aaron Ruben	Bob Sweeney
#93	4/22/63	Dogs, Dogs, Dogs	Jim Fritzell and Everett Greenbaum	Bob Sweeney
#94	5/6/63	Mountain Wedding	Jim Fritzell and Everett Greenbaum	Bob Sweeney
#95	5/6/63	The Big House	Harvey Bullock	Bob Sweeney

WRITERS AND DIRECTORS
THE FOURTH SEASON

Eps	Air Date	Title	Written By	Directed By
#96	10/28/63	Briscoe Declares for Aunt Bee	Jim Fritzell and Everett Greenbaum	Earl Bellamy
#97	11/4/63	Gomer, the House Guest	Jim Fritzell and Everett Greenbaum	Earl Bellamy
#98	10/7/63	The Haunted House	Harvey Bullock	Earl Bellamy
#99	10/14/63	Ernest T. Bass Joins the Army	Jim Fritzell and Everett Greenbaum	Dick Crenna
#100	10/21/63	The Sermon for Today	John Whedon	Dick Crenna
#101	9/30/63	Opie, the Birdman	Harvey Bullock	Dick Crenna
#102	11/11/63	A Black Day for Mayberry	John Whedon	Jeffrey Hayden
#103	11/18/63	Opie's Ill-gotten Gain	John Whedon	Jeffrey Hayden
#104	12/2/63	Up in Barney's Room	Jim Fritzell and Everett Greenbaum	Jeffrey Hayden
#105	11/25/63	A Date for Gomer	Jim Fritzell and Everett Greenbaum	Dick Crenna
#106	12/16/63	Citizen's Arrest	Jim Fritzell and Everett Greenbaum	Dick Crenna
#107	5/19/64	Gomer Pyle, U.S.M.C.	Aaron Ruben	Aaron Ruben
#108	12/30/63	Opie and His Merry Men	John Whedon	Dick Crenna
#109	1/6/64	Barney and the Cave Rescue	Harvey Bullock	Dick Crenna
#110	1/13/64	Andy and Opie's Pal	Harvey Bullock	Dick Crenna
#111	1/20/64	Aunt Bee, the Crusader	John Whedon	Coby Ruskin
#112	1/27/64	Barney's Sidecar	Jim Fritzell and Everett Greenbaum	Coby Ruskin
#113	2/3/64	My Fair Ernest T. Bass	Jim Fritzell and Everett Greenbaum	Earl Bellamy
#114	2/10/64	Prisoner of Love	Harvey Bullock	Earl Bellamy
#115	2/17/64	Hot Rod Otis	Harvey Bullock	Earl Bellamy
#116	2/24/64	The Song Festers	Jim Fritzell and Everett Greenbaum	Earl Bellamy
#117	3/2/64	The Shoplifters	Bill Idelson and Sam Bobrick	Coby Ruskin
#118	3/9/64	Andy's Vacation	Jim Fritzell and Everett Greenbaum	Jeffrey Hayden
#119	3/16/64	Andy Saves Gomer	Harvey Bullock	Jeffrey Hayden
#120	3/23/64	Bargain Day	John Whedon	Jeffrey Hayden
#121	3/30/64	Divorce Mountain Style	Jim Fritzell and Everett Greenbaum	Jeffrey Hayden
#122	4/6/64	A Deal Is a Deal	Bill Idelson and Sam Bobrick	Jeffrey Hayden
#123	4/13/64	The Fun Girls	Aaron Ruben	Coby Ruskin
#124	4/20/64	The Return of Malcolm Merriweather	Harvey Bullock	Coby Ruskin
#125	4/27/64	The Rumor	Jim Fritzell and Everett Greenbaum	Coby Ruskin
#126	5/4/64	Barney and Thelma Lou, Phfft!	Bill Idelson and Sam Bobrick	Coby Ruskin
#127	5/11/64	Back to Nature	Harvey Bullock	Coby Ruskin

WRITERS AND DIRECTORS
THE FIFTH SEASON

Eps	Air Date	Title	Written By	Directed By
#128	10/26/64	Barney's Bloodhound	Bill Idelson and Sam Bobrick	Howard Morris
#129	10/5/64	Family Visit	Jim Fritzell and Everett Greenbaum	Howard Morris
#130	10/19/64	Aunt Bee's Romance	Harvey Bullock	Howard Morris
#131	10/28/64	Barney's Physical	Bob Ross	Howard Morris
#132	9/21/64	Opie Loves Helen	Bob Ross	Aaron Ruben
#133	10/12/64	The Education of Ernest T. Bass	Jim Fritzell and Everett Greenbaum	Alan Rafkin
#134	11/2/64	Man in the Middle	Gus Adrian and David Evans	Alan Rafkin
#135	11/9/64	Barney's Uniform	Bill Idelson and Sam Bobrick	Coby Ruskin
#136	11/16/64	Opie's Fortune	Ben Joelson and Art Baer	Coby Ruskin
#137	11/23/64	Goodbye, Sheriff Taylor	Fred Freeman and Lawrence J. Cohen	Gene Nelson
#138	11/30/64	The Pageant	Harvey Bullock	Gene Nelson
#139	12/7/64	The Darling Baby	Jim Fritzell and Everett Greenbaum	Howard Morris
#140	12/14/64	Andy and Helen Have Their Day	Bill Idelson and Sam Bobrick	Howard Morris
#141	12/28/64	Otis Sues the County	Bob Ross	Howard Morris
#142	12/21/64	Three Wishes for Opie	Richard M. Powell	Howard Morris
#143	1/4/65	Barney Fife, Realtor	Bill Idelson and Sam Bobrick	Peter Baldwin
#144	1/11/65	Goober Takes a Car Apart	Bill Idelson and Sam Bobrick	Peter Baldwin
#145	1/18/65	The Rehabilitation of Otis	Fred Freeman and Lawrence J. Cohen	Peter Baldwin
#146	1/25/65	The Lucky Letter	Richard M. Powell	Theodore J. Flicker
#147	2/1/65	Goober and the Art of Love	Fred Freeman and Lawrence J. Cohen	Alan Rafkin
#148	2/8/65	Barney Runs for Sheriff	Richard M. Powell	Alan Rafkin
#149	2/15/65	If I Had a Quarter Million Dollars	Bob Ross	Alan Rafkin
#150	3/1/65	TV or Not TV	Ben Joelson and Art Baer	Coby Ruskin
#151	3/8/65	Guest in the House	Fred Freeman and Lawrence J. Cohen	Coby Ruskin
#152	3/15/65	The Case of the Punch in the Nose	Bill Idelson and Sam Bobrick	Coby Ruskin
#153	3/22/65	Opie's Newspaper	Harvey Bullock	Coby Ruskin
#154	3/29/65	Aunt Bee's Invisible Beau	Ben Joelson and Art Baer	Theodore J. Flicker
#155	4/5/65	The Arrest of the Fun Girls	Richard M. Powell	Theodore J. Flicker
#156	4/12/65	The Luck of Newton Monroe	Bill Idelson and Sam Bobrick	Coby Ruskin
#157	4/19/65	Opie Flunks Arithmetic	Richard Morgan	Coby Ruskin
#158	4/26/65	Opie and the Carnival	Fred Freeman and Lawrence J. Cohen	Coby Ruskin
#159	5/3/65	Banjo-playing Deputy	Bob Ross	Coby Ruskin

WRITERS AND DIRECTORS
THE SIXTH SEASON

Eps	Air Date	Title	Written By	Directed By
#160	10/4/65	Aunt Bee, the Swinger	Jack Elinson	Larry Dobkin
#161	9/13/65	Opie's Job	Ben Joelson and Art Baer	Larry Dobkin
#162	10/11/65	The Bazaar	Ben Joelson and Art Baer	Sheldon Leonard
#163	9/20/65	Andy's Rival	Laurence Marks	Peter Baldwin
#164	9/27/65	Malcolm at the Crossroads	Harvey Bullock	Gary Nelson
#165	11/5/65	Aunt Bee on TV	Fred Freeman and Lawrence J. Cohen	Alan Rafkin
#166	10/25/65	Off to Hollywood	Bill Idelson and Sam Bobrick	Alan Rafkin
#167	11/1/65	Taylors in Hollywood	Bill Idelson and Sam Bobrick	Alan Rafkin
#168	11/8/65	The Hollywood Party	Fred Freeman and Lawrence J. Cohen	Alan Rafkin
#169	10/15/65	A Warning from Warren	Fred Freeman and Lawrence J. Cohen	Alan Rafkin
#170	11/29/65	A Man's Best Friend	Ben Joelson and Art Baer	Alan Rafkin
#171	12/6/65	Aunt Bee Takes a Job	Bill Idelson and Sam Bobrick	Alan Rafkin
#172	11/22/65	The Cannon	Jack Elinson	Alan Rafkin
#173	12/20/65	Girl-shy	Bill Idelson and Sam Bobrick	Lee Philips
#174	12/13/65	The Church Organ	Paul Wayne	Lee Philips
#175	1/3/66	Otis, the Artist	Fred Freeman and Lawrence J. Cohen	Alan Rafkin
#176	1/10/66	The Return of the Barney Fife	Bill Idelson and Sam Bobrick	Alan Rafkin
#177	1/17/66	The Legend of Barney Fife	Harvey Bullock	Alan Rafkin
#178	1/24/66	Lost and Found	John L. Greene and Paul David	Alan Rafkin
#179	1/31/66	Wyatt Earp	Jack Elinson	Alan Rafkin
#180	2/7/66	Aunt Bee Learns to Drive	Jack Elinson	Lee Philips
#181	2/14/66	Look, Pa, I'm Dancing	Ben Starr	Lee Philips
#182	2/28/66	Eat Your Heart Out	Ben Joelson and Art Baer	Alan Rafkin
#183	2/21/66	The Gypsies	Roland McLane	Alan Rafkin
#184	3/7/66	A Baby in the House	Bill Idelson and Sam Bobrick	Alan Rafkin
#185	3/14/66	The County Clerk	Bill Idelson and Sam Bobrick	Alan Rafkin
#186	3/28/66	Goober's Replacement	Howard Merrill and Stan Dreben	Alan Rafkin
#187	3/21/66	The Foster Lady	Jack Elinson and Iz Elinson	Alan Rafkin
#188	4/4/66	The Battle of Mayberry	Paul David and John L. Greene	Alan Rafkin
#189	4/11/66	A Singer in Town	Howard Merrill and Stan Dreben	Alan Rafkin

WRITERS AND DIRECTORS
THE SEVENTH SEASON

Eps	Air Date	Title	Written By	Directed By
#190	9/12/66	Opie's Girlfriend	Budd Grossman	Lee Philips
#191	9/26/66	The Barbershop Quartet	Fred S. Fox	Lee Philips
#192	9/19/66	The Lodge	Jim Parker and Arnold Margolin	Lee Philips
#193	10/17/66	The Darling Fortune	Jim Parker and Arnold Margolin	Lee Philips
#194	10/10/66	Aunt Bee's Crowning Glory	Ronald Axe	Lee Philips
#195	10/3/66	The Ball Game	Sid Morse (story by Rance Howard)	Lee Philips
#196	12/19/66	Goober Makes History	Paul David and John L. Greene	Lee Philips
#197	11/14/66	The Senior Play	Sid Morse	Lee Philips
#198	11/28/66	Big Fish in a Small Town	Bill Idelson and Sam Bobrick	Lee Philips
#199	10/31/66	Mind over Matter	Ron Friedman and Pat McCormick	Lee Philips
#200	11/7/66	Politics Begins at Home	Fred S. Fox	Lee Philips
#201	12/26/66	A New Doctor in Town	Ray Brenner and Barry E. Blitzer	Lee Philips
#202	11/21/66	Opie Finds a Baby	Stan Dreben and Sid Mandel	Lee Philips
#203	12/5/66	Only a Rose	Jim Parker and Arnold Margolin	Lee Philips
#204	12/12/66	Otis the Deputy	Jim Parker and Arnold Margolin	Lee Philips
#205	1/2/67	Don't Miss a Good Bet	Fred S. Fox	Lee Philips
#206	1/9/67	Dinner at Eight	Budd Grossman	Lee Philips
#207	1/30/67	Andy's Old Girlfriend	Sid Morse	Lee Philips
#208	2/20/67	The Statue	Fred S. Fox	Lee Philips
#209	2/2/67	Aunt Bee's Restaurant	Ronald Axe and Les Roberts	Lee Philips
#210	2/13/67	Floyd's Barbershop	Jim Parker and Arnold and Margolin	Lee Philips
#211	1/16/67	A Visit to Barney Fife	Bill Idelson and Sam Bobrick	Lee Philips
#212	1/23/67	Barney Comes to Mayberry	Sid Morse	Lee Philips
#213	2/27/67	Helen, the Authoress	Doug Tibbles	Lee Philips
#214	3/6/67	Goodbye, Dolly	Michael L. Morris and Seaman Jacobs	Lee Philips
#215	3/13/67	Opie's Piano Lesson	Leo and Pauline Townsend	Lee Philips
#216	3/20/67	Howard, the Comedian	Michael L. Morris and Seaman Jacobs	Lee Philips
#217	3/27/67	Big Brothers	Fred S. Fox	Lee Philips
#218	4/2/67	Opie's Most Unforgettable Character	Michael L. Morris and Seaman Jacobs	Lee Philips
#219	4/10/67	Goober's Contest	Ron Friedman and Pat McCormick	Lee Philips

WRITERS AND DIRECTORS
THE EIGHTH SEASON

Eps	Air Date	Title	Written By	Directed By
#220	9/11/67	Opie's First Love	Doug Tibbles	Lee Philips
#221	12/25/67	Goober, the Executive	Seaman Jacobs and Michael Morris	Lee Philips
#222	10/16/67	Howard's Main Event	Earl Barrett and Robert C. Dennis	Lee Philips
#223	10/23/67	Aunt Bee, the Juror	Kent Wilson	Lee Philips
#224	9/18/67	Howard, the Bowler	Dick Bensfield and Perry Grant	Lee Philips
#225	10/9/67	Opie Steps Up in Class	Joseph Bonaduce	Lee Philips
#226	10/2/67	Andy's Trip to Raleigh	Joseph Bonaduce	Lee Philips
#227	9/25/67	A Trip to Mexico	Dick Bensfield and Perry Grant	Lee Philips
#228	10/20/67	Tape Recorder	Michael L. Morris and Seaman Jacobs	Lee Philips
#229	11/6/67	Opie's Group	Doug Tibbles	Lee Philips
#230	11/13/67	Aunt Bee and the Lecturer	Seaman Jacobs	Lee Philips
#231	11/20/67	Andy's Investment	Michael and Seaman Jacobs	Alan Rafkin
#232	12/11/67	Suppose Andy Gets Sick	Jay Raymond	Peter Baldwin
#233	11/27/67	Howard and Millie	Joseph Bonaduce	Peter Baldwin
#234	12/4/67	Aunt Bee's Cousin	Dick Bensfield and Perry Grant	Lee Philips
#235	12/18/67	Howard's New Life	Dick Bensfield and Perry Grant	Lee Philips
#236	1/8/68	Emmett's Brother-In-Law	James L. Brooks	Lee Philips
#237	1/1/68	The Mayberry Chef	James L. Brooks	Lee Philips
#238	1/22/68	The Church Benefactors	Earl Barrett and Robert C. Dennis	Lee Philips
#239	1/15/68	Opie's Drugstore Job	Kent Wilson	Lee Philips
#240	1/28/68	Barney Hosts a Summit Meeting	Aaron Ruben	Lee Philips
#241	4/1/68	Mayberry, R.F.D.	Bob Ross	Peter Baldwin
#242	2/5/68	Goober Goes to an Auto Show	Joseph Bonaduce	Lee Philips
#243	2/12/68	Aunt Bee's Big Moment	Dick Bensfield and Perry Grant	Lee Philips
#244	2/19/68	Helen's Past	Doug Tibbles	Lee Philips
#245	2/26/68	Emmett's Anniversary	Dick Bensfield and Perry Grant	Lee Philips
#246	3/4/68	The Wedding	Joseph Bonaduce	Lee Philips
#247	3/11/68	Sam for Town Council	Dick Bensfield and Perry Grant	Lee Philips
#248	3/18/68	Opie and Mike	Doug Tibbles and Bob Ross	Lee Philips
#249	3/25/68	A Girl for Goober	Bruce Howard and Bob Ross	Lee Philips